Marching
Through Babel

To Rosemary:
Remembering our book
discussions at the Greencroft
Book Club.
Bill Reyburn
Sept. 16, 2003

D1430611

Marching Through Babel

True Tales from the
Life of a Linguist

William D. Reyburn

This book was printed in the United States of America.

To order additional copies of this book, contact:
Xlibris Corporation
1-888-795-4274
www.Xlibris.com
Orders@Xlibris.com
15147

Contents

ACKNOWLEDGMENTS 11

THE EARLY YEARS

Zoolalia 15
The Martínez Gang 19
Hairs in the Soup 22

WORLD WAR II

Pataskala 27
Bombs and Boredom 30
Mama Agancho 32
Sasebo 35
Kiyoshi Kamagawa 38
Nagasaki 42
Easter Morning 46
Good-Bye 50

CHEROKEE AND LATIN AMERICA I

Mexico and Beyond 55
Qualla Reservation 68
Cherokee Wedding 74
Gentlemen Wanted 81

Annie 90
Toba 96
The Long Trip 101
Burro 106
The Resurrection of Mariano Cumbal 116
Patrón 124
Anybody Here Speak English? 130

FRANCE AND AFRICA

France 135
The General Mangin 138
Aloum 142
Elephant 150
Susie 162
Kambélé Station 168
Gwe Nemeno 170
Lolo Village 174
God, Space and Sputnik 180
Bushfire 183
Incest, Sex and Adultery 186
Say It from the Heart 189
God Hears 192
Overboard, Almost 197
On to Europe 200
David 203
Bibles and Beer 207
Maria 212
The Hollowed Bible of Edouard Ewutu 217
Translators School 221
Travel Risks 227
Blessed are the Peacemakers 235
Hausa 240
Diamonds for Ramadan 246
Out of Africa 250

EUROPE

The Eternal City 257
A Good Night's Sleep 262
Armenia and Mittens 267

MIDDLE EAST

On to Lebanon 275
A Provocative Act 281
How to put out a Fire 284
Monastery 288
Visa for Vietnam 293

CANADA AND LATIN AMERICA II

Peace Pipe 299
Marching to a Different Drum 305

Therefore, it was called Babel, because there the LORD confused the language of all the earth; and from there the LORD scattered them abroad over the face of all the earth.

Genesis 11.9

ACKNOWLEDGMENTS

I owe a deep debt of gratitude to many people, some living and many dead, who, without knowing that I would one day write this book, have inspired these pages with their love and friendship. My companion Marie has sustained me with her trust and affection in every episode from **Cherokee Wedding** to the end of the book. Her careful editorial eye has guided me on many occasions away from pitfalls of my own making. Without her keen memory of many events, this book would have suffered greatly.

Myrna Grace Reyburn, my mother, saved, without my knowing it, every letter I wrote from the time I entered the Marine Corps in World War II until her death in 1984. These letters turned out to be an archive of memories and saved me from guessing many dates, facts and names.

Our children Annie, Susie, David and Maria have taken an active interest in this project and shared with us their many insights. Betty Sellers, Georgia's poet laureate, graciously read the entire manuscript and encouraged me with her literary wisdom. Likewise, Robert Bratcher and Heber Peacock, translators of the Good News Bible and colleagues of many years, read and shared their knowledge with me.

I am indebted to Albert and Lois Buckwalter for all matters relating to the Toba Indians. I owe much to Juan Litwiller of Argentina and my beloved German friend Walter Trobisch. The untimely deaths of these two colleagues have left us all spiritually impoverished. I shall always remain respectfully grateful to the memory of Annie Oocuma and Jess Youngdeer for their patient collaboration in my study of the Cherokee language. I also thank Frank Bradley of Cherokee, NC for statistics he supplied regarding the Qualla reservation.

Quechua Indians Vicente Cuzco and Carlos Bawa helped me understand what it meant to be an Ecuadorian Indian just as I had gained some insight into the life of a Japanese war-time family through the friendship of young Kiyoshi Kamagawa. My work as a Bible translations consultant with the Lebanese poet Yusuf El Khal and the Egyptian Catholic Bishop Antonios Naguib live in memory as the highpoint of my years in the Middle East. I never knew personally the Nigerian child who copied into a notebook the words of Matthew 5.9 "Blessed are the peacemakers . . . ," for that child's life was brutally cut short. Still, his written message lives on.

I am especially indebted to Guahar Masih who accompanied me on my many visits to translators in Pakistan and who regaled me with many hours of delightful stories. I wish also to thank Tateos Michaelian of Iran, a faithful friend whose life was taken by zealous and fanatical people. Personal friends in Ecuador who inspired me and who lost their lives were Mission Aviation pilot Nate Saint, and missionary Jim Elliot. I am grateful for the lessons I learned from Thomas Miyauchi of Japan, Fouad Accad of Lebanon, John Fafalios of Greece and Albert Isteero of Egypt. I owe much to former colleagues William Smalley, William Wonderly and Eugene Nida for their intellectual stimulation.

My life, as well as that of my family, has a deeper meaning for having lived among the Quechuas of Picalquí, the Tobas of Nam Qom, the Bulus of Aloum, the Kakos of Lolo, the Hausas, Yorubas and Igbos of Nigeria, the Lebanese Arabs of Beirut and Brummana, and the Egyptians of Maadi. The list in full would be a roll call of Babel.

I have attempted to keep the chronology clear and have in a few cases changed the names of persons to avoid causing problems for them or their offspring.

THE
EARLY
YEARS

Zoolalia

Loveland, my home town, lies nearly a mile above sea level at the foot of the front range of the Colorado Rockies. Loveland is hardly on one of the ancient crossroads of civilization and is certainly far removed from the great polyglot cities of the world. It may seem surprising, therefore, that this rather insular western farming community would provide the stimulation necessary for a young boy to develop a love affair with language and grow up to become a linguist. Nevertheless, the area has a diversity of its own and to travel to Loveland by road is to experience through local place-names the taste and feel of the American frontier.

Highway 76 enters the northeast corner of the state at Julesberg and passes through Sterling, Brush, Fort Morgan and Greely—all rather anglo-sounding names. However, if you come up from the South on Highway 25, you will notice the names take on an Hispanic flavor: Ratón, Trinidad, Águilar, Pueblo, Aurora. From the North in nearby Wyoming you may pass through what was once Indian country: Medicine Bow, Cheyenne, and Pawnee. Out of the West you can reach Loveland by passing near Rabbit Ears Pass and Muddy Pass. Dinosaur, Elk Springs, Deer Ridge and Bear Lake awaken the mind to the wealth of wildlife cradled in the embrace of these majestic heights.

East of Loveland the earth flattens out and rolls away to the uttermost horizon. Here farms are laid out in sections or blocks of square miles and all roads run east-west or north-south. In the country as well as in the towns people give directions by the cardinal points of the compass. Thanks to the towering Rockies no one is ever in doubt about West.

Likewise never in doubt is the season of the year. Summer is fiercely hot, winter is bitingly cold and fall and spring mark the transitions. During my boyhood the graveled streets of summer snaked beneath massive cottonwood trees and in winter, following the autumn leaf-falls, house chimneys spewed out smoke from wood and coal fires into the icy air. In summer, street sprinklers—elephantine water tank-trucks—groaned ponderously about town subduing the choking dust. In winter—often as early as October—snowplows clearing the streets heaped up snow across driveways that had to be shoveled away to get the family car out to the road.

But what I liked best about Loveland was what lay between the streets—the alleys. In those days Loveland was part town and part farm. The town perspective could be seen from the streets where flourished trees, ornamental bushes, and lawns framed by sidewalks. The country view was seen from the alleys, dingy roads behind the houses with cow or horse barns, rabbit hutches, chicken pens, and rusting farm machinery and where an occasional windmill creaked and flapped when struck by the north wind. These barnyard quarters provided their households with milk, eggs and meat and bathed the neighborhood in the pungent fragrance of country life.

Furthermore, the presence of so many domestic animals greeting each dawn in a cacophonous chorus made me feel I was part of a joyful celebration of sunrise. The mooing of cows, the nickering of horses, the crowing of roosters, the cackling of hens seemed to say to all that life was good and it was time to arise and face the new day with hope. It was a very special message, for the times were hard; the Great Depression was piteously impoverishing, and people everywhere needed work and encouragement.

I am not sure why this early morning barnyard orchestration captivated this small boy's imagination. I guess I had convinced myself that it was not just noise coming from the alleys, but rather when the Blackstones' old bay mare whinnied and Judge Rogers' stately Tennessee walking horse a block away replied, I conjectured there was some kind of a horsey conversation going back and forth. Roosters did the same and over much greater distances. I felt bad that a donkey at the Harris house in the next block could arouse no respondent. He, or perhaps she, hee-hawed or she-hawed itself into breathless exhaustion. It seemed entirely logical that if I dedicated myself to sufficient practice, I should be able to understand and communicate with these neighborly creatures. I would eventually become, like a latter-day Doctor Doolittle, able to talk with the animals. Accordingly, with single-minded devotion I plied the alleys seeking out the horses, mules, ducks, roosters, chickens, cows, pigs, goats, sheep, dogs, cats and even cocked an ear to catch the honking of a high-flying formation of Canadian geese bound for the sunny South.

The linguistic education of Billy was underway: "Animals of the Alley 101."

Conversation with animals can be called **zoolalia** from the Greek noun for animal and the verb to speak. The study of this phenomenon may be termed **zoolalialogy** and the one who speaks with animals a **zoolalialogist**. If anyone had ever proposed such academic jargon to me, I would have let go with a resounding earful of pig squeals.

Years later I was to learn that people speaking different languages ascribe different sounds to their animals. For example, in English *cock-a-doodle-doo* is supposed to represent what a cock says, but in spite of the fact that in America where we have roosters in place of cocks, we still march to the drumbeat of *cock-a-doodle-doo*. If the American rooster had a chance to proclaim its independence from its British ancestors, I suspect it would want us to say that he sings out *rooster-rooter-roo*. The French rooster says *coquerico*, the German says *kikeriki* and the

Portuguese sings *cocoricó*. The Danes claim their roosters sing *kykeliky* and the Hispanic bird crows *quiquiriquí*. Although each has four or five syllables with stress on the final lengthened vowel, anyone who has traveled from Boston to Bangladesh or from Juneau to Johannesburg knows that mature roosters all sound about the same and none sounds like the onomatopoeic sound imitations ascribed to them in a thousand languages.

In 1929 I was old enough to enter Garfield Grade School, and had become a seasoned habitué of the alleys on the west side of town and had by that time perhaps a more detailed knowledge of backyards and their contents than anyone. Many of the animals I regularly called on paid little attention to a small barefoot boy peering at them from a fence top and showed no interest in the animal-like noises I ejected in their direction. However, there were others that mooed, whinnied, baaed, oinked, or quacked spontaneously when I greeted them in their native voices. I concluded that animals, like human beings, were not all equally bright. The clever ones recognized their own tongues, even when spoken by a foreigner—who might have just a tinge of accent.

It always disturbed me a bit that my animal friends seemed not the least interested in imitating the sounds of other animals. All of their conversations were kept within their own kind so that a barnyard was a little United Nations without interpreters. I even tried to teach old Mike, my faithful alley-dog companion, to meow but gave up when he brought home a dead cat and proudly deposited it at our back door.

The Martínez Gang

The Great Depression was a time when the citizens of Loveland turned to finding things to sell. A large market was set up in a field on East First Street and people brought firewood, tools, home canned goods, livestock and some even sold the furniture from their homes to obtain some badly needed cash. My mother often bought a load of firewood and I climbed the stockpen fences to listen to the sing-song chatter of the auctioneer.

It was at these sales I first heard the staccato rhythms of Spanish spoken by the Mexican-Americans bidding on the animals. I pushed my way into their midst and watched with fascination their energetic gestures and heard *doce cincuenta por la negra . . . oye, Pedro, no vale tanto . . . ofrécele diez cincuenta . . . apúrate hombre.* I understood nothing but was enthralled with the sights and sounds of it all.

When the auction had ended and the animals were being loaded onto trucks, I found myself alone gesticulating to the absent auctioneer and bidding on the animals in a gibberish that sounded to me like Spanish. Within a few days I realized that I had a thirst to learn this language and the only way to quench it was to find some Mexican-American kids to play with. Just as I could locate a pen full of geese, I was able to find the children I was looking for. The Spanish education of Billy slowly displaced his **zoolalia**. In fact, I began to understand that the **zoolaliamania** (love for talking with animals) was an expression of a love for language, real communication where meaning instead of mere sound imitation was all-important.

The Martínez house stood on a slope above a cattail swamp on West First Street. The walls were made of pine slabs from a derelict sawmill and had at some time been painted red, but the bright color had become covered by the dust of vehicles going to and from the city dump. A wobbly stovepipe carried out the smoke from the wood stove where señora Martínez busied herself making tortillas to feed her husband and six children.

I called through the open back door and in a moment heard a rumble of running feet approaching. Six pairs of dark eyes materialized in the doorway. I lifted a handful of marbles from my pocket and motioned to one of the older boys. There was no response and the dark-eyed faces continued to stare silently until señora Martínez, a short, stout woman with cornmeal flour on her hands, came to the door and looked out at me over the heads of her brood. *Quiere jugar bolas* "He wants to play marbles," she announced and shuffled back to her stove. Two of the boys came out and I drew a circle in the dirt, made a small mound on which I placed an old chipped marble. I motioned for them to do the same, but they shrugged and patted their empty pockets. To each I gave a shooter and one marble, their dibs. When we got on our knees to shoot, it became clear they did not know how to play. They wanted to stand and throw their shooters. That was not going to work.

I then pointed to myself and said my name. Pointing to the older of the two boys, I asked "You name?" "Miguel," he answered. The smaller boy dropped to the ground and began laughing. When I asked his name he said *perro* then *gato* and finally *gallo*. As he said the word for "rooster" he began to flop around in the dust, flap his arms and crow. The other four had now come out of the kitchen and were standing around their brother shouting *gallo, gallo*. I now had hold of the word for rooster and so I let go with a lusty crowing which was met by shouts of *gallo, gallo*. When I switched to oinking all shouted *chancho, chancho*. When I mooed the chorus sang out *vaca,*

vaca. Before long I had exhausted my entire repertoire of zoolalia. The problem now was how to remember the Spanish names of these birds and animals. To help me I called out *chancho* or *perro* or *pato* and the Martínez gang made the appropriate noises. By the time señora Martínez called us in to sit on the kitchen floor and eat tortillas, the Martínez kitchen reverberated in the pandemonium of a discordant barnyard.

As I trudged home, I had a keen awareness that a door to a new world had opened for me and I would never again be the same. Like the Creator who brought all the birds and animals to Adam to see what names he would give them, I had paraded all of mine before the Martínez kids and they had given them Spanish names. With stubborn determination and much effort I was eventually able to talk with the Martínez family and other Hispanics. I then realized how often they had a different viewpoint on life than the majority anglo population. Seeing matters from their perspective made me less prone to judge others, and to examine my own way of life more objectively.

Hairs in the Soup

The 1936 marriage of my older sister, Barbara, to Bob Pegau in New Mexico opened a new door for my acculturation in the Hispanic lifestyle and language. Brother-in-law Bob managed a farm for L.R. Allison, a highway contractor. The farm lay in the fertile Rio Grande valley north of Albuquerque. The laborers were all Spanish-speaking New Mexicans.

I had little difficulty conversing and understanding these men, all considerably older than myself. But I was soon to learn that my knowledge of Spanish had a gaping hole that would need to be filled if I was going to interact in a meaningful way with them. For example, when one of the men confided to me that his wife was always "looking for hairs in the soup," I thought he meant it literally. I pictured her bent over a bowl of soup fishing about with a spoon. He was, of course, speaking metaphorically and his expression had nothing to do with literal hairs and soup. It was simply a way of saying that she was one who found fault with everything.

Figurative language like the example above causes problems of comprehension for children in all languages. When the American child hears his father say "I think granddad is losing his marbles," the child may be a bit surprised to learn that granddad is still playing marbles. It takes a degree of maturity in the language before the child understands that this expression is a way of saying that granddad is getting senile. Or when the child comes into the house and asks where dad is, the mother may answer: "Leave him alone; he's sawing wood," meaning "he's asleep." Until the child learns the sense of this expression, he or she will interpret it literally and perhaps search for dad out at the wood pile.

On one occasion I was told by the foreman to go to another field and give a message to José Ramos. I did not know José so asked the foreman to describe him. "He's a half bottle" was his curt reply. I didn't know if this meant he could drink a half bottle of booze—something that was very common—or if he might be carrying a half bottle of liquor in his pocket. When I found the man, I saw that he was almost a midget—a half bottle, indeed!

I had been accustomed to hearing anglos say, after someone had had a haircut, that "he had had his ears lowered." When I heard the same expression in Spanish, I assumed, quite wrongly, that it meant the same as in English. Nothing could have been further from the truth. The saying in Spanish means that a person is crestfallen, has a disappointed look. When I reported to my work-gang that I had heard on the radio that Hitler had made a treaty with the Russians, one of the men smiled patronizingly and said "Oh, that has got a beard." It was already old news to them.

One morning while on my way to the fields I passed the house of Natividad Gallegos, who had once lived in Costa Rica. Although it was time to go to work, I noticed Natividad was still sitting on his porch. I greeted him and asked what he was doing. *Matando la culebra* "killing the snake," he replied. That caught my attention; so I walked over to him and asked to see the snake. He looked at me blankly and asked, "What snake?" "The one you were killing," I replied. "Oh, that snake," he said. "That's not a real snake." I was confused and asked how he could kill an imaginary snake. Perhaps Natividad had been drinking too much and was seeing snakes. "Was it a whole bunch of snakes or just one?" He was clearly becoming annoyed with me by now. He laughed, "Look, Guillermo, *Matar la culebra* is what we call a *modismo*, an idiom. It is just a way of saying that I am not busy.

`I'm killing time,' as you gringos say." He must have seen a light turn on in my head for he then asked. "Tell me, when gringos `kill time' do they do it with a machete or a club?" I thanked Natividad for the lesson and went on to work.

I worked on the Allison farm until 1940, nearly every day learning the pathways that led to competence in New Mexican Spanish. My teachers, like the Martínez kids, were unschooled but graciously patient and endowed with intuitive wisdom. I did not realize until later that they had given me both an invaluable education and also insights on being a teacher.

WORLD WAR II

Pataskala

The opportunity to teach came while I was a Marine Corps trainee in a college V-12 program in central Ohio. While hitchhiking to Columbus, I was stranded at a crossroad when I noticed a gang of men at work on the Pennsylvania railroad. Although too far away to hear them, their gestures and body language were unmistakably Mexican. I crossed a field and walked along the tracks until I was near them. They looked up to see a figure in uniform approaching. Thinking perhaps I was a railroad boss, they picked up their tools and began working silently.

I called out *Buenos días.* The sledge hammers stopped and their faces turned toward me. Still uncertain who this stranger could be, they began to whisper among themselves. I introduced myself and we all shook hands. I explained that I was a Marine trainee in a college nearby and they explained that they had been recruited in Mexico and brought to Ohio. Their wives and children, they said, were in the small town of Pataskala. "It is very difficult for us here because we don't understand English. Our wives have trouble buying food because no one in Pataskala speaks Spanish. We feel like children lost in a forest."

I learned that they had no newspapers and no radio—television was still some years away. One man said they had a few old magazines, but nothing modern. I asked if I could get some Spanish books, what would they like to have. After a short conference, they agreed they would like to have a Spanish Bible.

They again went into a huddle and when they emerged they doffed their hats and their spokesman said, "If your mercy could come and teach us English, our hearts would be full of joy." The others nodded in agreement. As I pondered their request, I thought of all the Mexican-Americans who had taught me. It was time to return the favor.

The following Saturday I arrived with a blackboard and chalk. We organized our classroom in an empty train car that stood on a siding. Our classroom quickly filled with nearly all the railroad gang plus many of their wives and children. What we lacked in pedagogical materials we made up for in enthusiasm. The children were the best students and soon were helping their parents. My students shared their food with me and placed a cot in our classroom where I slept on Saturday nights, after an evening of guitar playing, games and singing. One of the men led a brief worship service each Sunday morning and then our classes continued until it was time for me to hitch a ride back to the college.

José López who read the Bible to the group on Sunday mornings often stumbled, mispronounced words, freely substituted others and often left his listeners confused. In some cases the errors in reading were minor. For example, John 15:1 says in Spanish *Yo soy la vid verdadera* "I am the true vine." José might substitute *vida* "life" for *vid* "vine" and the sense became "I am the true life." In other cases the misreading was more serious; for example, Luke 11:25 says *y el postrer estado del aquel hombre viene a ser peor que el primero* "and the final state of that man is worse than the first." Here José might substitute *potrero* "horse pasture" for *postrer* meaning "final" and the sense would become "and the horse pasture state of that man would become . . . ." Little known words like *alfa* and *omega* in Revelation 21:6 were predictable sand traps for José who would turn them into *alfalfa* and *ombligo*, the latter meaning "navel."

The wording of the Reina Valera traditional version was sometimes obscure, even when read correctly. For example, in

Acts 26:24 Festus accuses Paul of being beside himself and says "much learning doth make thee mad." This version has *letras* for "learning" meaning "letters of the alphabet" to José's listeners. Festus' condemnation of the apostle was hardly a great motivation for my students who were trying very hard to learn their *letras*. The folks at Pataskala expected the Bible to be difficult to understand and José did not disappoint them.

It became apparent that the Reina Valera version was often obtuse, perplexing, if not downright unintelligible, to the railroad crew at Pataskala. Eventually, I was able to get José to select in advance the passage he planned to read on Sunday. I would then go to the college library and prepare notes on the problems. By having him read it aloud to me the next Sunday morning and by explaining to him the difficulties, his listeners improved in both attention and comprehension. The lesson became clear to me: these folks needed and deserved a clear, idiomatic translation in popular Spanish. Four years were to pass before some selections from the New Testament were available and the entire New Testament (Versión Popular) did not appear in print until 1966, some twenty-three years after Pataskala.

Bombs and Boredom

At the end of six months, I had completed my training and it was time to move on to Parris Island, South Carolina, for boot camp. It was not difficult to leave the college, but to say *adios* to my Mexican family in Pataskala was a heart-rending farewell.

August 6 1945 an atomic bomb exploded over Hiroshima and three days later a plutonium bomb fell on Nagasaki. By this time I had become a second lieutenant and was a platoon commander in F Company, Second Battalion, Twenty-fifth Regiment, of the Fourth Marine Division based on the island of Maui. We were running military exercises in the hills of Maui preparing for the invasion of Japan when we learned of the fate of these devastated Japanese cities. Then, came the news of the surrender of Japan. Our maneuvers ceased and we waited for word from the top about going home or going elsewhere. The troops became restless and heavy boredom settled on us like a thick fog. I was one of the fortunate ones who had interests that kept my mind occupied. In a bookstore in the town of Wailuku I had found two books that I have kept with me these fifty-four years: H. L Mencken's *The American Language* and Frederick Bodmer's *The Loom of Language, A Guide to Foreign Languages for the Home Student*. Along with the Bible, these were my constant companions that refreshed and renewed my spirit through the most wearisome and tedious hours of camp life.

Although I recognized and enjoyed the literary beauty of the psalms, I was frustrated in my reading of the King James Bible by the many archaic expressions and the literal renderings in the gospels and particularly in the epistles. I could not help but believe that these obscurities could be cleared up and made lucid and meaningful. Little did I know at that time that I would eventually become a member of a team of specialists whose purpose and mission would be the translation of the Scriptures into the popular languages of people everywhere.

I was also to learn later that Albert Schweitzer, while on military maneuvers in Alsace in 1894, carried his Greek New Testament so he could prepare for his examinations at the University of Strasbourg.

Mama Agancho

When orders came for those lacking sufficient points to return to the States, I was sent to Guam and assigned to a military police unit responsible for supervising the unloading of supplies from merchant ships at Apra Harbor. On many occasions I sat at night near the hold of a ship to see that the merchant seamen did not loot the cargo. Under a bright light I cradled one of my books in my lap and read until it was time to go below and inspect the holds. I am sure the seamen thought I was studying a volume of disciplinary action and punishments for persons caught pilfering cargo. If that is what they thought, I never sought to disabuse them.

Guam, which lies at the south end of the Marianas group of islands, is some thirty miles long and four to eight miles wide. It was discovered in 1521 by the Portuguese explorer Ferdinand Magellan and had been a Spanish colony for more than three hundred years when it was ceded to the United States in 1898 after the Spanish—American war. The Japanese captured Guam three days after the attack on Pearl Harbor and the US Marines invaded the island on July 21, 1944.

But Guam offered me a much more significant challenge than policing merchant ships. The people of Guam, at least in 1945, were still going about speaking their native language, Chamorro, a Malayo-Polynesian tongue. I wanted to learn Chamorro and watched with nostalgia when I passed huts where children played. These kids could be the island's Martínez bunch, but I was too old to be crowing and oinking, not very dignified for a

Marine officer. Instead, I drove my jeep to a Catholic church in Agat village and found the local priest, who listened with interest when I told him I would like to study the language and therefore needed a mature person to help me. He said he did not know any teachers of the language, but could send me to an elderly lady who knew the history of the people.

In Agat village I located the hut of Mama Agancho, who appeared barefoot in the doorway puffing on her pipe and puzzled by my presence. With the assistance of her son-in-law, I managed to get her cooperation, aided in no small degree by a promise to supply her with tobacco from the P.X. Our sessions, held on the tiny porch of her house, were begun by my pointing to pictures in a magazine and writing down her responses as best I could. It turned out that she could speak Spanish which warmed our relationship and improved our communication.

I was surprised at the time to discover the extent Spanish vocabulary had been taken into Chamorro. Numerous tropical fruits had Spanish names as did the ubiquitous goat but not the pig. Even some body parts such as the chest was a Spanish word but not, for example, the head or shoulders. The word "to smoke" a cigarette or pipe was the Spanish word meaning "to suck." Even some colors were expressed in Spanish as was the word for "air." I was not surprised to learn that Mama Agancho had learned Spanish from the Spanish missionaries as she would have been nearly twenty years old when the island was turned over to the United States. Spanish missionary influence continued and Father Jesús Baza Dueños was tortured and beheaded by the Japanese on July 12 1944, only nine days before the US Marine invasion.

My word list grew with each session, but it had nearly all nouns and no verbs. However, by acting out eating, drinking, pointing, sitting, standing, and many other actions, I was able to gather some verbs. My actions attracted a group of children who joined our theatrics by standing on their heads, jumping up and down, pushing, pulling and carrying each other. The vocabulary grew but I was not always sure of the meanings.

One day as I drove into Agat village several people were gathered around Mama, who was holding a book in her lap and reading slowly. I soon realized that she was reading from one of the gospels. This was the first time I had seen a book in Chamorro. From time to time she paused while her neighbors contributed their comments. When she had finished the reading, she carefully closed the small book, wrapped it neatly in a newspaper and tied string around it. It was clearly something of value to her. She had been reading in Luke's gospel the parable of the woman who lost a coin then lit a lamp and swept the floor until she found it. Standing, she danced about singing "Be glad with me because I have found my coin." Her neighbors responded "We are glad with you that you found your coin." Then Mama added "Jesus tells us there is joy in heaven when one sinner repents; God finds her."

As the neighbors began to leave, one woman said to me in broken English "Mista marine, when you catch our language, help us get whole God's book in Chamorro." Her encouragement urged me forward in my first steps in Chamorro in spite of my evident lack of training in linguistics. I was making good progress in the language when I received orders transferring me to Japan.

Sasebo

Sasebo, Kyushu, one of Japan's largest deep water harbors was my new post. Assigned to the Second Pioneer Battalion, a construction and demolition outfit, there was no demand for my qualifications as an infantry officer nor as a military policeman. I certainly had no expertise to offer these engineers and when I reported to the commanding officer, I thought it prudent to lay my cards on the table. I had no brilliant record in math and had barely eked through mechanical drawing. I rehearsed my confession until it sounded positively disarming. When I delivered it to the C.O., who peered at me incredulously—at least it seemed so—through a pair of dark shades that hid his blood-shot eyes, he rocked back in his swivel chair and in his south Georgia idiom allowed as how "all the finer things of life depend on getting the numbers right." He emphasized his point by thumping his desk top with a well-worn riding crop. "We all owe it to the great men of science to follow their habit of exactness." I was certain by now that I would be given orders to move on to a more suitable assignment, perhaps a cooks and bakers school. Then the creaking chair shot forward and the face behind the glasses froze in mid air. "Like I always say, lieutenant, it's science that won the damn war. Men like Oppenheimer and Einstein and professor what's-his-name from Iceland; they are the trail-blazers of our future. If we don't climb aboard, we'll be discarded on the junkheap of history. Ya heah?" The riding crop slapped again. I was feeling like flotsam in the wake of a vanishing civilization.

The colonel stopped to light a cigarette. He seemed to be running out of steam as he hoisted the dark shades, rubbed his eyes and blinked me into focus.

"Well . . . Reyburn," he squinted at my orders to get the name right, "that's all very true, but if truth be told, the only science in this battalion is poker, and the only mathematics is the order from one pair to five of a kind." He now allowed a grin to play across his face. For the first time since entering his office I relaxed. I felt like I had just been welcomed into the colonel's private club.

Standing up and stretching he marched smartly to the window and gazed out upon a field of bulldozers, trucks and dredges. "We've got enough equipment here to push this whole island into the sea, but that's not what I have in mind." His tone became serious. "We're standing at the crossroads of history, mister, and I don't want us to fail when the great judgment trumpet blows." The colonel was beginning to sound like a southern evangelist. "We must save this society from its samurai tradition, root out its warlord tendency, and you know, Reyburg, where to begin?"

Before I could marshall my thoughts, the colonel was off under a full head of steam. "You begin with the kids. Teach the kids how to play fair, and there is nothing like good old American baseball to do the job," he said swinging an imaginary bat. "Look what we did in Central America. Sure we invaded and took over down there; the Nicaraguans may hate us but they love baseball. Even in the halls of Montezuma those Indians were batting 'em out of the ball park."

The C.O. sat down and swiveled toward a shelf on the wall by his desk. What he said next came forth in the form of a private confession to a photo of his wife and children. "I swear it, Rebecca Lee, I will come home a happy man when I know every nip kid in Sasebo can swing a bat." His voice became prophetic "One day there will be Japanese leagues playing each other and the old war lust will have been put out like a slow runner to first base." He reached out his left hand and drove his right fist into it. "He's

out!" The chair whirled back again and his finger flashed at me.
"Fairburn, I'm counting on your cooperation, ya heah? See the
adjutant on your way out."

Kiyoshi Kamagawa

The Pioneer Battalion occupied a camp that previously had been a Japanese artillery base. The marines were billeted in a two story cement barracks and the officers in a crumbling wood building with outdoor toilets where the honey dippers came weekly to fish up and carry away the night soil for gardens. The motor pool was a hodge-podge of wooden repair sheds spread among several acres of vehicles of every sort for moving earth. I went there in search of Corporal Adams, said to be the man who could teach me how to handle any piece of equipment on the lot.

We began with the bulldozer and when I felt competent, we moved on to the road grader then the power shovel, and finally the road roller. By the end of a month, I was able to drive any of this heavy equipment out of the camp and to the various baseball fields under construction. Moving these behemoths through narrow winding roads without ripping the side out of a Japanese house required a high degree of skill. It was not uncommon for the members of a household to gather around their threatened structure and shout all manner of abuse at the driver to keep his iron dinosaur from taking a bite of their house.

I was carefully maneuvering a bulldozer between two rows of houses when I came to a sharp bend in the road. If I turned too sharply to the left, the rear of the machine would swing around and take out a wall on the right. I paused to study the problem and was relieved that none of the inhabitants seemed to be at home. Then I noticed a small figure ahead in the road. From his visored cap to his small feet he looked like a miniature policeman without a sword. He wore a black jacket with an even row of bright buttons to his chin and was carrying a backpack supported by straps that crossed his chest. Standing at attention with his arms rigidly at his sides, he raised his left arm and motioned me forward. Halfway into the bend, he signalled me to halt and back slowly, showing me the room I had behind me by measuring the distance with his two hands. He watched carefully as I reversed then motioned me to go forward keeping to the left. Step by step we inched the big dozer around the narrow curve and left the houses unscathed. I throttled back and leaned over. My guide came alongside and called up.

"Good afternoon, Sir. May I inquire you name, please?" His English was far superior to that of most of the kids I had heard on the newly-leveled playing fields.

"Would you say that again, please?" I called down to him. He repeated what I thought I had heard.

"Reyburn," I shouted back. "May I inquire who you are, please?"

"I am Kiyoshi Kamagawa, thank you."

I was eager to learn more of this curious youngster, so motioned for him to climb up. He wriggled his way up onto the track then to the seat. He sat beside me, his canvas-shoed feet dangling freely.

"I enjoys learning English," he offered as he looked up smiling. His upper front teeth were long and gave him the appearance of a wiskerless pet rat.

"I'm going to the marine camp," I explained, "but I want to thank you for helping me get around those houses."

His feet swung back and forth "Vely well, I show you way to you camp," he volunteered.

"I think I know the way"

"Maybe two head better than one," he said as his rodent grin spread across his face. He was pleased with his humor and as the big engine roared again, he grasped the sides of the seat with his small hands and we were off.

When we reached the main road and could go faster, Kiyoshi reached up and tapped me on the shoulder. He was pointing to a Shinto temple we were passing. "You like go there I take you." I shook my head. "These places are off bounds for us."

I could see he was mouthing the phrase "off bounds," registering a new bit of vocabulary in his mental dictionary. He told me the names of each of the bridges we crossed, the buildings that once occupied the bombed-out spaces, how many trains used to arrive daily at the Sasebo station and other trivia that were lost in the purring of the big cat. He was still pointing and talking when we roared into the camp.

Sitting on the silenced bulldozer, I asked how old he was and if he would teach me Japanese. After a bit of reflection, the twelve-year-old suggested it would be better for me to teach him English.

"But you know English," I objected.

"Not enough I go university," he retorted.

"University? That is years from now."

Kiyoshi straightened and looked directly ahead "Uncle say all Japanese go learn English now." He paused for a moment then looked up at me. "You go Amelica and talk Japanese with you father? You father speak Japanese?" His toothy grin revealed that he was sure he had me cornered.

"OK, Kiyoshi, I'll help you with English if you'll help me with Japanese." I extended my open hand. He hesitated then carefully laid his soft hand in mine. "We call that a deal," I said.

"Deal for playing cards," he corrected.

"Yes, that too, but language is a lazy thing. It uses one word for many things." I cast about for an illustration. "Here, this machine is called a 'bulldozer.' Do you see the bull, horns, hoofs, hide? No, it is strong like a bull, but there is no bull animal."

We agreed to meet each day on his way home from school. I wrote him a pass to show the gate guard. As he walked away I could hear him mumbling "bulldozer, no bull, no horns, no hide, bulldozer no bull . . . ." He turned to face me and saluted as he called out *Leyburn-san, sayonara.*

Nagasaki

"Lieutenant, I'm tired of hearing this squeaky damn wheel of yours. How many times do I have to tell you that Nagasaki and Hiroshima are off limits? Good God, man, think about the atomic radiation. He swiveled his chair away from me, hoping no doubt when he turned back again I'd be gone. It was true; I had badgered the man repeatedly to give me a pass to Nagasaki. The chair creaked once more under his weight and he peered out at me over the top of his smoked glasses, raised his brows and seemed ready to strike a deal.

"Tell you what I can do: give you a pass to Omura, that's about halfway to Nagasaki."

When he saw the hollow disillusionment in my eyes, he hastened to add, "Now, if you just happen to come home the wrong way . . ." He paused to let me cogitate. "Well, if you do, you're without a pass and if the MPs find you . . . and, by the way, get yourself back here before dark . . . ya heah?"

At dawn the following morning I pulled out of camp headed for Omura and points beyond. Nagasaki lay only some thirty-five miles to the south. It had snowed lightly in the night and the weather was bitterly cold, particularly traveling in an open jeep. The route took me along the east side of Omura Bay where the wind was churning up whitecaps and hurling foaming waves over the road. Splashing through deep holes, the engine drowned out and I had to dry the plugs before going on.

In Omura I nudged my way through knots of pedestrians,

rickshaws, two-wheeled carts, bicycles, and occasionally passed a charcoal-burning bus. On the southern outskirts of the city and lining both sides of the narrow road were tens of thousands of Japanese soldiers who, I later learned, were being repatriated from China. These troops were no doubt catching a passing glimpse of the first American they had seen occupying their homeland. I steered the jeep slowly between the endless columns of staring, stone-faced soldiers and breathed easier when finally clear of them.

As I neared Nagasaki, the sun was shining out of a cloud-streaked pale blue sky. The morning air was still frosty. In a few minutes I would be face-to-face with the annihilation of a third of one of Japan's great historical centers and port city where the gigantic Mitsubishi shipyards had produced ships for the Japanese navy. Nearly six months had passed since the fateful day of August 9 when some four square miles of the city had become vaporized in a single instant. The military police at the entrance of the city waved me through without asking for a pass.

As I made my way slowly into the part that was the wasteland of Nagasaki, its overpowering desolation, a vastness of crumbled emptiness, left me breathless. All around lay a dead sea of rubble in which a few cobblestone roads had been partially cleared. No sign of life existed in any direction, no human moved, not a scavenging dog nor vulture. Everywhere lay shattered stones, bricks and roof tiles. The earth had been scorched black and every combustible object had left behind only its ashes. The few trees standing had been shattered and their limbs ripped away. I was aware that I was beginning to feel sick and wanted to vomit.

In the midst of the charred debris there stood a blackened wall, the remains of a building, roofless and windowless. Here and there smokestacks rose up, moribund sentries standing guard over this valley of the shadow of death.

I steered slowly over a bumpy road where building stones had been heaped along the roadsides and came finally to a bombed-out building still recognizable as a church. The steps leading up to it had been ripped up and scattered. The doors had been blown away as had the windows and the roof. The remains of the steeple hung upside down above the entrance like a grotesque dunce's cap. Inside the sanctuary everything had been burned and even the roof tiles lying on the ground had melted in the heat of the blast.

The horror that atomic warfare had visited unmercifully on this place caused my mind to reel. My legs grew weak and I squatted on the ground, not unlike the ancient Job in his ash heap. I felt I was staring eye-to-eye into the face of evil. Was I witnessing what could become the future of humankind, the final solution? Could anyone be an eyewitness to this scorched earth and his soul remain unscarred? Was it only a matter of time until our planet, our only home in the universe, would be cast into this desolate grave? My brain burned with questions and found few if any answers. One thing, however, was clear: I could never again think of atomic annihilation in the abstract. It was here and real and held me in its sickening embrace. The question was not what will the Russians and Americans do next, but what must I do now? For me there was no getting in my jeep and driving away, putting it all behind me like a bad dream. In this bombed-out church I bowed my head in repentance and committed my life to the way of peace and nonviolence. I have never for a moment forgotten that at age 23 in this place of death I experienced spiritual awakening.

When I confided to a fellow officer that my visit to Nagasaki left me with no choice but to repent for the evil loosed upon that place, he ridiculed the very thought of a contrite spirit, adding "If it weren't for those damn bombs, your bones and mine would have been scattered on these hills." At that time I did not know of another penitent soul—Albert Einstein—who for his role in helping to develop the bomb later said, "If only I had known. I would have become a watchmaker."

As I reflect on this pivotal day fifty-two years ago, I realize how vast was our ignorance of what we had witnessed. We did not know that, according to Japanese figures, 74,000 people had been killed and 77,000 wounded. We did not know that the Nagasaki bomb was plutonium and more powerful than the uranium one that destroyed Hiroshima. We were ignorant of the struggles between the warlords and the peace factions in the Japanese government. Only much later as reports and studies were published was it possible to comprehend some of the many facets that led to the atomic bombing of the two cities and their subsequent effects.

In 1970, twenty-four years after seeing the devastated Nagasaki, I returned there accompanied by a Japanese friend, the Reverend Thomas Miyauchi. By that time the city had been rebuilt, a modern city with a peace statue and atomic bomb museum. When we went to the museum, my Japanese friend excused himself and remained outside. The horrors on display brought back memories most Japanese of his age were still struggling to escape. Along one wall were jars containing terribly deformed human fetuses, photos of screaming people whose burned flesh left them with sheets of skin dangling from their bodies. There was the image of a policeman at a street corner imprinted on a wall by the searing intensity of the light. A brochure obtained in the museum contained a colored photo of the memorial erected at the center of the blast. The description concludes with these words: "This landmark at the Epi-center is a record of stupidity and brutality of human being."

When I rejoined Mr. Miyauchi, I recalled the thought expressed by Robert Oppenheimer, father of the US atomic bomb, who said, following the successful detonation of the first atomic device at Alamogordo, New Mexico on July 16, 1945: "In some crude sense which no vulgarity, no humor, no overstatement can quite extinguish, the physicists have known sin; and this is a knowledge they cannot lose."

Easter Morning

The sky over the Sea of Japan was losing its stars to a pale pink dawn as I swung my feet to the floor and groped for the light switch. Outside the birds were beginning to chirp and the weather was warming. The cherry blossoms were in full bloom and the air of the camp that normally reeked of gasoline and oil now smelled fresh and clean following a downpour in the night. Dressed, I tiptoed quietly down the stairs, passed the Colonel's quarters and made my way to my jeep, which I had parked the night before near the camp gate. I had told the guard that I would be leaving at daybreak. When the motor cranked, the guard appeared, saw who it was and waved me through. I had been looking forward to celebrating Easter sunrise on a high hill overlooking the city and the harbor.

The darkened camp receded behind me as I began to wend my way in and out of bombed-out lots between fragile wooden houses that clung to the slopes. Occasionally I passed rock fences stacked around small garden plots where cabbages and onions grew. The houses that had survived the American bombing raids had been built with ventilation more than insulation in mind. Kyushu had brief cold winters but the summers were long and intense. Japanese cedars, pines and oaks grew between the buildings and along the maze of paths that linked one level with the next. Here and there a dog leaped to the side of the road and snarled as I passed.

As I neared the summit, the early morning air bathed the

hillside in a refreshing breeze. The houses gave way to scrub bushes, weeds, and heavy artillery emplacements the Japanese had hauled up to protect the Sasebo harbor and repulse an American invasion that never took place. We had disabled these big guns that now lay inert and silent like the bones of some prehistoric monsters. Forested glades trailed downward toward the city.

I pulled my jeep to a stop facing east at the head of a thickly wooded ravine and turned off the motor. The only sounds were the distant barking of dogs, the crowing of roosters and the crackling of the cooling engine.

Far below, the ninety-nine islands of the Bay of Sasebo were faintly concealed by a shifting fog. As the haze began to lift, I could make out the forms of merchant ships and an aircraft carrier. On the eastern horizon the sun like a great golden disk pushed up from the glassy sea and climbed until its full and resplendent shape cast a glistening beam across the water.

Captured by the sight of the sunrise, I failed at first to notice a sound that wafted up to me from the woods below. When I listened carefully it seemed to be soft feminine voices, but as the breeze shifted the distant music vanished before returning again. For a moment I thought I was hearing an Easter hymn, but then decided I was simply hearing the wind, and because I knew it was Easter Sunday, my mind was serving up what I would have loved to hear. "If what I hear is Easter singing," I reasoned with myself, "there must be people celebrating Easter sunrise somewhere down in one of these ravines." Before I could give it further thought, I was making my way down the steep descent. It was as though my legs were not willing to wait for orders from my brain.

Deep into the wooded gulch, I jumped across a small stream and caught a glimpse of my reflection and came abruptly to a halt. It was time to stop and ponder. "Was I hearing an Easter morning hymn or were these singing voices an oriental version of the female sirens in Greek mythology who lured ancient sailors to their destruction?" That thought gave me pause and I stood motionless among the dark trees and waited for a sign to go forward or to retreat.

However, again I found my feet had made their own decision and my head seemed helpless to stop them. "Don't be foolish," I caught myself saying, "do sirens sing Easter hymns? There has to be someone down here." I figured that if there was, then they had climbed up from the city to celebrate Easter sunrise the same as I. Surely, they would not mind if I joined them. The woods became thick and I lost track of the singing. The ravine seemed to widen and I wondered if soon I would myself be lost. I crossed to the other side and began to return from where I had come. Suddenly the singing became very clear and I realized that I was again above them, whoever they were. In another moment I had come to the edge of a clearing and found myself behind a group of school girls sitting on the ground and singing under the direction of a woman who appeared to be dressed like a scout leader.

No one saw me until the hymn finished. Then the director, who was facing the girls and me, became hushed and visibly stiffened. The girls must have suspected something, for two of them turned to see what was claiming their director's attention. There was a murmur and a dozen faces turned toward me, startled.

I could now bow and withdraw, leaving them fearful and perplexed, or try to set them at ease. I decided on the latter. Removing my cap I went to the front where the director had stood only moments before and bowed from the hips, a very deep bow and all the while trying desperately to think what I could say in my impoverished Japanese. I was even resenting Kiyoshi for not teaching me more than his usual greeting forms. We never met in the morning as he only came by in the afternoon when school was over, and so I was not sure how to say "good morning." Still bowing with my palms together I greeted them *kon-nichiwa* "Good afternoon." I expected to see them laugh or at least giggle. They did neither and returned my greeting. I next tried *Omeni kakarete ureshii desu* "I am pleased to meet you." Again there was a response and stony, unsmiling faces were beginning to light up. Assuming they were students, perhaps they would know some English so I asked *Anata-wa eigo-o hanashi masuka?* "Do you speak English?" I was not at all sure if I had said it correctly, but a girl about Kiyoshi's age stood to her feet and replied "Yes, we speak Engrish. We girls from Kwassui Jogakko Methodist school Nagasaki. We hope you happy Easter." She dropped back to the ground folding her legs beneath her. I thanked her and there was again an awkward silence. Then a second girl stood "Atomic bomb bloke Nagasaki. We hope go study again Nagasaki."

I asked the director if I could sit with them while they sang again. The director came to the front and said "They know to sing their school song," which they then sang with verve and gusto, ending it by raising their arms and shouting *banzai!* By now everyone was smiling broadly.

When the singing finished, I wrote my name and gave it to the director who said her husband would come to the camp "and take rutenant Leyburn to their house," which he did. As I made my way back up through the ravine, my mind was besieged with questions about the stupidity of war and hate between nations. I felt that if people of different nations could simply know each other as people, we could solve lots of problems. I had gone out to celebrate Easter morning alone and little did I know that a whole community would be there to share it with me.

What an Easter morning this had been!

Good-Bye

Kiyoshi listened carefully when I related my story from Nagasaki. And when I told him I had been spiritually awakened by it, he suddenly stood up and said "You like Buddha. When people ask Buddha if he god or saint, he say 'No, he not god or saint; he awake.'" Kiyoshi was of the opinion that Nagasaki had been good for me and offered to take me to meet his uncle who would show me the way to become, as he put it, "with light on," meaning 'enlightened.'

From Uncle I learned the Four Noble Truths that the Buddha revealed after his enlightenment and the Eightfold Path, the steps for training in right living. Again and again the teachings of Buddhism and the Judeo-Christian faith commingled. The instruction in Right Conduct, for example, is the equivalent of the ethical parts of the Ten Commandments: do not kill, do not steal, do not lie, do not be unchaste. Concerning the last, I inquired of Uncle if young girls learned these. He replied that they were supposed to. I wondered, because on several occasions as Officer of the Day, a twenty-four hour duty, I was ordered by the commander to go through the barracks at night and chase out all the girls.

Kiyoshi also listened quietly as I related my Easter morning experience to him. He had not heard that Christians like to gather for worship at sunrise on Easter, but thought it a good idea in Japan where the emperor was the descendent of the sun. He covered his face and laughed with embarrassment when I told him I had greeted the girls with "good afternoon." He had not heard of the Methodist girls' school in Nagasaki.

He continued to read my Bible when he visited and often asked me to explain how the moon could turn to blood, and what was the meaning of *the pollution of idols* and how did one go about *soothsaying*, which he called "toothsaying." When he ventured into the epistles the language often became even more opaque and I was little help deciphering it. When he read 2 Corinthians 3:10 he pulled off his cap and scratched his head *For even that which was made glorious had no glory in this respect, by reason of the glory that excelleth.* He looked up in desperation and said "Christian religion hide behind hard word." The lesson I had learned from José López in Pataskala was back again. However, Kiyoshi had an alternative to offer: "I think Leyburn-san be happy follow Buddha way."

With the coming of summer Kiyoshi invited me to visit his family—mother, two older brothers and a younger sister. There was no father present, and not wishing to probe, I felt he would tell me if he cared to. Once when he asked about my family—he had written several letters to my mother—I told him that my father had died when I was an infant. He then said "My father die too, maybe Okinawa, maybe Iwojima."

Visits in the evenings with his family, their graceful gentleness, generosity of spirit and quiet composure contrasted radically with the daily clatter and ribaldry of a battalion of marines. In the beginning of our relationship I quite naturally felt paternalistic toward him, but before I left Japan, I had come to think of him as a younger brother. There were eleven years difference in our ages, but we had both matured.

The night before we sailed out of Sasebo heading back to San Diego, I said farewell to Kiyoshi's mother and siblings and thanked them for being my surrogate family. Kiyoshi slipped quietly from the room. I waited for him to return, but he chose not to and finally I left.

Early the following morning en route to the harbor, I recalled a scene that had occurred as the 69th replacement draft was loading aboard ship and heading for the Pacific. My platoon was the last to board. The first squad, sea bags hoisted on shoulders, were going up the gangway when I caught sight of two anxious looking marines dressed in khaki—the rest of us were in dungarees—hurrying down the ladder. The moment their feet touched the dock, they turned and ran. It was all too obvious: these two were jumping ship. They had carried their equipment to the first secluded spot, pulled out khaki uniforms from the top of their bags, changed clothes and got off the ship. I was behind them in hot pursuit. The dock at San Diego was long and straight with no place to turn or hide. Within a hundred yards I had overtaken the slower one who gave up without resisting. An approaching jeep of military police caught the other one. Both were taken aboard ship and locked up in the brig.

I knew that scene would not be repeated here on the Sasebo docks where some three thousand marines could not wait to get aboard the General G. M. Randall and sail for home. It was a joyful time, yet a bit sad for some. Girls had come to tell their lovers good-bye. Marines with fresh lipstick smudged on their faces waved from the decks.

Watching from the lower deck, I noticed a man on a bicycle pedaling slowly toward the ship. As he drew near, I could see he had a passenger behind him. Someone on the ship called out "Reyburn, your boy has come to tell you good-bye." Kiyoshi was shielding his eyes and scanning the shipside. Hurrying down the gangway I caught up with them. We had only a minute before the Randall's horn bellowed and the gangway began to lift.

From the stern I watched through moist eyes a boy and man standing beside a bicycle grow smaller and smaller until they faded from my vision, but never from my heart.

CHEROKEE
AND
LATIN
AMERICA I

Mexico and Beyond

While still on Maui with the Fourth Marine Division, and before being sent to Guam and Japan, I had begun to make plans to attend graduate school at the University of New Mexico in Albuquerque. From the telephone office in Wailuku I put through a call to the Modern Languages Department and was connected to Professor Francis Kerchville who encouraged me to have my undergraduate records sent to him. It would be October 1946 before I was discharged and able to enroll.

After completing the Master of Arts program and teaching college Spanish for a year, I was anxious to take up linguistics and anthropology at the University of Pennsylvania in Philadelphia. However, I had the summer of 1949 free and decided to make a land trip from Ciudad Juárez, Mexico to Lima, Peru. My itinerary would take me across Mexico and Central America to Panama where I would have to go by boat or air— there was no road through the Isthmus of Darien—then across Colombia, Ecuador and half of Peru. I took ample notes on the places I wanted to visit, equipped myself with a backpack and a US army hammock complete with canopy and mosquito netting, and on July first crossed the bridge over the Rio Grande River between El Paso, Texas and Mexico.

A second-class train ticket costing six dollars—there was no third-class—bought me the right to share a wooden bench with my traveling companions for the twelve hundred miles to Mexico City. The trip that took approximately forty-eight hours worked out to 23.5 miles per hour, which is a bit slow, but the cost, even in 1949, was hard to beat: .005 cents per mile. Although the train speed probably picked up to forty miles per hour at times, countless stops cut down our speed and gave the engineer and brakeman a chance to visit family and friends and to take on an occasional invigorating glass of tequila.

The wooden coach was painted a ghoulish grey and where the first-class cars enjoyed windows, ours were louvered wooden shutters. These could be placed in two positions: flapping in the wind or fastened shut. The closed position made the car too hot and the open position gave the roiling dust free entry. The tiny room labelled "W.C." had no water and the ablutions of the passengers took place along the tracks during stops. Experienced travelers carried their own water; the rest of us could buy warm beer and soft drinks from railside vendors whose menu consisted monotonously of hard-boiled eggs, tortillas rolled around fried beans, fried plantain, rice and overripe bananas.

It was always pleasant to feel the train wheels grind to a halt and hear the gurgling of the boiler, for it meant a reprieve from the constant shower of cinders that poured from the smoke stack and entered the coach.

Dawn found us north of Torreón where the mesquite covered hills gave way to a lovely fertile, irrigated valley, some of the best agricultural land in Mexico. By this time there had developed a warm camaraderie among the passengers who vied with each other in buying for their seat companions the best food and drinks sold by the catering crowd. After eating, the endless rocking motion of the train brought sleep and loud snores up and down the benches. The conductor never announced the name of the next stop, and no doubt did not always know where the engineer might plan to rein in his iron horse.

Near midnight on the second day the train jerked to a halt at Aguascalientes where I watched a man, three women and five blond children climb aboard. I observed them closely for some time. They spoke American English and the children were polite and well behaved. My curiosity having been aroused, I moved over and sat down next to the man. I learned from him that they were Mormon missionaries, a polygamous household who had been teaching Mormonism in Mexico for six years. When I remarked that polygamy was against the law in both the US and Mexico, the man replied "We don't teach that; we just live it." I must have dropped off to sleep, for when I awoke later they had detrained.

It was nearly 4:00 p.m. on July third when the train reached Mexico City. After entering the Federal District, it took nearly an hour to arrive at the central station. I hoisted on my pack and pushed my way through the Sunday afternoon crowds until I reached the small Hotel Museo. The dusty tramp who stared back at me from the bathroom mirror was soon in the shower watching the coffee colored water swirl down the drain. Back on the street again in a change of clothing, I found a small restaurant and had a hot meal and later slept profoundly with a rolling sensation until after ten the next morning.

On the street the morning newspaper headlines accused the PRI, the dominant political party, of scandalous and fraudulent elections of two senators. I spent three days visiting museums, the Teotihuacán ruins, and getting tourist passes for Central American countries.

My next stop was Oaxaca via Puebla and Tehuacán. The owner of the small hotel in Oaxaca, Nueva China, was indeed Chinese, señor Jam, married to a Mexican wife and having seven children. Alberto, señor Jam's twelve-year-old son, reminded me of Kiyoshi. Together we hiked the hills around Oaxaca and visited the ruins of Monte Albán. I was now one thousand four hundred miles south of my starting point at Ciudad Juárez and everywhere had met only friendly and helpful people.

While returning to my room after watching a game of jai alai, I came across two policemen standing over a body at the entrance to a park. One of them stopped me and asked if I knew the man on the ground who appeared to be either drunk or asleep, and, according to the police, had been assaulted and robbed. I knelt down and looked at the man's face and shook my head at the police. They handed me his moneyless wallet and I fished out his driver's license that identified him as sixty year old Stephen George Deblois of Philadelphia. The police, not anxious to take him to jail, asked if I would care for him. I agreed to do that if they would help me carry the man to the Nueva China where señora Jam brought a pad and blanket to make a pallet for him on the floor of my room.

After several hours of groaning, my ward began to sober up and needed to use the bathroom. I stood him to his feet and guided him to the bathroom, all the while he was muttering "who the hell . . . what the hell . . . ?" In the bathroom he fell to the floor so I dragged his pallet there and rolled him on to it.

By 2:00 a.m. his drunken stupor had abated enough that he got to his feet and groped about until he found a light switch. Seeing that I was asleep in the bed, be began to curse me and order me out of his room. It took some time for him to understand that I had not kidnapped and robbed him. He soon became very sick and vomited on the floor. Eventually he surrendered again to sleep. In the morning I returned his wallet and took him downstairs for coffee and tortillas. Remorseful for having allowed himself to get drunk and robbed, he seemed to be in need of some kind of confession. With tears in his eyes he told how his dear father, Kennedy Deblois, had been a former president of Eastern Baptist Theological Seminary in Philadelphia, and "would turn over in his grave if he knew about me . . . . Did you ever read the book John Bunyan, the Man?" I confessed that I had not read it nor heard of it. He became tearful again "My father, my own dear father, wrote that book." Eventually I was able to confirm his story.

I accompanied him to his hotel—quite swanky compared to the Nueva China. So that he could telegraph home for money, I gave him twenty dollars and departed. This was my first and only encounter with a prodigal American tourist.

On July 17 I reached Guatemala City where the streets were crowded and busy like in other large cities. The following day as I was leaving the hotel to walk to the city center, I was told that two of the main figures in the nation had been assassinated: General Araña, head of the army, and a Colonel Sandoval, chief of police. When I reached the capitol six blocks to the north, there was a large crowd milling about in the plaza. No one seemed to know if there would be trouble until about 4:00 p.m. when a single fighter plane began circling overhead and the plaza quickly emptied, people scurrying away in all directions. A light tank rumbled into the plaza firing over the heads of the crowds.

About midnight shooting broke out in the streets as insurgent forces were attacking the national army headquarters. Much of the firing came from rooftops where nationalist forces were attempting to keep people indoors to prevent them from joining the rebels. By 8:00 a.m. the firing had ceased and I ventured out with my camera to get a firsthand evaluation of the situation. I was making good progress in the direction of the capitol again when a burst of machine gun fire sent plaster cascading down about me. Crouching behind a large column, I was able to get a few photos of nationalists returning the fire of rebels up the street. When the incoming shots were too close, I managed to slip inside a nearby door standing ajar. This turned out to be a private residence and the owners, thinking I was a news correspondent, were anxious for me to tell them what was going on and what would happen next. They graciously served me coffee and we chatted while outside a machine gun was spitting hot shell cases against their door.

Calm returned to the city about 10.00 p.m. and the lights that had been off for two days came on again. In the morning people were out gathering up spent cartridges and observing bullet holes in their walls. Some shop windows had been broken by looters and many cars parked on the streets had shattered windshields and holes in their metal. This was my introduction to "revolution," but the Reyburn family, which did not yet exist, was to survive several major civil and military clashes as we marched through Babel in the years ahead.

The Panamerican Highway came abruptly to a halt at the edge of a forest some fifty miles south of San José, Costa Rica, at a small town with the large name of San Isidro del General. Anyone planning to go south of this point had to walk or fly. If you walked, you were best advised to ford the countless rivers in the morning because the summer rains let loose about 2:00 p.m. and raised the water level of even small streams to raging torrents, making it impossible to cross. Funds from Washington to continue the highway construction had dried up and engineer Russ Philips and his Costa Rican crew were kept on to look after the equipment. He had good maps of the projected highway and was able to advise me how best to plan my itinerary to Panama, some eight to ten walking days to the south.

A local Pentecostal preacher secured a guide, Don Bruno Quesada, and two skinny nags which I saw as poor descendents of Don Quijote's loyal Rocinante. Their bones were prevented from protruding only by the grace of their taut hides. Over the next three days I was to learn how tough these bony little beasts really were. Don Bruno was to accompany me as far as an area known as Buenos Aires, where, I was told, I would meet an American cowboy with a Costa Rican wife. Four hours south of San Isidro we met another American, Alexander Scotch, a biologist from New York state who had a collection of exotic birds, flowers, plants, snakes and insects. His small house was filled with his nature friends and he asked us to please avoid stepping on ants as we traveled south.

The first day on the trail the rains came early and I discovered what the local people meant when they spoke of the swollen streams becoming "bravo." Most of the streams were forty to fifty feet wide and only a foot or two deep before being transformed into turbulent and tempestuous rampages. My pack containing the hammock was tied securely behind the saddle and I could see the river in front of me was far swifter than I had expected.

Don Bruno had stopped to adjust his saddle. I remembered from seeing western films that cowboys often had to cling to their mount's tail to reach the other bank. I thought I heard Don Bruno call to me just as my little horse stepped into the rushing river. In less than a heartbeat he lost his footing and was swept away with the current. Out of the saddle but with one foot caught fast in the stirrup, I struggled to free myself as we were pitched up and down in the flooding rush of water. When finally my foot was free, I fought to reach the opposite bank, even while being whipped about like a helpless log. My only hope was to make it to the far bank and hope my poor beast would do the same, but I had lost sight of him in the churning waters.

I suddenly realized I had been carried to the far side by the current in the curve of the river and could grasp branches that hung out from the bank. I clung to them and bit by bit was able to haul myself to the shore where I climbed out and dropped exhausted to the ground. Pulling off my soaked clothing, I wrung out my shirt and pants and dumped the water from my shoes. As soon as I was able, I started downstream to look for the pony. After making my way in and out of trees and bushes for some time, I finally caught a glimpse of my little horse, his head down near his front hooves, his nose cut and bleeding. My pack that had been tightly secured behind the saddle now hung beneath his belly. His reins were torn away from the bit and the saddle hung on his dripping flank. As I approached, he bravely lifted his head and snorted. It was a joyful reunion, one I had almost lost hope of seeing.

Dark was closing in when we reached the place opposite our nearly fatal entry into the river. Don Bruno had gone; he had returned to tell Mr. Scotch that his compatriot had been washed away. With some sticks and banana leaves I managed to build a lean-to, wrapped myself in the wet hammock and settled down for a cold and hungry night. The rains had ceased and in the morning I looked up to see Don Bruno crossing the now calm stream. From his saddle bag he brought out a chunk of bread and a banana and handed them to me. Then he crossed himself and gave thanks: *Padre nuestro te doy gracias por haber salvado a Don William y a este caballito, guíanos . . . amen.*" This dear man never scolded me, but each time thereafter when we neared a stream—bravo or calmo—he made certain that he was in the lead.

That afternoon we came across several palm-thatched huts half hidden among banana trees. In a shelter where there were several other horses, we put our ponies and approached a hut whose door stood partly open and where smoke was oozing from the thatch. A woman appeared and looked out at us.

"*Buenas tardes, señora,*" my guide greeted her, "*¿Puede servirnos un cafecito?*"

The woman nodded and motioned us in as she disappeared into the smoky darkness of the windowless hut. The fire felt comforting against my damp clothing.

"What do you call this place?" I asked Don Bruno. From somewhere in the room several voices responded as one "*El Volcán.*" As my eyes adjusted to the dark, I noticed several pairs of bare feet dangling above me. These travelers had mounted a raised platform where the rising air could warm them. Someone inquired how far we were going, where we had come from and did we know how much rice was selling for in San José, the capital. Don Bruno answered all their questions. When he said we were headed for Buenos Aires, several voices said "*Saludos a Don Jorge,*" referring to George Burbage.

Assured that we planned to pay for our victuals, our inn keeper eventually produced two enamel plates of boiled eggs, rice, beans, fried plantain, and a tin cup of *agua dulce,* hot sugar cane juice. No five star hotel could have quenched my hunger pains better. We staked the horses where they could graze and I hung my hammock in the shelter where now goats and chickens had gathered to pass the night. Before sleeping, the last sounds of the tropical night were the croaking of frogs and the screech of a hoot owl.

Daybreak was greeted by the crowing of a rooster that had mounted the roof of the shelter just above my head. I lay quietly recalling the early morning sounds of my childhood so very far in the distance and yet so near in memory. After a cup of *agua dulce,* we were again heading south through the jungle. The sun, when there was an opening in the trees overhead, poured down rays of soothing delight, but in those pools of warmth insects were rife settling in eyes, ears and nostrils and causing the ponies to blow and shake their heads until they would stumble and fall to their knees.

About noon we came to the ranch house of a Maxwell Cone of Baltimore. He owned more than five thousand acres and kept an airstrip and plane to inspect his spread. Here again we were reminded to look up Mr. Burbage in Buenos Aires that turned out to be a vast expanse of rolling grasslands with forests growing only in the lower valleys. We passed a dilapidated wooden church that apparently had never been painted. The few Costa Ricans living there all knew Don Jorge and how to find his house, a plank building with corrugated metal roof and standing alone at the crest of a hill.

I was ill prepared for what I was to find at the Burbage household. However, being a student of languages and interpersonal communications, I was about to observe a new style for living. Mrs. Burbage was on the front porch of the house waiting for an Indian to decide he wanted to make a purchase at her little store. She explained later that the longer an Indian waits, the more serious are his intentions to buy something. Not being an Indian, I walked up to her porch and introduced myself.

"I am traveling through to Panama, and would like to know if the Burbages could give me meals and a room for two or three days." She shook my hand warmly and excused herself saying in Spanish that she would call Don Jorge who was milling some rice in the barn. I heard the electric generator go silent and in another minute Don Jorge entered through the back door of the house.

Without his ten gallon hat and cowboy boots, Burbage was well over six feet. I could not say how much over because he so seldom removed the hat or the boots. His companion, Josefina, came just above his elbow. A lively four year old girl named Sulma, whom Josefina was careful to identify as her niece, completed the Burbage family.

"Well, what the hell brings you down here?" Burbage asked as he extended his hand.

"I'm traveling through to Panama and would like to find a place to stay for a few days while I wash my clothes and get them dried." Josefina had returned to her client on the porch.

"You're welcome to stay here if you don't mind paying a dollar a day for your grub. I'll throw the room in free."

I agreed and went out to pay Don Bruno Quesada the amount we had contracted for before leaving San Isidro. We embraced, then he mounted and rode away to the north leading my pony. Burbage and I sat on the porch looking across the vast empty spaces to the east rimmed by hills that took on a bluish hue in the late afternoon. As he chewed on a cigarette he told me how he had gone from his home in California to the Panama canal before the war, saved his money and after the war came north to Costa Rica and now owned five hundred acres, a rice milling machine, a generator and several other pieces of machinery, some of it flown to him in bits and pieces. "The way I see it—what dja say your name was?—someday they will get this Panamerican Highway built, if them people in Washington will get off their asses, and you can ship a cow on the hoof right down to the canal or up to San José. Who knows, buddy, if I do well, I might even get me an airplane like Maxwell Cone. You meet him?"

Burbage lowered his voice and slid his chair closer. He was

in a confidential mood. "I've noticed if an American comes down in these parts, he's had trouble with a woman or with the law." He pushed his oversized hat back on his head, no doubt expecting to hear my confession as out-law or woman beater.

"So what was your trouble?" I asked.

He spat out his butt and wiped his mouth with the back of his hand. "Me, I ain't never had no trouble with the law." He winked and said no more. The Indian bought some colored beads and left. Burbage looked back at Josefina in the doorway and rubbed his stomach "Mama, chop chop." I realized I had as yet heard no conversation between them.

"You speak this damn spañol?" he asked. And when I asked him the same he replied "Hell no, anybody that's gona work, as I did, for the US government can damn well speak American. Josefina understands me and I understand her. There ain't a thought in her head that I don't know about. She deals with the locals and keeps our accounts. Spañol is a pretty good lingo for singing and getting drunk, but not much else." With that he pointed his fingers at his open mouth and Josefina called back "'OK.'" Supper would soon be on the table.

I was fascinated by the way they communicated with truncated words reinforced with hand signals and it was apparent to me that the Burbage household was living on the edge of something halfway between a deaf school and a Trappist monastery. After the meal Burbage poured himself a pint size glass of *aguardiente*, wolfed it down and dropped into his favorite rocking chair and was soon snoring under the brim of his hat. Josefina took advantage of her man's slumber to explain to me in detail that her relatives were making life miserable for her because she and Don Jorge were not properly married.

"I must tell you the facts and ask you to speak with Jorge. Perhaps the saints will open his heart and he will do what he should." She went on to explain that in two days a priest would come to the church in Buenos Aires and marry all the couples "who like Jorge and me are living without the blessing of the church." Her voice dropped to a whisper "and Sulma who I said was my niece," tears now moistened her dark eyes, "she is our daughter." She grasped my arm and pleaded "Please, oh please, convince Jorge that I cannot go on living in sin like this, lying about Sulma and saying I am a married woman. I am just a simple country woman without education, but our parents raised us children in the church to honor the saints and to know right from wrong. Oh please help me, Don William." Sulma, clutching her rag doll, came skipping into the room just as Josefina wiped her eyes and slipped into the kitchen.

I went out to the porch, perplexed, and began to reflect—*Dear God, did you send me down here to help a drunken tourist in Oaxaca, did you let me escape being shot on the streets of Guatemala City, rescue me from drowning in a flash flood then bring me here to convince this cowboy that living with a woman requires the rituals of a priest? Quite frankly, God, don't you have something more important that I can do to bring peace to the world?*

As I meditated the night hurled its darkness across the distant hills. All was silent save the snuffles inside in the rocking chair. Here and there a tiny light was visible. Overhead were the countless sparkling stars. *What about my little light? Wasn't I supposed to let it shine? Isn't my neighbor a person in need? Look at Burbage, he needs to sober up and Josefina needs a sympathetic spokesman in this household of grunts and gestures.* I knew what I needed to do.

It was late when George stirred and called out "Mama, coffee, coffee." When he had downed several cups and Josefina had retired, I went over my list of reasons why my hosts should be joined in holy wedlock. Two days later with mother and daughter astride the family horse, we marched to the church.

July 1980, thirty years after my intervention in the Burbage wedding, we read in the San José papers that the unsolved disappearance of George Burbage had, after a number of years, been cleared up. His private plane, which had crashed and burned in the jungles, had been located and his skeletal remains identified. The Panamerican highway had been built, and cattleman George had become a success and owned his own plane, just as he had said he might do.

Qualla Reservation

September 1949 I registered as a graduate student in the linguistics department of the University of Pennsylvania and very quickly realized how much linguistic science could have helped me in my efforts to study Chamorro and Japanese, and even Spanish. Moreover, in the years ahead I would be greatly aided by pursuing linguistic studies as I tramped my way through language after language on five continents.

In the spring of 1950 I was sent by the anthropology department to the Tuscarora Reservation at Sanborn in upper New York State to transcribe a legend known as "Crossing the Ice," a story that suggested the ancestors of the Tuscarora Indians, an Iroquois tribe, found their way to their present home by crossing a great body of ice. Before I could get down to work with Dan Smith, the raconteur, Clinton Rickard, the chief, clad in the vestments of a Plains Indian, complete with feathered headdress and bells that tinkled with his every step, escorted me to Niagara Falls and introduced me to the editor of the local newspaper. From the moment we entered the editor's office I was "the specialist in the Tuscarora language." Never mind that I had not yet heard one Indian speak a word of the tongue. Photos were taken of the chief and me and the paper printed an article explaining how I was about to prove that the Tuscarora had crossed the Bering Strait and had migrated from Siberia to New York State. Such was my introduction to Indian public relations exercises.

Having gathered vocabularies and narratives from Tuscarora,

Kiowa, Hopi, Laguna and Navajo, it was felt that I was ready to undertake a serious study of Cherokee in the field. Professor Zelig S. Harris, who had worked with Cherokee informants, knew this was a language with many unsolved problems and would be a challenge to anyone who was willing to tackle it. I was willing. He lent his own materials for me to study, supported my application for a grant from the American Philosophical Society, and gave generously of his time when, finally, I was putting together my doctoral dissertation on Cherokee verb morphology.

The Qualla reservation, home of the eastern band of Cherokees, lies in the heart of the Great Smoky Mountains of southwestern North Carolina. The eastern Cherokees were originally some three thousand who, at the time of the removal to Oklahoma (1838-39), escaped into the mountains of North Carolina and were eventually granted a reservation there. The Qualla reservation or boundary consists of fifty-six thousand acres. Today, there are about 11,800 people officially registered as Cherokee but only 7,000 reside on the reservation. In 1951 it was apparent that many of the younger generation were no longer speaking the language, and today it is estimated that not more than 600 still speak Cherokee. However, the language is taught to all in grades 1 through 6 and is optional in high school. Only a very few adults are able to read the syllabary.

The first problem a linguist faces in gathering language data, just as I had learned on Guam, is to obtain the help of a native speaker. A language informant needs to have a deep interest in his or her language, and patience to endure the stumbling attempts of the linguist to imitate and to record, particularly in the first few weeks, what the informant says. It is important, if the informant is good, that he or she persevere to the end of the project. If, on the other hand, the informant proves to be unsatisfactory, it is best to make a change early rather than late.

My two Cherokee helpers were superb, especially the second one, Annie Oocumma. Her patience and steadfastness contributed immensely to the success of our efforts. The first helper was Jess Youngdeer who as a youth had been an outstanding athlete and a teammate of the great Jim Thorpe when the two were students at the Carlisle Indian School in Pennsylvania. Jess was without a home when we met and was living with various relatives on the reservation. His sojourns with his kinsmen lasted a month or two and then he became restless and moved on to another. Because it was often difficult to locate him, I was delighted that he accepted my invitation to move in with me in Hoot Owl Cove where we shared the cooking and cleaning, such as two bachelors might attend to.

Jess had reached the age when older men are more given to memories than thinking of the present and making plans for tomorrow. Sometimes it was necessary to listen to tales of his youth before we could return to the task at hand. After supper in the evenings he often told me of his life, people he had known, opportunities he had failed to take and other disappointments. Occasionally he would fall asleep in his chair and I would not hear the end of the story for several days.

After two months together, Jess began to talk about relatives living in Big Cove and wondering how they were getting on. I suggested we drive to Big Cove to visit them and thus let him know if they were all right. (No one in Hoot Owl Cove or Big Cove had a telephone at that time.) When we were ready to make the trip, Jess appeared with the few worldly goods he had brought with him to my cabin. I did not need to inquire of his plans and he did not say anything about not returning with me. Our lives together had been a pleasure for me, but it was clear that Jess was ready to move on again.

Several times Jess had mentioned Enoch Welch as a person who read and spoke good Cherokee, but I did not realize that he was in this way giving me notice of his plan to leave. When later I found Enoch, he was holding forth in a small Wesleyan Methodist church and preaching in Cherokee, until I entered. He then switched to English so I would understand. When I asked if he would be interested in helping me with the language, he referred me to his sister, Annie. I later realized that Enoch seemed to have one subject that never escaped him. Years earlier while drunk he had crushed a man's skull with a rock and had served time in the penitentiary. In nearly every Sunday sermon Enoch reached a point where he retold the skull crushing episode, tears streaming down his cheeks.

Annie, who was in her mid fifties, lived alone in a hillside cabin within walking distance of the Cove. She seldom left her cabin and her only neighbors were a few chickens and a cat. She daily read the Cherokee New Testament, was intelligent and, when she understood what I was attempting to do, was able to provide a wealth of illustrations for each grammatical point I was working around. Although she had little formal schooling, she had a good command of English and a healthy respect for her own language. Sometimes while in the midst of trying to ferret out some obscure verb suffix, she would rock back in her chair, breathe deeply and ask "Is there such a thing as `psychology' and can you explain to me what it is?" I was glad for opportunities like this because in this way we were often teaching each other. I suspect she was disappointed that I did not become a speaker of Cherokee, but she admitted once that "before working with you, I had no idea my language was so difficult."

To give just a taste of Cherokee difficulties consider the following: English has seven subject pronouns: I and we, you singular and plural, he, she, it, and they. By contrast Cherokee has eleven: I, I and another person (we 1), I and more than one other person (we 2), I and you singular (we 3), I and you singular plus others (we 4), you singular, (you 1), you dual (you 2) and you plural (you 3), he/she animate, it inanimate, they animate and inanimate. To make these eleven subject pronouns more difficult, each form changes according to a complex set of rules. English has one way to say "we" but in Cherokee the speaker has to choose one out of four, depending on the persons that must be included or excluded.

Again, Cherokee has twelve object pronouns. Consider, for example, the verb *hit* to illustrate: "you hit me and one other" (us 1), "you hit me and several others" (us 2), "he hit me and you singular" (us 3), "he hit me, you and several others" (us 4), "he hit you singular" (you 1), "he hit you dual" (you 2), "he hit you plural" (you 3), "he hit him or her animate," "he hit it inanimate," "he hit them plural animate" (them 1), "he hit them plural inanimate" (them 2). In this case *us* has four definitions, *you* has three, and *them* has two.

In English we speak of *having* something and the verb *have* does not change if we say we have a stick, a paper, a book or a drink. But in Cherokee many verbs like *have* change their form if the object is animate or inanimate and the inanimate objects are thought of as long (stick), flexible (paper), indefinite (book) or liquid (drink). Corn whether eaten on the cob or after being cut from the cob is considered long. Accordingly the verb to eat a long object has one form. When you can corn the verb to can expresses processing a round object. The word to remove corn from a can is still expressed in terms of removing a round object. However the verb to eat the corn taken from the can is to eat a long object because the original corn came from a cob and was thought of as being long.

All Cherokee verbs have prefixes and suffixes and the stem of the verb is often a compound word made up of various meaningful parts. Even nouns are most often made up of component elements having individual meanings. For example, the word for horse is literally 'he carries-heavy-things,' a possum is a 'smiling-pig' and my wife is 'she-cooks-for-me.'

The Cherokee writing system is a syllabary meaning that each letter represents either a vowel or a combination of a consonant and a following vowel. Accordingly, the Cherokee "alphabet" has eighty-five letters or signs. The creation of this writing system was the work of a Tennessee Cherokee named Sequoya. At first this uneducated man tried to create a sign for each word, but eventually realized that he could not remember what his bags full of wooden symbols represented. He then developed a sign for each syllable and thus eighty-five symbols were adequate and could easily be learned. He suffered for his efforts for he had given up farming and hunting to concentrate on his alphabet. Enemies thought him crazy and burned his house down. In all, he spent nearly twelve years getting what he called "singing pages" for his people. By 1825 he had mastered his project and the syllabary was complete. There followed a period of years in which the Cherokee slowly took to the reading and writing of their language.

Books of the New and Old Testaments were translated between 1829 and 1953. The entire New Testament was printed in 1860 and revised in 1951. The Cherokee writing system was used in nearly all publications, which were numerous. For example, during the forty years following the completion of the syllabary, the printing press of Dr. Samuel A. Worcester, one of the principal translators of the Cherokee scriptures, turned out some fourteen million pages of Indian language texts, mostly in Cherokee.

Cherokee Wedding

I awoke early, excited by the news in Marie's letter that she expected to arrive in Cherokee that very day. The cabin in Hoot Owl Cove had been swept and mopped, the cobwebs brushed from the corners and a roll of toilet paper had replaced the pages of the Asheville Citizen in the outhouse. The mossy old stones around the spring had been replaced by clean ones from the creek; the back door now had bright brass hinges holding it straight, and the leaky roof above the table had been patched. Never had Henry Otter's cabin been more ready to welcome a bride.

The day seemed endless until about dusk when a car made its way slowly along the rutted road toward the Bradley barn. The path from the cabin to the road went by the spring and led out into a large pasture where cattle grazed. The land rose and fell and finally the path ended beside the barn where a stile put you over the fence and on to the roadside.

Six year old Liz Bradley, who had watched the approaching car and had seen me running across the pasture, recalled this scene many years later: "I was watching that thar car comin up our road. I figured they was lost, but then I seen this gal get out jess as Bill jumped down from the stile. Boy, I seen some huggin and kissin! I yelled for my older sister Midge to come and look. Wow, we'uns didn't get to see goins on like that much. Bill waved for us to come down to the road. He had smiles all over his face. We knowed it was Marie, the gal he'd been looking for. She gave each of us a big hug and we knowed Bill had picked the right kind of a gal. As soon as that car drove off, Bill scrambled over the stile and Marie follered him. When she was on the other side, she jess jumped right into Bill's arms and he toted her off across the pasture. We'uns stood thar with our mouths open. Ain't never seen nothing like that before or since."

Marie was the second child and only daughter born to Nurse Pearl Lateer and Doctor Paul Williams Fetzer. Later Pearl died giving birth to their fourth child, a third son. Growing up between brothers, Marie learned to defend herself and beat boys at their own games. She became an outstanding basketball player, swimmer, tennis player, and was elected president of the Reidsville, North Carolina, high school graduating class of 1942. She began college with the aim of going, like her father, into medicine, but after observing her first surgery in the Cook County Hospital in Chicago, she became convinced that medicine was not her calling.

Raised in the South long before the civil rights movement, Marie found herself in opposition to the racism in America. Growing up in the Bible Belt she became aware of the conflict between the ideals of Christian brotherhood and the harsh realities of segregation. Being a people-oriented person, she found the study of anthropology gave her insights into human behavior and was an early advocate of cultural studies for prospective missionaries. With this in mind she pursued graduate studies at Columbia University in New York before teaching at Wheaton College.

Marie and I had met in the summer of 1950 while studying linguistics in the Summer Institute of Linguistics program at the University of Oklahoma. After resigning her teaching post, and completing the second summer course at Norman, she had come to Cherokee to join me in a pilgrimage that would span many years, five continents, and bring us four children, and a myriad of experiences, some of which are recounted in this book.

The first item on our agenda was the planning of the Fetzer-

Reyburn wedding. There was the usual formality of a marriage license obtained at the Swain County courthouse in Bryson City, and a Wassermann test at the public health department. The Reverend J. Dennis, resident Methodist missionary on the Qualla reservation, allowed as how he could make himself available on Friday afternoon "not before four in the afternoon and not after five. I'll be on my way to the Piggly Wiggly in Bryson—Henrietta don't like for me to be gone too long. Y'all know how that is . . . No, I guess y'all don't." We agreed to be at the Birdtown Methodist church not later than four.

Our next job was to decide who would be willing witnesses to this august occasion. We had many Cherokee friends, but we also wanted this to be an interracial affair. For that purpose no one could help more than Matilda Mathis, an elderly mountain Caucasian woman and neighbor who had a household of white, Indian, and black offspring. She had never explained how this integrated family came about and we saw no point in inquiring. Our closest neighbor in the cove was Lizzy Cucumber, an oak strip basket maker, who had a number of children and grandchildren and we would not know how many would want to go to the wedding until they started piling in the old Willys jeep. Our most important guests would be Annie Oocumma, Bill's language helper, her brother Enoch Welch and his family and the Homer Powell family. Homer and Fanny Powell were Cherokee singers, a vital element in any church event.

Having the only vehicle in the cove, we organized a shuttle service between Hoot Owl and Birdtown and by 4:00 p.m. six benches of the little church were packed The church stood in the woods well off the highway beyond a stream. It was a typical country church with belfry, one that had once been white but had slowly turned grey with age. The shingles that had once served their purpose were now beginning to slide away and leave openings in the roof. The front door was entered by mounting four fragile wooden steps, somewhat dislodged from the foundation.

Inside, the center aisle was flanked by rough pine board benches, the kind that dig into the backbone and keep people awake. A potbellied castiron stove darkened one corner under a stovepipe that wormed its way through a yawning hole in the south wall. Phoebes that darted in and out of the hole had built nests near the stovepipe. Even in the heat of summer, the entire room smelled of last winter's smoke and ashes. It was this odor that reminded us that we had done nothing to decorate the church, not even to bring a vase of wild flowers. Nevertheless, we were happy that the Birdtown church would remind us in years to come of the simple way of life we aspired to.

By four-fifteen the ceremony was ready to begin, that is, all except the Reverend Dennis. By four-thirty we were thinking that the Reverend was probably pushing his shopping cart somewhere. Suddenly like a theophany, he materialized, book in hand motioning for Marie and me to take our places before him. Eyes heavy with sleep began to open and babies, who had howled on mothers' laps, were now nursing peacefully. It looked at last as though this marital journey was ready to set its course.

"Dearly beloved: We have come together in the presence . . ." From the rush of his reading, it was clear the Reverend Mr. Dennis had other promises to keep. *". . . of God to witness and bless the joining together of . . . in Holy Matrimony."* Behind us we heard a stirring, then a creaking of the floor boards. *"The union of husband and wife in heart, body . . ."* I felt a hand grasp my left arm. Matilda Mathis was at my elbow with a panicky look in her one good eye. I lowered my head to hear what she had to say, but it was unnecessary. In a rattling screech she reminded everyone that she had been sitting as long as she could without her snuff. "I wasn't gonna say nothin bout it but this feller (she motioned toward the preacher) took all day gettin' here. I been to church where people comes in late, but ain't never been to one where the preacher don't 'member to come." The Reverend Dennis kept his cool and squint-eyed Matilda over the tops of his specs. She

put her mouth to my ear and whispered "Get out thar to your car and look for my snuff now."

I excused myself and slipped out the side door. When I rejoined the happy throng, Matilda cuddled her snuff can to her breast and the solemn service swung once more into action. Behind us the door opened and closed several times and I was afraid some of our guests had decided to go outside. When at last my curiosity could no longer be restrained, I turned to see that none of our friends had moved. On the contrary, they had been joined by a bench load of tourists who had noticed the little church and had decided to drop in.

The *will-you-have-this-man-to-be-your-husband* question sailed forth smoothly from the Reverend's lips and was answered in the affirmative. The pastoral bifocals rotated toward me, "*Will you, William, have this bedded woman to be your wife . . . ?*" I scanned the preacher's face for some admission of humor and waited a moment for him to amend the question. His face, however, was expressionless and he plowed straight down the row, his eyes trailing his finger through the text. I felt an elbow nudge me in the right side and thought perhaps Matilda had run out of snuff again. Then I saw Marie biting her lip to retain her besmirched dignity—bedded woman, indeed!

The Reverend was again rushing toward the finish line and would not be deterred. "*Will all of you witnessing these promises do all in your power to uphold these two persons in their marriage?*" The Indian congregation replied with stony silence and the preacher clapped his book shut, a shot that reverberated across the room sparking slumbering babies into screams. Ejecting himself from his clerical robe, Mr. Dennis shook our hands and waved good-bye as he hurried out the door "Y'all enjoy your marriage, won't you. I'd stay but this is Friday and my wife likes me to get the shopping done early." His car rumbled away, clattering the loose boards in the bridge. The Cherokee singers, led by Homer Powell, tuned up and soon the little congregation was clapping and singing. At last there was something to be in church for.

In 1968 we returned from Africa to Cherokee with our four children, having told them they would see the little church where mom and dad were joined in the bonds of holy wedlock. It was a bright sunny afternoon when we walked from highway 19 over to the Birdtown Methodist church. The bridge was new, the river only half as wide, the trees were gone. The church, we learned, had burned to the ground and the only remnant were some concrete steps that had replaced the earlier ones and now stood half hidden in a cornfield. We mounted them, mom and dad full of memories, and four laughing children not at all certain there had ever been a church.

In the village of Lolo in Cameroun, West Africa, the old men of the clan had been explaining to me the details of their marriage ceremonies: the paying of the bride price to the family of the bride, the long and complex negotiations required to transfer the ownership of the offspring to the groom's family, the days of preparation for the wedding feast, and many other such events.

After hours of describing a typical wedding in Lolo, a clan elder silenced his brothers: "Now, we will learn how a white man takes a wife." Pointing at me with his lower lip, he added, "Our ears await your words."

It was clear that I was about to relate something that would be beyond their imaginations. I had already failed in my attempts to explain the Russian Sputnik that was then in the news, and I was certain my marriage would be equally obtuse. Even to explain how many days down river in a dugout I was from my father's village could only impress them as a poor attempt to tell a lie.

At any rate I tried to tell them in some detail how I had met my bride, how I did not meet her brothers first, did not negotiate a bride price with her village fathers, did not prepare a feast of goats and pigs, did not take her to live in my father's village and confessed the many other failings that cast serious doubts on the legitimacy of my children, the worth of my wife and the morality of my very existence.

All the while I spoke there was a continuous sigh of grief and despair, hands clasped to the crowns of heads in a gesture of shame. When I finished, the clan elder hoisted his cane and a hush fell over the men's club house. "We all know," his eyes moved from person to person, "that a woman fish lays eggs in quiet waters then swims away and does not look back." He lifted a long finger in the air to make his next point. "Who comes then? A man fish swims to the eggs and lays his sperm on them." He made a wide sweep with his arm. "That man fish too swims away and does not look back. Not long later, these baby fish start wiggling away. Some are eaten by big fish, some get sick and die, and a few grow up to become big fish and they start that kind of life all over again."

The elder watched the faces of his audience while he scooped a hot coal from the fire to rekindle his pipe. "Our old ears have heard something new today." Spitting with distaste into the fire, he concluded, "We have heard that white men marry just like fish."

Gentlemen Wanted

The four-wheel drive jeep station wagon that had shuttled our friends to the wedding at the Birdtown church had been offloaded on the customs dock in Guayaquil, Ecuador and appeared to be in satisfactory condition. However, a closer look inside revealed that my tools, tire jack and other items for the road that had been carefully packed under the seats were no longer there. When I reported our loss to Marie, she showed me in a newspaper report that tons of steel had disappeared from the New York docks. At least, we still had the car, the wheels and even the spare.

While waiting for the car, Marie was busy studying Spanish and I was again delving into an Indian language—Quechua, spoken by several million people in the Andean region of Ecuador. In fact, this vast language in its various dialects extends from Colombia in the north to Northern Argentina in the south— a considerable contrast to the six or seven thousand Cherokee speakers on the Qualla reservation.

As soon as the car had cleared customs and arrived in Quito, the capital, I made arrangements to obtain an Ecuadorian driver's license, thinking I would simply fill in a form, present my U.S. license and be given a new one. When, however, I presented myself to the license bureau in downtown Quito, I learned that the Ecuadorian system would require time, money, a test and, most of all, lots of patience. When at last I obtained the application form, there were fiscal stamps, revenue stamps, road safety stamps, municipal stamps, and treasury stamps to be affixed and each stamp was sold in a different building that was open for business at different hours and located in different parts of the city. There being no city maps, it was necessary to inquire from one place to the next and hike up and down the hilly cobblestone streets of the capital whose elevation is above eight thousand feet.

The streets were a challenge to the pedestrian as well as the motorist. They were narrow, crowded, and busy with donkey carts, Indian bearers, exhaust-spewing trucks, cars, and people going in every direction at once. Horns blared ferociously in the midst of a sea of exhaust fumes. Before pasting half the stamps on the form, I questioned the desirability of driving and was about to give up the whole idea.

For three mornings I had presented myself in this bureaucratic jungle waving my application, now colorfully decorated, at one office and then another. No one seemed to know where I should go next or cared to inquire what I was after. To gird up my courage for yet another assault on this beehive of bureaucracy, I marched up and down a dimly lit corridor wishing I had brought my marine corps uniform to Ecuador. Perhaps then I would have become visible.

That was the case of my friend Hector Masih in Pakistan who had taken his son, Salim, to the Lahore drivers' examination office to apply for a license for each of them. Arriving sharply at 8 a.m., they found the office jammed with applicants shouting, pushing and waving forms at two harassed clerks. Seeing that it was futile to wait, Hector and Salim went home and, after putting on their military uniforms, returned to the bedlam that was the motor vehicle department. Immediately one of the clerks spotted the two officers and disappeared only to reappear in a moment with his superior in tow.

While Hector and Salim watched, the clerk mounted the counter and shouted over the heads of the crowd. As he motioned for the two to come forward, the sea of aspiring drivers parted and the two officers passed through to the front where they were then escorted to a V.I.P lounge and served tea.

Hector, the father, sipping his tea, asked if a road test would be required. The superintendent's eyes blossomed with surprise. "Sir, how could I require a pilot in the Pakistan Air Force to prove he can drive a car? Is not the flying of a fighter plane at the speed of light in defense of our country a much greater feat?"

Hector, who had been an educational officer before retiring, had never flown a plane. When the stamps were affixed to the forms and Hector had scratched his name on them, he informed the eager bureaucrat that his son also needed a license. The man replied, all the while ogling the row of ribbons on Salim's chest, "I am very certain if the father can fly a plane, the son can drive a car." He laid his hand on his heart. "It is only logic to know its conclusion, don't you agree?"

When the papers were in order, the sea of faces ebbed back again. Father and son plied their way through to the street and to their waiting car.

I was reluctant to leave my application for fear it would be swallowed into the stacks of dusty papers that lined the office shelves. So, I marched into an office and held it out before a clerk who eyed it as if I were slipping him some recondite piece of revolutionary propaganda

¿Es Usted William?

Sí, señor.

Turning the form over he pointed to the place where the examining officer was to sign. Then he pointed straight up and said, "*Oficina 103b.*"

In room 103b I found six or seven men seated along one wall reading newspapers. I assumed they were waiting in line, but if they were, it would be the first such line I had witnessed. At the only desk in the room, also hidden behind a newspaper, was someone, I perceived, because of a column of cigarette smoke drifting ceilingward.

I addressed the smoke, *Buenos días.* There was no response so I tried again. Slowly the paper descended, revealing a figure in uniform but who continued to read until finally he folded the paper and called out: "Son of a whore, Gonzalez. The Peruvians are stealing our country again." Curses and condemnation burst forth from along the wall, condemning the Peruvians as thieves, cutthroats, brigands and cowards. When the excitement subsided, I dangled my application before the officer's eyes.

¿De qué se trata, Señor? he asked, lighting up again.

"I need a driver's license," I replied.

"Don't you have one?"

"Yes, but it is from the United States" I explained and showed it to him, hoping he would accept it in lieu of an examination.

He scanned it as he arose slowly from his chair "You know that it is not lawful to drive in this country with a foreign permit?"

"Yes, sir, that is why I have made out this application," still bobbing it like bait before him.

"You need to know that our examinations are more strict than in most countries. We require a thorough road test and proven knowledge of all rules and regulations pertaining to the operation of a vehicle." Examining me carefully he inquired, "Is your vehicle equipped with a certified operational fire extinguisher?"

I was surprised by the question and asked if he could supply me with a manual of the rules.

"A manual?" He hesitated as if trying to recall if he had ever seen one. "Certainly not. You learn from experienced drivers." Motioning toward the row of newspapers, he said, "Myself and these officers are at your service to guide and instruct you in the proper handling of any vehicle, be it truck, bus, van, sports car or other."

"Thank you, sir, when can I take the exam?"

He removed a stub of a pencil from his inside shirt pocket and tapped it against the visor of his cap. "Would you be ready in two weeks?"

I was getting tired of being put off. "What about today?" I asked.

He took a step back, "Today, this very same day?"

"Yes, right now."

He pulled a small notebook from his jacket pocket and flipped through the pages, then turning to the row of readers, he asked, "*Señores*, is there anyone who would be free to examine this man?" Several of the papers were lowered "What day would you expect to be examined?" one of the men asked looking my way.

The officer replied, "The *señor* has asked that it be done today, *ahora mismo.*" The wall of newspapers went up again. Then one man slowly folded his paper. *"OK, estoy listo."* By the time we reached the outside door there were two examiners, their papers tucked under their arms, and the uniformed policeman.

Out on the street I invited my examining board to climb in. The two plainclothesmen got into the rear seat but the officer walked around the car inspecting it carefully and noting the foreign license plate and the size of the tires. Then he motioned for me to unlatch the hood. He lowered his head into the engine compartment and I thought surely he was searching for the fire extinguisher which, fortunately, he did not mention again.

When the engine cranked, and I was waiting instructions, an attractive woman approached the car and spoke softly to the officer. She said she had not seen him for several days and wondered how he was. Would she be seeing him soon? He agreed that she would and tipped his hat to her. As we pulled into the busy street, he confided, "She is what we call `a lady of the night.' Rather lovely, don't you think?"

We shared the narrow cobblestone street with donkey carts, Indians trudging along under massive loads strapped to their backs, buses, cars and trucks. It all brought back memories of my driving through Omura, Japan, on my way to Nagasaki, six years earlier. At the first intersection I was instructed to stop and allow pedestrians to cross. A line of vehicles behind me, anxious to keep moving, began blowing their horns until the noise was

deafening. The officer thrust out his arm and motioned for them
to cease, but they continued. He got out and walked back along
the street casting threatening looks at each driver. His maneuver
brought a break in the din until, as we started forward, a donkey
cart piled high with merchandise stalled in the intersection. The
driver attempted to get the little beast to move by jabbing its
flank with a stick, but the small burro, after lunging forward
several times, slipped on the smooth stones and sat down in its
traces, closing its eyes to the beating and cursing laid on it by its
driver. By now vehicles from all four directions unleashed the
full ruckus of their trumpets. Tapping the policeman beside me
on the knee, I shouted "Why don't you go assert your authority?"

"My authority?" he called back. "I am not a traffic cop." He
calmly put another cigarette into the holder and settled back to
wait for the world to put itself right. "This kind of thing is the task
of the traffic department." He turned for support from two heads
in the back seat that were bobbing in agreement.

Since it was evident that we would be delayed, my examiners
decided to talk business. "What make of vehicle is this? What
year of manufacture? Does it have four—wheel drive and how
many kilometers has it run, and, if you want to avoid traffic like
this, we will give you a thousand Sucres and you can peacefully
ride the bus or take a taxi." I did not respond. The hullabaloo in
the street blared on. The burro managed to get to its feet and
bellowed out a pitiful hee-haw, a cry for help to one of its own
kind. The driver unhitched the animal and dragged it to the side of
the street. Four Indians pushed the cart to the side and the traffic
began to trickle forward amidst the stink of manure mixed with
choking exhaust fumes. My front seat companion put his hand on
the steering wheel. He seemed to be urging me to make a decision.

"Wait, this is an important moment for you. We offer you a
reasonable price for the car." Cars were hard to obtain and
extremely expensive. "We will take you to the bus station so you

can go home." He shook his head in despair as he waved away the scene before us. "It is a shame for a *caballero* 'gentleman' to have to drive in this uncivilized place, don't you agree?"

"No, not at all, I rather enjoy it; it teaches me patience."

He turned his head away from me and moaned to the other two "It teaches me patience!" Nothing more was said about buying my car.

We soon found ourselves confronted by a religious procession streaming out of the San Francisco church. The three removed their hats and crossed themselves as the figure of the saint was carried through the street. The cop at my side was stirred by the religious pageant unfolding before us. He began to discourse:

> "Look about you, my friends, what you behold is the grandeur of the ancient city of Quito whose roots go back to our Inca ancestors. Think of the magnificent city square bounded by the cathedral, the palaces of the president of the Republic, and the archbishop of our mother church, and the municipal house. Think of the gold that covers the altar of the Compañía de Jesús." He began to chant, "Ay, Quito, most ancient of all the South American capitals. Ay, Pichincha, our majestic volcano that has not erupted since . . ." He paused and pointed to the two men. One said 1667 and the other said 1665. An argument broke out. The officer fumbled in his jacket pocket until he drew out a whistle and blew it. "The correct answer is 1666."

Feeling that I had long been forgotten in my quest for a driver's license, I continued driving without commands until well into the countryside. Then, as if he suddenly remembered, the front seat examiner ordered me to pull to the side of the road and turn off the motor. The pair in the backseat had fallen asleep and were propped against each other.

"Now suppose," he said, "it is night, a very dark night, and you see another vehicle—could be a bus, a truck, another car—coming toward you. What are you required to do?"

Having driven in Ecuador and having ridden in buses, I replied, "Well, sir, I would turn off my lights, put on my park lights and proceed with caution." A snore from the backseat unsettled the examiner who snapped his fingers and scolded his colleagues for falling asleep while on the job.

"Pay attention to our candidate's responses. You may learn something about why there are so many nighttime accidents on the road." Turning again to me he said in a remorseful tone, "*Señor*, that is not the correct answer." He carefully snuffed out his cigarette, slipped it from the long stem holder and placed it in the cup of his hand, thus saving it for a later smoke. "Now pay close attention to what I tell you; it will save your life and avoid all manner of road tragedies." He coughed and spat out the window, not noticing that it was closed. "If you are a gentleman," he accented each syllable of *ca-ba-lle-ro* by thumping the back of his cupped hand against my shoulder, "you will pull your vehicle to the side of the road and come to a full stop." He rammed both boots firmly against the floorboards and reared back in his seat. "Like this, then what do you do? It is at this precise moment that you turn out your headlights."

Twisting his misshapen cigarette butt back into its holder, he lit up and relaxed, pleased that he had rescued me from my wretched ignorance of the rules of the road.

"I understand, *Capitán*, but is there not still a problem?" I asked.

"*¿Problema?* Not in the least if you follow my instructions. Did I not tell you back in the office that experience is the manual of instruction? We learn from those who know."

"But what if the other driver follows those same instructions? How can one gentleman meet another in the night and still reach their destinations?" I was genuinely perplexed.

The examiner pulled his cap over his ears and exhaled a sigh of exasperation. Would this feckless gringo never understand? *"Señor,* you still fail to comprehend the rock bottom fundamental upon which all other truths repose." I was now expecting a philosophical discourse. "You must understand that in this country there are no gentlemen!" He brushed off his hands in a gesture of finality, then added, "It has been a most trying examination and the Adam's apple is suffering from the most severe drought." He turned back to his two drowsing companions. "What must we do to redeem the day?"

A conference ensued and it was voted three to nil that we should return to the city by way of the *Cantina Los Tres Caballeros* where dry throats could be refreshed and my application signed and approved.

Annie

Before the death of the Inca Huayana Cápac, the great empire was divided between his two sons. Huáscar, who was given the southern region, ruled from Cuzco, and Atahualpa, who inherited the northern kingdom, reigned in Quito. The two brothers fought over control of the empire and Atahaulpa was victorious but the Spaniards arrived in 1533 and put Atahualpa to death. The first cry of independence was heard in Quito on 10 August 1809, although independence from Colombia was not achieved until 1830. Nevertheless, Independence Day has always been celebrated on *el diez de Agosto*.

10 August 1953, was the day Annie Reyburn decided to celebrate her independence from her mother's womb. We passed the word to Dr. Paul Roberts of the medical department of radio station HCJB and to nurse Carol Rosales of the Lutheran mission, and by noon we were all at the private clinic in Quito known as *La Clínica Pichincha*, bearing the name of the highest volcanic peak in the area of the capital. By 2:00 p.m. everything seemed set for the delivery. Labor pains were down to a minute apart. Marie was calm, but then we saw the doctor rush by with an irritated look, hesitate, as if wanting to tell us something, and then hurry off. In the hall I met Carol, the nurse, who also seemed agitated. "Carol," I asked, "what's going on? Roberts is in a stew about something." Carol was reluctant to answer. Then she whispered, "They can't find the keys to the delivery room."

After all, it was the national holiday. Most of the clinic staff was home or out celebrating. Who knows where the keys may have been put or who had carried them off? Roberts soon came along with the cleaning man who had a batch of keys chained to his belt. In Ecuador people in the cities have an obsession with keys and locking things up. The man tried key after key while we joined the cue at the door, hoping each next key would be our *abracadabra.* He pulled, pushed and shook the door as he neared the end of his wad. Finally, with one last key and one last shake the reluctant door obediently swung inward.

I had hoped to stay beside Marie, but the doctor, not wishing to add to the septic conditions of the place, ushered me out and closed the door. Standing by a window and gazing upward to the great extinct volcano, the words of the Psalmist seemed so real:

> *I lift up my eyes to the hills*
> *From whence does my help come?*
> *My help comes from the LORD*
> *Who made the heavens and earth*
> *. . . The LORD will keep*
> *your going out and your coming in*
> *from this time forth and*
> *Forever more.*

When finally the door opened, I went in and found Marie sweating, but smiling. Carol was holding the tiny girl sucking determinedly on her little fist. We had agreed, if it was a girl, she would carry the name Annie in memory of our beloved Cherokee friend. In contrast to Annie Oocumma, who had never traveled outside of Swain County, North Carolina, this little Annie would travel up and down South America, cross the Atlantic to Europe and grow up in Africa. She was the first of four children to join Marie and me on our march through Babel.

In the eastern jungles of Ecuador I had been recording the Quechua dialect to compare it with that spoken in the Andean area. We had made arrangements with missionaries Jim and Betty

Elliot to send a dugout canoe and two polers to meet us and transport us downriver six hours to their location at the confluence of the Puyo and Pastaza rivers. The Pastaza is one of Ecuador's largest rivers and has its headwaters high in the Andes where the snows of Mount Chimborazo feed it before it flows southeasterly out of Ecuador and into Peru to the Marañón that empties into the Amazon.

The Puyo River, in most places thirty to forty feet wide, was at times wild and strewn with boulders. Other parts were calm and we often moved along carried by the current and the expert steering of our two Quechua boatmen. Although the differences between the Quechua spoken in the Andes and that spoken here in the jungles were considerable, we were able to communicate.

Indians living along the riverbanks often stopped their activities to watch as we passed and curious children ran to the bank to get a better look. Our polers told us that people in this area had never before seen a white baby. Annie, six months old, sat peacefully in her mother's lap even when water was splashing over the sides. Marie, the expert swimmer, had no fear or doubt of her ability to keep the two of them afloat if we were pitched into the river. Only once did anyone go overboard. I was getting to my feet to change position when the dugout turned sideways and was rammed into a submerged rock. In an instant I was in the cold water to my neck and the stern poleman reached out his pole and pulled me to the boat. I clambered over the side soaked like a wet cat, all the while watching Marie doubled over with laughter and Annie excitedly clapping her tiny hands. I made certain that I never stood up to change positions again. Our Indian guides were too polite to join in the laughter, but I have no doubt they told the story around the fires at night and all delighted in the scene of this landlubber being fished out of the cold water.

After a most enjoyable two-day visit with Jim and Betty, we said farewell to Jim for the last time. A year later, he, along with four colleagues, was killed by Waorani (Auca) Indians while attempting to establish friendly relations with them.

We were again in the same piragua but now headed upstream hugging the bank of the mighty Pastaza while making our way slowly against a violent river that could snatch and twist us into its current and hurtle us downstream wildly out of control. The very sight of this savage river was enough to strike terror in the heart of the most seasoned river traveler. I was relieved to think that I had seen nothing like it in my travels through Central America.

Our boatmen had fixed a rope to the bow and while one manned the pole at the stern, the other strained against the line, planting his feet among the rocks along the bank and heaving his strength against the rope to move us slowly along. The lead man with the rope tied to his waist was not unlike Chinese trackers harnessed to hawsers hauling boats up the Yangtze. This was tiring labor and it was necessary to pull into coves often to rest.

By late afternoon we had reached Lushin, a small settlement of huts where two young women of the Wycliffe Translators were studying the language in preparation for translating the Bible. We spent the night with them and in the morning the sky was overcast and rainy. The airstrip was short and the surface blotched with puddles. There seemed little chance for the small mission plane to fly in. While I turned the hand-operated generator, Marie spoke on the radio with pilot Nate Saint who explained that he could not take off with the three of us, even if the ground were dry. Therefore, he suggested that Marie and I hike out to his base at Shell Mera, a one-day trip, and that we leave Annie for him to bring out the following day when the weather promised to be better.

This was a painful decision; for no one could be certain that the weather would be clear the following day. Furthermore, to leave a six-month-old baby with two maiden ladies with no experience caring for infants was not for Marie and me a comforting thought. However, we had to decide soon. While Marie gave the ladies a few lessons in baby care, I bade our two boatmen *adios* and, accompanied by another guide, we set off by foot in the rain and just at dusk we came out of the jungles, crossed the airstrip to the Saint's house where Marge Saint welcomed us and served up a hot supper. Then it was a shower and to bed.

The next day we scanned the sky for omens and by mid afternoon, Nate took off with several stops to deliver mail, spare parts and things jungle missionaries had come to expect. Later, we gathered around the radio and heard Nate say that he had Annie aboard and was ready to take off. Marie and I ran out to the airstrip and searched the eastern sky until finally a small yellow spot could be seen above the roof of the jungle. The drone of the motor increased until the plane was over us. The engine went silent and the plane, bearing our most cherished possession, glided gracefully onto the grass runway. When the cabin door opened, we peered into a wooden crate to see a mosquito-bitten little girl smiling up at us.

When we told Nate Saint good-bye, we were also speaking with him for the last time. He was with Jim Elliot and the other missionaries a year later when the Waorani Indians speared them to death.

Annie took her next steps through Babel at age three when the three of us landed in Paris preparing to go to French-speaking Cameroun. Her Spanish soon drifted away as she spent her days in a French-speaking playgroup. During these months she began speaking to us entirely in English. After six months in France, we moved on to West Africa where Annie began to hear and absorb Bulu in the village of Aloum where mom and dad were making serious efforts to acquire a working knowledge of this Bantu tongue. By the time she was six years old, I was studying at the university of Heidelberg and Annie was adjusting to a German kindergarten and her fifth language. She seemed to be able to adapt to all new linguistic environments without signs of frustration or anxiety. This may have been due to the fact that she picked up languages and dropped them when she no longer heard them being spoken. The language of mom and dad was American English and on this she could rely. However, she had not forgotten Bulu, for when we arrived in New York after six months in Germany, she greeted some African American children, assuming that all black children spoke Bulu, and was quickly rebuffed. She confided to us with grave concern in the hotel lobby, "Those kids over there don't speak Bulu!"

By age 13 Annie had attended no less than eight schools on three continents, had been in 29 countries and had been exposed to a greater or lesser degree to five languages. Looking back at her childhood, she says, "Throughout my childhood I was vividly aware of the physical and human environment. This consciousness separated me from nearly all my peers in England who had little interest in people and places beyond their own lives. The sounds or words of a language I recognized or a custom I knew about or a far away place name I could identify would catch my interest while my friends would no longer be listening."

In 1972 Annie was offered a place at the University of Essex to pursue Latin American Studies, but turned it down because she wanted to qualify to teach and the subject she wanted to teach was Religious Education. In England this refers to comparative religion and includes Judaism and Christianity among many others. "I was fortunate," she says, "to grow up in a family where there was an atmosphere of openness and acceptance toward other cultures and the non-Christian religions. This enabled me to learn how, for example, Muslims, Hindus, animists and others interpret their own existence."

Annie obtained a teaching certificate in Education and Religious Studies after three years at Keswick Hall College, Norwich, and later a Bachelor in Education from the University of East Anglia. Annie is the mother of a son Joss and daughter Leila. She teaches Religious Education at the Hetherset School in Norwich, Norfolk, England.

Toba

In the spring of 1954, we were invited to assist a Mennonite mission in the northern Chaco province of Argentina. There were two problems that required outside help. The first concerned the Toba language, that had never been reduced to writing and there were no written materials to help the missionaries learn the language. The second problem, and no doubt more difficult, was the need to examine cultural and religious developments among the Indians, and recommend ways in which the Mennonite mission might find a meaningful role through which to serve the Toba people.

After making preparations to leave Ecuador, we flew from Guayaquil in late May and headed south in stages, there being no direct flight to Buenos Aires. In Asunción, Paraguay, we stayed several nights at a mission guest house, and, among other things, saw the opera *Madame Butterfly* performed in Spanish. President Alfredo Stroessner, Paraguay's longtime dictator, was in the presidential box and no one was allowed to leave the building until the president and his party had departed.

We flew into Buenos Aires at night, and, after passing for several hours over the dark abyss below, the illumined capital came into view like a sparkling sea. Unlike many modern cities today, Buenos Aires in 1954 had no flashy colored neon lights. Rather, the vast metropolitan area was a monochrome of luminous beauty, a bright replica of the starry skies overhead.

To reach the Chaco we traveled north from the capital on

board a river steamer that plied the Paraná river and deposited us at the city of Corrientes where our host, Albert Buckwalter, met us and took us by road to his station at Nam Qom in the heart of the Chaco. Albert's vintage car had the steering wheel on the right side, although the traffic drove on the right and not on the left, as is customary for such cars. With a right-hand drive vehicle, it is difficult and often impossible to see the on-coming traffic. Fortunately, this was not a great problem in the Chaco where there were few cars.

El Chaco, a province with some forty thousand square miles, is a large lowland plain covered mostly by scrub forests and grassy savannas. The summers are hot and humid, the land flat, and the drainage poor, causing frequent flooding. In the rainy season the unpaved roads turn into impassable quagmires and cars and trucks are forced to wait, sometimes for days, for the sun to dry the roads. Fences are few and cattle roam the country, often devouring entire fields of cotton plants.

In this inhospitable land, the semi-nomadic Toba Indians were settling down and attempting to raise food, cotton and cattle, often with devastating results. However, their spiritual lives were alive and thriving. Thousands of Tobas had turned to a Pentecostal expression of their new faith and thereby often appeared bizarre and incomprehensible to their Mennonite missionaries.

Residing on the mission property was an extended family of Tobas named Rodríguez, who showed an intelligent interest in having their language put into writing. Some of the young men spoke Spanish and Cristóbal Rodríguez, especially, was a patient and capable helper. Cristóbal and I met each morning in a small schoolroom where I asked in Spanish how to say words, phrases and sentences in Toba and recorded hundreds of pages of texts. In the afternoons I would sort and file my materials and prepare questions for the following day. By the end of four months, I had put together a grammar of sorts that would enable the missionaries to get hold of the language. Fortunately, while he was on study leave in the U.S., Albert took courses that would help in his further study and analysis of the language. Lois Buckwalter, mother of three energetic children, had been raised in Argentina and was able to assist Albert in countless ways.

A serendipitous reward for me in the Chaco was the presence of Lois' brother, Juan Litwiller, who, like his sister, had grown up in Argentina and was more at home in Spanish than in English. On various occasions, Albert, Juan and I visited Toba communities located in places with names like *Pampa del Indio, Legua 17 and Legua 15*. We had many opportunities to sit around the fires at night under the bright heavens and share our thoughts and hopes with each other. Juan, who later became dean and then director of ISEDET, a united theological seminary in Buenos Aires, was a person with a keen inquiring mind coupled with a subtle sense of humor. He delighted in pursuing questions about the relations between Toba culture, the Bible and theology. He introduced me to the writings of Dietrich Bonhoefer, Karl Barth, and especially Emile Brunner, who I would visit a year later in Zurich. My contact with Juan Litwiller had a lasting effect on my life and work for it broadened my vision and helped me to see implications in my work that I was not fully aware of. Juan's untimely death in 1971 at the age of forty-three was a tragic and painful loss to theological education in Latin America.

In order to make certain that the Rodríguez Toba I was collecting at Nam Qom was the same as that spoken in other areas, I needed to visit outlying communities such as Legua 15, some four hours north by horse. Albert had taken a sleeping cot and some supplies by car and left them there for me. I preferred to travel by horse so that I would not be stopped at a road barrier if the road was closed by the rains.

One evening about dusk in late July when the air had cooled, I left Nam Qom on a spirited horse and made my way north. The sky soon glittered with stars, the southern constellations splendidly lucent. The dirt road, straight as an arrow, cut through the forests and dipped occasionally to cross a shallow stream. My horse, that needed no commands from its rider, was surefooted and kept up a steady fast walk while I feasted on the luminaries overhead, sang to myself, and was enchanted to be alone in this boundless, silent corner of the planet. Several times my horse swerved suddenly and rolled its head and ears toward the trees where no doubt it had heard the growl of a wildcat.

About midway in our journey through the night, a strange phenomenon occurred. A great circle of light surrounded us on all sides. It appeared without sound, as though a powerful searchlight overhead had been switched on. My horse came immediately to a halt, its ears rotating forward and backward as if waiting my instructions. The light was so brilliant the smallest pebbles in the road were remarkably visible. I turned in the saddle to look to the rear and could see the edge of the light some fifty yards away circling into the trees on either side of the road. Ahead, about the same distance, the glow was identical. Within the confines of the circle it was bright daylight in the otherwise darkness of the Chaco. Searching the sky overhead, I could see no evident source of this light and the stars remained as bright as before.

As I sat on my horse and perceived everything around me bathed in daylight, I became aware of being without shock or fear. Strange as it may have been, I felt assuredly at ease, as though the light out of darkness was a friendly presence. I had not touched the horse's flanks but he now began moving forward, all the while turning his ears to the right and to the left, and as we approached the front edge of the circle, it vanished as quickly and silently as it had appeared.

At Legua 15 I lay on my cot reconstructing the strange event and asking question after question. Surely, it had to be some kind of natural phenomenon, or was it? Didn't the apostle Paul while approaching Damascus see a light from heaven flash about him? But a voice spoke to him. No sound came from our light and yet it was not in the least frightening to the horse or to me. I was well aware of the important metaphor of light versus darkness in religions and then, just as I was about to fall asleep, I recalled

Kiyoshi saying that his uncle would show me the way to become "with light on." Was I being enlightened? If so, about what? My efforts later to learn if the Toba had such experiences brought no new insights and I know nothing more today that I did that July night in 1954.

Annie celebrated her first birthday at Nam Qom with the Buckwalter children and I think they must have impressed upon her that Spanish was the language of children, for her first utterances were in Spanish and continued in that language until we had been several months in Paris.

The Mennonite missionaries reoriented themselves and their work to serve the Toba churches in translation of the scriptures and discovering the Tobas as fellow members of Christ's church. Over the years the Buckwalters forged ahead with their Toba colleagues and together translated the New Testament for the growing Toba church. Albert also guided two other groups of Chaco Indians: the Mocoví, and Pilagá and produced the New Testament also in those languages.

Satisfied that we had done what we had come for, the Reyburn trio headed overland back to Ecuador.

The Long Trip

In September 1954 we returned to the port city of Corrientes, Argentina, where we boarded a river steamer and traveled north on the Paraná and then on the Paraguay river to Asunción, capital of Paraguay. Near the capital the Pilcomayo converges with the Paraguay. We had learned, while with the Mennonite missionaries in Argentina, that several colonies of Mennonites had settled in the interior of the Paraguayan Chaco and so we were anxious to visit them, for these east Europeans had proven that they could adjust to the rigors of the Chaco's harsh environment, raise commercial crops and maintain their European Mennonite lifestyle.

The Mennonites in Paraguay had emigrated mostly from Russia to Germany and then to Paraguay in 1930. From Asunción they had traveled north on the Paraguay river to Puerto Casado where they made a three-day train trip to a point where they were met by Canadian Mennonites who had emigrated from Canada in 1927. The Canadians welcomed the new arrivals with ox-drawn carts and led them for sixty-six miles into the heart of the Chaco to lands which the Mennonite Central Committee had purchased for them on credit. The new settlers had chosen Paraguay because that government granted them self-government, freedom of religion, control of their own schools, use of their own language (German), and exemption from military service.

Their first cash crop was cotton, which they hauled by ox and horse carts to the railhead sixty-six miles away. Over the years they developed a number of industries, a radio station, printing plant and electric plant. They maintain their own educational system in the German language, although today Spanish is taught as a foreign language beginning in the third grade. In addition to cotton they raise sorghum, sugar cane, peanuts, manioc, sweet potatoes, watermelon and citrus fruits. They supply sixty percent of the nation's milk supply. Today these products are transported over the Transchaco Highway to the capital.

When we flew to the colony of Fernheim "distant home,"— there were no adequate roads and no land transportation to the colony—we discovered that news about our work among the Toba had gone before us and we were soon put to work by Herr Gerhard Giesbrecht, one of the immigrants, who had been serving as a missionary to the Lengua (Enxit) and Chulupí (Nivacle) Indians. These languages are quite different from each other and very different from Toba. In fact, all three belong to different language families. To complicate matters even more, I was unable to work with the Indian informants in Spanish. The reason for this was that the informants Herr Giesbrecht recommended had learned the low German dialect from the Mennonite settlers. However, with the help of Giesbrecht we were able to obtain a good linguistic sample and determine what the necessary sounds were that had to be written. After our departure from Fernheim, we corresponded with Herr Giesbrecht as he pursued his analysis of the Lengua language.

From Asunción we continued by boat on the Paraguay river which, in part of its course, forms the boundary between Paraguay to the west and Brazil to the east. It was a hot and humid Sunday afternoon when we docked in Corumbá, a tiny, rustic village on the Brazilian side. The customs and immigrations shed was closed and no one was available to let us debark. We were prepared to by-pass this formality, but the boat captain warned me to do so could land the three of us in jail. When I suggested to the captain that he blow his boat horn and let the local officials know we had arrived, he explained in considerable detail that I would be required to pay for this special Sunday service. A fellow passenger called me aside and urged me to pay nothing, that this boat docks there every Sunday at this time and that it was the responsibility of the boat company to pay. When I passed this bit of news to the captain, he became furious and started the motor and said we would just have to remain with the boat and get off at another port tomorrow. While the boat was churning the water as if to depart, two officers suddenly appeared at the customs shed. No doubt this was a regular Sunday afternoon ritual. When our passports were stamped, I turned and threw a kiss to the irate captain.

We spent the night in a tiny hotel in Corumbá where we tasted the best coffee we had drunk in Latin America. The Brazilians, it seemed, were keeping the best quality coffee for domestic consumption and sending the rest to the world market. On Monday we sat on a small ferry boat that crossed the river only when there were ten or more passengers. It took several hours to accumulate the requisite number. In Puerto Suárez, Bolivia, we waited for four days for the train that would haul us through the jungles to Santa Cruz.

Puerto Suárez was a mosquito infested village half of which was regularly under water due to the poor drainage and heavy rains that pelted the area like clockwork every afternoon about 2:00. On the edge of the village I located a German catholic missionary, Fray Angelo Schmidt, who had been the sole missionary in the place for nearly seven years. From his tonsured head to his sandalled feet, Fray Angelo was not about to make any concession to the blistering steaming heat of the jungle. His vestments were heavy wool and he perspired profusely. We had long talks each day and he seemed genuinely happy to have me visit him. He appeared at the railroad the day we boarded the train and wished us *eine gute Reise.*

The train to Santa Cruz, a full day's journey, was almost a perfect replica of the second-class coaches running between

Ciudad Juárez and Mexico City. The benches were wooden but here in the jungle the shutters were open completely and the locomotive, fired with wood, dragged along through the forests at almost pedestrian haste. At times to relieve the monotony, I walked beside the train and had to slow down in order not to get too far ahead. The train snaked along through the heavy forest and crossed numerous wooden truss bridges. At times the vegetation grew so close to the tracks it brushed the sides of the train cars. Houses along the railroad were few and many of them were thatched huts standing on poles to keep them out of the water where pigs were often seen wallowing about. Railside vendors were seldom seen but fortunately we had been advised by Fray Angelo to carry our own food and drinks. Occasionally we passed clusters of huts where purple bougainvillea grew in abundance and where papaya and mangoes flourished.

The railroad through the eastern jungle was of vital importance for Bolivia which had lost its outlet to the Pacific to Chile in 1883. A raillink from the capital, La Paz, to Santa Cruz and on to Corumbá would allow Bolivia to ship its produce by train all the way to Sao Paulo, Brazil. The section Santa Cruz-Cochabamba was still under construction in 1954 and so we had to fly over that part. Thirteen years after our passage through this area, Bolivian troops killed a revolutionary here who was attempting to organize the overthrow of the Bolivian government. His name: Che Guevara, who had been Fidel Castro's second-in-command in Cuba.

After visiting the tin mines at Oruro and spending a few days in La Paz adjusting to its 12,000 ft. elevation, we rode the bus north to Lake Titicaca. (Among the Reyburn children where Spanish *caca* refers to excrement, the combination of *titi* and *caca* always produced the giggles.) Lake Titicaca is said to be the world's highest navigable lake (12,507 ft.) It is 110 miles long and is crossed by a steamer overnight. Amazingly, the ship was disassembled on the coast and carried by donkey caravans to the lake before being reassembled. The lake connects Bolivia with Peru and at the port of Puno we were again on a bus destined for the ancient Inca capital of Cuzco.

The return trip to Ecuador, nearly a month of travel, gave us an excellent opportunity to compare the dialects of Quechua spoken from northern Argentina to northern Peru. Moreover, we were able to see how each nation's history had determined the way in which Indians and non-Indians had developed along separate lines. For example, in 1952 Bolivia's president, Paz Estensoro, broke up the large estates and provided land for hundreds of thousands of Indians who for centuries had been landless peasants and sharecroppers.

Once again in Ecuador we were able to write a number of articles including the booklet *The Toba Indians of the Argentine Chaco, An Interpretive Report* published by the Mennonite Board of Missions and Charities. We had settled down, at least for awhile, in the Andean town of Riobamba, almost in the shadow of Ecuador's highest peak, Chimborazo. The apartment house, owned by a local baker, was built around the four sides of an open patio graced by colorful flowers. One family had lots of children and Annie's Spanish increased daily.

Burro

From Indians in the Riobamba market I had learned that traveling merchants spent the nights in hostels as they went from town to town. They would buy tomatoes, potatoes, oranges, wheat, corn, barley and beans in one area and transport these things on donkeys to another where the demand was greater and the price higher. As a result of the constant moving of food to markets, the need for cheap accommodations for traders and fodder for their animals developed, even in the smallest hamlets.

Hostels performing this function were normally an extension of the cantinas or bars on the outskirts of the towns. For about twenty-five cents a night, a traveling trader could get feed and shelter for his animal, and for himself a barn floor with straw shared with fellow travelers.

What a perfect set-up for an undercover Indian such as I! Of course, when I talked it over with Marie, I realized that I could not pass as an Indian—clearly not in speech, size, color, or, for that matter, anything else. Nevertheless, with a good disguise, I might get by as a cholo, a term used in some parts of the Americas to refer to a person of mixed Spanish and Indian ancestry. That was it; the old hat, well-worn poncho, *alpargata* sandals, patches-sewed-on-patches pants were all I needed for a good exterior. I was soon to learn that the interior could not be so easily papered over.

The plan I had put to Don Carlos Bawa, an elderly Indian carrier, was to hike over the roads some fifty miles down to the semitropical zone in which lay the town of Baños, famous in Ecuador for its hot springs and mineral baths. The trip, I estimated, would take three days and since we would spend time in the markets of the smaller towns, we would need five days to reach Baños. And above all, we would need a strong little donkey. That's why Carlos showed up at our door not long after sunrise one morning.

Don Carlos never knocked. People who knock on doors only want to know if the owner is away so they can burgle the house. Instead, Carlos would clear his throat, cough or, if that got no attention, call out *"Patrón, Guillermo, imanallataj cangui?"* When I opened the door on this occasion, Carlos, who never looked directly at me, said in Quechua, "He's a good donkey; he can walk." A small burro stood behind Carlos flicking its ears and swishing its tail. Like Carlos, it never looked at me either.

An Indian leading a donkey through the cobblestone streets of Riobamba was as common as a dog on the streets of Dodge City or a cat crawling through the garbage of Beirut. But an Indian leading a donkey into the patio of Señor Brito, the town baker, brought curious children running along the verandas, pointing and shouting "¡*Burro, mamá, mira burro!*

Children tugged at their mothers' skirts to take them to the enclosure behind the building so they could pat the burrito. However, there was much less joy among the neighbors when this small domestic ass relieved himself at dawn of half a dozen prolonged hee-haws.

Billy, as I soon christened him, would carry two sacks of *raspadura*, hard blocks of cane sugar eaten by peasants of the countryside for quick energy and used in all kinds of recipes. We would sell *raspadura* in the markets and at night, if I could remain awake, I would listen to the secrets of the heart that traders unveil to each other in the stillness of night.

Having no telephone, and with telegrams delivered only to post office boxes, Marie suggested we have a plan for the homebound journey. Marie always operated with foresight and knew my limits better than I did. Setting aside the very real possibilities of being run over, coming down with a debilitating illness, or being waylaid by brigands, Marie proposed that she and daughter Annie drive over the mountain roads to Baños on our fifth day out. The thought of leaving Don Carlos to walk back with the donkey while I rode sat uneasily on my mind. I tried to dismiss it. After all, Don Carlos is a good Indian: he can walk.

Daylight was just breaking over Ecuador's highest volcano when Carlos, Billy and I reached the cobblestone road out of Riobamba. The rising sun soon gave the snow on Mount Chimborazo's summit a pinkish glow. To the east the volcano Sangay was still hurling fireworks into the heavens. I could read this as a warning to stop or as a sign of victory ahead. I preferred the latter.

Our order of march seemed entirely natural: Carlos in the lead, followed closely by Billy, who like Carlos never looked to the right or to the left. I brought up the rear or was the sweep, as hikers speak of the last person in the line who watches for things dropped or who helps stragglers. Don Carlos knew only one way to walk, his upper body tilted slightly forward and his legs keeping up a steady Indian trot. Billy never allowed a gap to open between them. I felt there was some kind of mystic communion between Indian and burro, a shared sense of time and movement born from their ancient coexistence.

There were moments of steep ascent when I reached out and coupled my hand to Billy's tail. This always made his ears swivel back and they remained that way until I released him. I sometimes had the impression that Billy was solicitous of my well being. Did he somehow intuit that I was a gringo in disguise?

It must have been about midafternoon when we reached a small hamlet with perhaps a hundred huts scattered over the mountain slope. I was uncertain about the hour, as a wristwatch was not part of my garb. I did not know the name of the place and, if I were to inquire of the local people, they would consider me to be someone who was very far from home and so to be treated with suspicion. There were cows, pigs, and sheep inside tamped mud wall enclosures. Smoke could be seen seeping through some of the damp thatch roofs. Stacks of reeds recently cut from the shores of a small lake we had passed were drying in the sun. At the side of the road a group of sheep all tied together were frightened by a passing truck. Each sheep tried to run in a different direction and all ended up in a woolly pile in the ditch. Two snarling dogs rushed out and snapped at Billy, who at the moment was busy with a horsefly biting his flank. Carlos cursed the dogs and drove them away.

We stopped opposite a small market stall where my eye had caught sight of a crate of bottled drinks covered with road dust. I bought two and asked the owner for an opener. While he was searching, Carlos took the bottles and pried the metal caps off with his teeth. Then without a pause, he poured the contents of one down his dry throat. I drank the other, after the fizzing stopped, then returned the bottles. Belching carbonated gas our little train puffed out of town.

It was nearly dark when Carlos stopped and began a conversation with an Indian woman spinning wool beside the road. I could see that she and her small daughter, almost a replica of the mother, were caring for her husband who was lying under a poncho nearby and waiting for him to awaken from his drunken dreamland. *"Maimantataj shamucungui?"* "Where are you coming from?" inquired the mother. When she heard we were traders, she asked what we were selling. She paid for an entire block of sugar from a handkerchief of coins knotted and stashed in her skirts. By the time we were ready to move on, night had closed in on us. I wondered if Billy felt any lighter now.

The village we soon entered had no electricity. We could see occasional cooking fires through open doorways and dark figures moving along the road. On a side road we heard a church bell and could see the flickering of candles inside. According to the lady we had spoken with, the Sánchez cantina was near the town square and was soon identified by the strumming of guitars and the voices of men singing. Their music endowed the darkened plaza with an air of friendly welcome. Watching Carlos and Billy in that moment, I could not but think of Joseph and Mary entering Bethlehem and looking for a place to spend the night. The difference was that I would have been disappointed if there had been a room for us in the Sánchez inn. I was on a mission to listen to travelers who spent their nights in the stable.

Finding the rotund Señora Sánchez busy at the bar, I asked for accommodation for Carlos, Billy and me. She wiped her hands on her apron and said, "This is not a hotel; it's merely a stopping place for the night, no beds, *comprende, Señor?*" I assured her I understood, that we were accustomed to such places and that we would be pleased to spend the night in the safety and comfort of her stable.

When Billy was unloaded, fed and in a dry stall, Carlos and I returned to the cantina for our supper—a bowl of hot potato and cabbage soup with bread. We occupied one table while the singers shared several bottles of rum at the other. I greeted them and they asked if they could provide a lively rendition of something I liked while we enjoyed our meal. I suggested they try a favorite Mexican tune of mine, *Guadalajara*. After several false starts, they managed to get it going and kept it going louder and louder for a long while.

Lifting the candle over my soup to inspect it—not always recommended—I beheld the head of a chicken complete with eyes, beak, and comb. One eye seemed to peer up at me from its watery grave. Carlos, whose soup had a few bare bones at the bottom, devoured his quickly and said he would go to the stable to sleep. I was in no hurry and was curious to see whatever might take place in this uncrowded Bethlehem inn.

I had been scratching away at the chicken head without any success, when I looked up and saw a tall military figure enter the cantina. His cap sat at the top of his heavy head of hair and was far too small to fit the crown of his head. He removed it and placed it under his left arm. The sleeves of his jacket ended several inches above his wrists and, although he was slim, his uniform appeared to have been tailored for one much slimmer than he. The riding breeches he wore disappeared below his knees into a pair of crumpled boots whose heels had been worn away on one side due to the turning of his ankles as he walked. The boots could be cleaned or shined, but they were neither.

He nodded to señora Sánchez, folded his arms and gave the shadowy cantina a disdainful glance. Standing imperiously in the entry he gave the impression of a German officer who was about to announce to a throng of French merrymakers that they had fallen under the dominion of the Third Reich.

I paid him no more attention until he stopped at my table. *"Buenas noches, Señor,"* he said in his official tone. "I don't think we have seen your vehicle pass through our town." "My vehicle? No, of course not. I didn't come in a vehicle."

I thought it best to be polite, so I arose and extended my hand. His hand was warm and limp. On one shoulder he wore the insignia of a captain. The other one was missing. When he sat he pulled his chair closer and leaned toward me when he spoke. His left eye locked on me while the right seemed to be fixed on the door. I had seen this chameleonic use of the eyes before and it disturbed me.

"I am Captain Morales of the *Guardia Nacional.*" The singers at the other table had by now downed most of their rum and their music had become soft and melancholic. Morales leaned in still closer and I could feel the flecks of his saliva striking my cheek. "I don't think we have had the pleasure of your visit before in our zone, *verdad?*"

I suspected this gaunt officer with a wolfish visage was hungry and that he was not going away soon. I clapped my hands for señora Sánchez who nodded when I ordered two bowls of *sopa de cebada.* When the soup was brought, the captain gave his spoon no rest until he pushed the empty bowl away and belched deeply, then lit up.

I admitted that I had never been in his village before. It

seemed safe now for him to focus fully on me. His right eye drifted back into position. "You will excuse me, I am sure, if I ask a few questions which is the nature of my responsibility. In the daytime we have soldiers on the road inspecting all vehicles, ascertaining the origins of all passengers and drivers, their destinations and much, much more. Your arrival after dark and on foot with one animal and one Indian makes our assignment more," he paused to shake the ashes off his cigarette, "more problematic. Do you not agree?"

I was not ready to agree with him about anything. On the one hand I thought I should just tell the man that I was in Ecuador with the authorization of the Ministry of Education to do linguistic and cultural research and traveling with an Indian and a burro on the road at night was part of the job. On the other hand, if I really wanted to learn how small Andean towns conduct their affairs, was not this an excellent way to do it? I refused to play the imperialist card. "Yes, my Captain, how can I serve you?"

"I must ask to see your identification." Reaching inside my shirt, I brought out my passport and handed it to him. He lifted it close to his left eye and held the candle near. "Oh, American? I thought you might be Argentinean. You don't speak gringo Spanish . . . ." He began turning the pages and saw visas for all of Central America, which did not particularly interest him until he saw stamps for Argentina, and then Peru. He now studied the visas, dates and signatures carefully. Tapping me on the knee with my passport, he said, "You understand why we in this part of the world must be eternally vigilant. Keep both eyes open day and night. The enemy can slip across the border and," he paused to let me reflect, then drew an unsteady index finger across his bobbing Adam's apple.

"Captain Morales, you surprise me. You sound like some Americans I know who see communists under their mosquito nets."

"Ah, Señor, the communists are nothing compared to these enemies of the state. They have already killed many of our brave soldiers, stolen our lands, and deprived us of our oil reserves."

"Oh, you mean the . . ." I pointed to the south.

"*Sí, Señor, los peruanos.*" Morales was now on his feet, thumping the table with his knuckles. "The Peruvian is our enemy and anyone who is spying for him will be given the cruelest punishment. You do admit that you have been in his country, do you not?" Shaking my passport in my face he added, "The evidence is right here."

The musicians were out in the street and, having run out of rum, their singing was becoming discordant. I paid señora Sánchez and asked her to inform Carlos in the morning that Captain Morales had invited me to visit his jailhouse.

Carlos entered the jailhouse hat in hand, wondering if he would be next. The jailor unlocked my cell door and handed me my passport. Morales was asleep at his desk. They had kept me up most of the night while we argued politics, democracy, justice, peace and religion. When Carlos and I were ready to leave, Morales was awake and standing at the door.

"Señor Reyburn, I can understand how being in Nagasaki made you decide against war and violence and I pray that no such bomb is ever dropped on my country, but for me personally, I would not hesitate to use such a bomb on the enemy who has stolen part of our *oriente*. Did not Mister Truman think the same as I?"

We shook hands. "I'm sorry that I failed to convince you or convert you. Perhaps we will meet again. *Adios.*"

When finally we reached Baños, I felt that my identity as a traveling trader had been rehabilitated and that I was raising few if any suspicions, that is, until I entered the *Cantina Dos Patos* and asked for accommodations for the three of us.

Two naked bulbs that hung over the bar illumined the cantina where a moonfaced madam overflowed her chair and rested her chubby arms on the bar. She told me where to find the stable and the feed for Billy. I paid her and we chatted about the warm climate in Baños, the biting of the midges and the recent rise in the price of rice and coffee.

Tipping my hat, I turned to go but before I reached the door, she called out, *"Meester, espere un momento."* I hesitated, almost ashamed to turn around. How had this woman seen through my disguise so easily and so quickly? My days and nights of passing incognito were now as nothing. In one moment, I had been stripped of my hard-earned new identity. She said I still owed her five sucres. I handed her the five and joined Carlos and Billy at the stable.

As soon as we had taken care of Billy's needs, Carlos and I went to the open market and bought our supper. That night the stable was full of animals and the sleeping floor occupied by many travelers. I lay down bone-weary yet comforted that tomorrow Marie and Annie would arrive. I was anxious to get home and take a shower. My body from the neck down was a mass of fleabites. While I lay awake hearing the snores of my fellow travelers, I tried to think of all the insights I had gained from these hostel crawlings. I had heard, for example, a few Indians grumble about how little money they had earned and how much they had to pay for a bowl of soup. I really only had learned how it feels to walk the roads and be covered by the dust of passing vehicles and to see how Indian traders fall asleep early each night.

I tried to refrain from scratching and thinking of that lady in the cantina who called me *meester*. I was determined to see her in the morning and clear up that mystery, if mystery it was.

I didn't hear another thing until very early when Billy began blowing his hee-haw trumpet, followed by half a dozen of his stable mates. When I returned to sleep, I dreamed I was the ringmaster in a great circus where even the gorillas, lions and elephants did the hee-haw.

Later, in the cantina I found the owner with a mop and bucket of water busily cleaning up. The water was running in rivulets into the street. *"Señora, buenos dias.* If you will permit me, I have a question." She leaned heavily on her mop handle and waited. "Yesterday when I came in here, you called me *meester*. I would like to know what it was that made you do that."

The barlady was embarrassed and I was a bit ashamed for putting her into this situation. She bent over and wrung out her mop and giggled then scratched her head. "I really don't know. Go outside and come back in just like you did yesterday," she said. I obeyed her orders and headed for the door when she called out, "Wait, wait. I think I know now. It is the way you walk. I never saw men from here walk like you *meesters* do, swinging your arms like you never carried a load on your back." She giggled again. I thanked her and left.

It was early afternoon when I saw Marie driving slowly along the upper end of the market. When we met, Annie was asleep with her head in Marie's lap but as soon as she turned off the motor, Annie sat up and yawned then jumped up shouting *"Papa, papito"* and reached out to me.

The three of us strolled through the market to where Carlos was sitting shooing flies from his remaining block of *raspadura*. I untied Billy, who nudged me affectionately with his head. Back at the car, I got out the tools and took out the back seat and strapped it to the roof. Marie said, "Uh-huh, I see what you are up to." I could not go off and leave these two fellow travelers to hike home. Through these five days and nights we had become *un ménage a trois,* risked our lives on the roads and survived the nights. We had to stick together. Through the open tailgate we lifted Billy and laid him gently on his side. Carlos then climbed in beside him.

As we drove out of Baños, Annie leaped up and down turning her mother's face to look back. *"¡Mamá, mira. Mamá mira Carlos y burrito, burrito!"* In a few more minutes Annie and our two backseat passengers were sleeping soundly.

The Resurrection of

Mariano Cumbal

Mariano Cumbal had fallen drunk in the road outside the town of Tabacundo and a loaded truck had run over his head, squashing it flat as a rotten pumpkin. In earlier times he would have been watched over by his wife, Rosa Imba, while she sat nearby spinning wool until he awoke, but Rosa had died from pneumonia and so Mariano had no one to drag him to the side of the road, to wait and watch beside him until his stupor abated. That's why on this cold night in the high Andes of Ecuador on the slopes of Cayambe I had joined Mariano's friends and relatives for the wake.

The hut we were in was crowded and the mourners, at least in the early hours, were respectfully silent. Mariano lay in a rough wooden coffin. His cousins had washed his body, dressed him in the only change of clothing he owned and nailed the coffin lid shut. There was no inquest, no complaint filed, no will to probate, no undertaker and no coroner summoned—just another drunk Indian found dead in the road.

Huddled inside their ponchos, the silent mourners waited for the first light of dawn before carrying Mariano's coffin to the Tabacundo church for mass and burial. Now and then someone would struggle to his feet and step over hats and ponchos until finally outside in the cold night air relieve himself, yawn and scrape the door open again.

Quechua Indian mourners were experts at wrapping themselves in their ponchos. From head to toe they covered themselves like beans under a wrapper on a merchant's shelf. Their woolen hats were pulled low on their heads and their necks sank into the collars of their ponchos as they themselves seemed to sink into the dirt floor of the hut. Under their ponchos their arms encircled their knees drawn up against their chests so that each one occupied the smallest possible space on the floor.

The one inviolate rule of etiquette at a wake, the Indians had reminded me, was to remain awake and alert at every moment, from the time a mourner wriggled his way into the crowded hut until the procession began to form up in the first light of dawn. To ensure that nobody fell asleep, two or three persons were charged with the task of setting fire to the hair of anyone who nodded off. To this end a pair of candles were kept lit, the only light in the room. The sight, sound and especially the smell of singed hair brought forth muffled laughter from the otherwise silent mourners. Persons with long braids hanging down the outside of their ponchos risked having their hair break out into a flame before they were aware of having dozed off.

Sometime after midnight, I noticed three women bearing large jars of fermented chicha enter the room and pass gourd cups of the intoxicating juice among the mourners. A figure in a darkened corner began a slow drumbeat and outside the plaintive wail of panpipes drifted through the dark valley.

As the moon flowed westward behind ominous clouds, I could see how the chicha awakened somnolent minds and loosened heavy tongues. People began to whisper, then talk in muffled voices. Someone going or coming from the door struck the coffin support and caused it to fall to the floor. There was a momentary burst of laughter then all became hushed while two relatives of the deceased lifted the coffin and set it straight again.

Somewhere in the village of Picalquí a rooster crowed, the first sign of approaching dawn. The drummer ceased his pounding, arose and attached his drum to his body. When he had worked his way to the outside, four of the dead man's relatives lifted the coffin, steadied themselves then carried the late Mariano Cumbal out of the hut. Outside a balaphone, two bass horns and a cornet joined the drummer. I heard one of the bass horn players complain that the pay was insufficient and the chicha served was of inferior quality. The band, he insisted would not play until the mourners were inside the church and would only play again while the body was being lowered into the grave. More than that, he insisted, would require fresh negotiations with Mariano's cousins.

To reach the road to Tabacundo, the funeral procession would cross several fields where cornstalks had been recently cut and then would follow footpaths hedged by century plants and eucalyptus trees. The path joined the road on the edge of the village, a place where water overflowed from a field and where stones were scattered in the road.

The eastern sky beyond the volcano known as Father Cayambe cast a raw umber glow across the sleeping valley. The four pallbearers hoisted the coffin to their shoulders and the band formed behind them. At the rear of the procession and scattered about like sheep, staggered the mourners. Crossing the fields, several of the mourners stubbed their feet and fell to the ground. Seeing their fellow mourners sprawled on the earth touched off great guffaws. At the place where the footpath joined the road one of the coffin carriers slipped on a smooth stone and went down on his knees. The others lost control and the coffin struck the ground with a cracking thud.

A woman bearing a huge jar of chicha rushed to the front of the procession and refreshed the carriers. By the time the procession had recovered its composure and was half the distance to Tabacundo, the four carriers had to put down their burden and relieve themselves. When they were ready to resume their journey, they were unable to hoist the coffin to their shoulders and it appeared they were going to take turns dragging it. By now all the mourners were present and demanding the musicians play.

Only the drummer was willing to beat his instrument. The coffin was too heavy. An argument broke out between some of the mourners and Mariano's cousins:

"Why," they demanded, "did you buy a coffin made of stone?"

"It is not stone. It is light wood, the cheapest rosas wood in the market. If these carriers are too weak, we will carry it ourselves."

I noticed that Vicente Cuzco had climbed on to the embankment and was waving his arms and calling for the people to listen.

"People of Picalquí, why do we go on year after year like beasts carrying our dead when they could ride in a bus?"

A voice responded: "A bus on this road? What owner of a bus would drive it in an arroyo bed? One trip to Picalquí and his tires would be dead, his bus a pile of junk."

For a moment or two a sober pause seemed to have settled on the Picalquians. The view was generously expressed and supported by affirmative shouts that the making of a proper road to Tabacundo would transform life as they and their forebears had known it. Trucks instead of human backs would carry the corn to markets, taxicabs would bring home the inebriated, no more Mariano Cumbals to have their skulls crushed under the wheels of the rich!

So impressed was the band leader with this expression of progress and communal spirit that he lifted his cornet to his lips and began to play a Spanish March. The two bass horns joined in and the drummer too. Four fresh carriers hauled Mariano to their shoulders and for a few moments the motley procession blossomed into a band of military peasants marching to overthrow the decadent bourgeoisie and plant the worker's flag in the public square. The revolutionary fervor faded in the next minutes when the cornet player ran out of wind and another chicha pause was demanded.

The procession reached the main road and the big stone church was now near. At the foot of the church steps, the carriers lowered Mariano to the ground and wiped their sweating faces. The band struck up a funeral piece just as the church bell clanged with loud, sustained, measured strokes. Surprised, we all gazed upward. Normally the sexton charged twenty sucres to perform this service, but Vicente Cuzco had climbed to the belfry to provide his neighbor with this special reception into the Christian burial, even if Mariano's soul was already well on its way to Taita Cayambe, the resting place of Indian souls.

When Vicente rejoined the procession, the *cura*, Father Antonio, appeared in the doorway waving his smoking censor, thought by the Indians to prevent evil spirits from entering the sanctuary.

Inside the great stone edifice, built by the Picalquians' ancestors a century earlier, the dim electric bulbs pulsated in sync with the vibrations of a small diesel generator at the rear of the church, hired on this occasion by Mariano's cousins for an undisclosed sum. The purpose of the electric lights was to illumine a monstrous mural that never failed to capture the attention and ruminations of Indian minds. Like a flock of frightened sheep they crowded into the pews along the wall. With their besotted and befuddled heads they stared with unblinking eyes upon a bewitching scene of hell that would have made Dante's depictions seem trivial and pedestrian.

There we beheld skeletons with bones burning in the flames, bodiless skulls whose mouths were contorted in expressions of anguish. Monstrous serpents coiled about fleshless bodies where flames and smoke consumed body parts scattered on the fiery earth. Inebriated eyes would stare at the scenes then look away only to see the hellish images metastasize like cancer to other parts of the foreboding sanctuary. The mourners dared not move for fear of finding themselves stepping among poisonous snakes and smouldering corpses.

Surely, the Spanish conquerors and their descendants

deserved a hell such as this and it gave the Indians pleasure to know that their own spiritual afterlife would be passed in the comfort and warmth of Cayambe's crater. In spite of five hundred years of Christian teaching, the Indians were not prepared to give up a restful hereafter for this eternal damnation and torment of body and soul.

The Indians had explained to me that a Christian mass for Mariano would protect him from the devil on his way to Taita Cayambe. After all, an Indian needed all the help he could obtain from Taita Dios to make certain his life in the spirit world was peaceful and free from the pain and suffering of this worldly life. The jars of chicha set out for Mariano would sustain and assure him a pleasant journey on his way to his final rest in Cayambe's crater.

When Father Antonio had collected his money for the mass, in spite of loud protests that he had cut corners, left out some words and did not call on San Pablo and San Pedro, the procession regrouped and tottered down the steps without incident and headed for the burial ground for Indians at the rear of the church.

I could see that the grave had yet to be dug, but fortunately there was now corn tostados, boiled eggs and bananas to shore up weakened bodies. The chicha provisions had miraculously multiplied and the band, playing now under a dull morning sun, entertained the mourners with spirited martial airs that kept the diggers working at a faster than normal pace. Soon a large mound of fresh dirt was heaped beside the grave. With no further ceremony, Mariano's coffin was lowered into the hole, but the grave diggers left the grave open so that Mariano would feel included in the fiesta of music, food and drink that ensued.

The band, feeling their contract with Mariano's cousins had been adequately kept, went among the mourners collecting tips. They then doffed their hats in a show of gratitude and disappeared. The mourners, resuscitated with food and drink, lay back on their ponchos and slept. José Chuncho, one of Mariano's closest neighbors, stretched himself out on the cool mound of freshly dug earth and fell into a deep slumber. Without waking, he rolled over and slid into the open grave where he lay face down and motionless on Mariano's coffin.

Later the cousins began to shovel dirt into the hole, but on hearing a groan they peered in to see what they thought was Mariano come to life and lying astride his box. Quickly they dropped to their knees to get a closer look. Dropping their tools, they ran to the church shouting for Father Antonio. Snatching off their hats and bowing they announced *"¡Señor Cura, viva la virgen santísima, Mariano es resucitado. Ya no está muerto!"*

Like many professional religious, Padre Antonio was skeptical about appearances of the Virgin and about people rising from the dead. I watched as he opened a side door and glanced out into the ancient cemetery. All the saintly departed were sleeping in peaceful repose. "Go and tell Mariano to come to the church and I will say a resurrection mass for him." The cousins hesitated for a moment until Padre Antonio added "for free!" The trio raced back to the grave. Down on their knees, they peered in cautiously and said, "Hermano Mariano, the *cura* says for you to come . . . ." The body lying on the coffin rose up and José Chuncho looked up bewildered. Standing on the coffin José held up his arms and the cousins pulled him from the grave. He bent over and rubbed his sore knees.

Several of the mourners now partially awake in their hangovers saw a figure rising out of Mariano's grave. They rubbed their tired eyes, crossed themselves and looked again. They saw José Chuncho stop beside the chicha jar, recharge himself and zigzag off in the direction of home. I was worn out from lack of sleep and decided to accompany him.

As we turned off the main road and started down the crooked byway to Picalquí, José hesitated then mounted an embankment and proclaimed loudly, "Today a miserable footpath for pigs, but tomorrow a great carriageway for those left behind by Mariano!" He removed his hat reverentially and held it out as if speaking to the dead man. "Long may you live, Mariano, and the Mariano Cumbal highway to Tabacundo!"

Exhausted by ceremonial strain and still pained where his knees had landed on Mariano's box, he lay down to sleep, and in his dream, he later told me, José beheld a great snake sitting in a toll booth charging the people of Picalquí who came and went on their new highway.

Patrón

The peasant Indian community at Picalquí discovered in 1946 that it had become the lower extension, although independent, of the American Protestant mission known as the United Andean Mission. After having purchased the hacienda, the mission's aim was to teach improved agricultural practices, heal the sick, educate the youth, and evangelize the lost. The Indians, plagued with parasites and infectious diseases, responded readily to the antibiotics and immunizations. They could see no harm, in fact they found it downright helpful, for their children to learn to read Spanish, the official language of the nation, and to do arithmetic. This knowledge was necessary if the next generation was to protect itself from exploitation by the non-Indian population. But improving the Indians' age-old farming habits and convincing them to change their religion were much more subtle matters. In these two areas the Picalquians' resistance was stubborn, steady and unyielding.

The United Andean Mission, an ecumenical American effort, had asked us to make a study of the life and ways of the Indians at Picalquí and to suggest how the mission could make its labors more effective.

To understand how Indians viewed their life from the huts and minuscule farm plots of Picalquí, we had negotiated with the community leaders who allowed us to live among them and learn from them. As the months passed, we gained an understanding of how vast was the chasm that stretched between the mission hacienda with its machines and purebred stock and the impoverished and dispossessed Indians.

We were permitted to occupy the one empty mud and thatch hut in the community that lay beside a footpath in the midst of tiny farming plots and within shouting distance of half a dozen other huts. The only thing that could be called furniture was a bamboo platform that served as a bed and a stack of mud bricks that we used as a stand for a two-burner Coleman gas stove. Our other departures from local lifestyle included a gas lamp, and a few pots and pans.

Since the previous occupant, now deceased, had cooked over an open fire on the floor, the interior thatch was blackened by smoke and stringy stalactite-like webs hung from the black thatch giving the inside the appearance of the roof of a bat cave.

Our toilet was a slit trench we had dug behind the hut, and the water, aside from some rain water we caught, had to be hauled by human toil from the great depths of a rocky ravine, a round-trip of nearly a mile. Marie, who made the trip a few times (but not carrying a water jar!), found it reminiscent of her college days when she had hiked from the south to the north rim of the Grand Canyon. Indian women trudged down and up the steep barranca two or more times a day to supply their households with water, carrying the precious commodity in locally made clay jars that weighed as much as fifteen pounds empty. When Marie became fully occupied working with the women in their fields, we engaged a local girl named Ciliana to keep our water jar filled.

Few Picalquians remembered Vicente Cuzco's appeal for a better road to connect their community with the town of Tabacundo, and the writer was the only one to hear José Chuncho dedicate the not-yet-built highway to the memory of the late Mariano Cumbal. Nevertheless, when the crops had been planted and several of the costly fiestas had been celebrated, people began remembering the talk of rebuilding the road. The rains had ended and, if the road work was to be undertaken, this was the time.

One morning when I had not been awake long—getting up from our rock-hard bed was always a relief—our neighbor, Alfonso Chorlango, called out: *"Patrón Guillermo, allillachu cangui?"*

I did not reply to his greeting immediately. Ever since we had moved into the village, the Indians had addressed me as *patrón*, the same as they would address the owner of an hacienda, a store owner, or a Spanish-speaking official in Tabacundo. *Patrón* meant bossman, chief, owner.

To enable the Indians to see that we lived on the brink of poverty, we never failed to let them come in and see that our house had far fewer goods than theirs. Their small huts were jammed with possessions, for example, sacks of grain, chicha jars, trunks with family heirlooms, mirrors, clothing, ponchos, chairs, and scavaging about the floor were a dozen or more guinea pigs that darted about underfoot making a ceaseless chirping that sounded like a bubbling brook. We had none of these domestic rodents, much to Annie's displeasure. Nevertheless, we were not fooling anyone, not even ourselves, for it was known that we had a four-wheel drive vehicle stashed up at the mission, something that was beyond the wildest hopes of our neighbors.

I dragged open the door and peered out. Alfonso's cheeks showed their slightly intoxicated color—a light dusting of rouge. His teeth were flaked with toasted corn bits and his hat sat sideways on his unsteady head. His face, half submerged into the collar of his poncho, rose to look in my general direction. *"Patrón, Guillermo,"* his eyes rolled and he could not make contact. "I have something very important to tell you."

I stepped closer so he could share the confidence.

"Patroncito, you cannot . . . ." He fumbled with his hands under his poncho, withdrew them, tried and failed to strike them together. He made a fresh assault on his sentence. "You cannot make a road with . . . ." He laughed and staggered a few steps then tried again ". . . make a road with your mouth." Having delivered himself of this bit of wisdom, he set about to explain

the meaning of his metaphor. "The people said they would build a road to Taba . . . Tab . . . acundo." He arched his eyebrows and asked "Did you see somebody build . . . make . . . cutting a road to Tabacundo . . . this morning . . . tomorrow morning?" He managed to liberate one hand from beneath his poncho. "No, not tomorrow and not yesterday." His head dropped and he swayed on his feet. "We will only make a road with our mouths. Not a bus road or a truck road, but a mouth road, unless . . ." He punched me in the chest with his finger to give his next point emphasis. ". . . unless *Patrón Guillermo* says we have to make a road!"

With it finally out, Alfonso lifted his hat, staggered backward a few shaky steps, turned and weaved his way down the path toward home.

Inside the hut I explained to Marie what Alfonso had revealed. Was it really true they had to have a patron figure to make them work on the road or was it Alfonso's personal and drunken opinion? Marie's counsel was that we wait and see. We were there to learn from the people, not to manipulate or direct them. We would wait until they took the initiative. In the meanwhile there were many jobs to be done. The most urgent was the thatching of roofs. The grass had to be cut, gathered and hauled in bundles up the two miles from the Pisque river. This kept us laboring from daylight until dark for two weeks.

During this time, as occasion presented itself, I asked my co-workers to explain why they insisted on calling me *patrón*. After all, wasn't I doing the same work as they, living in a hut even more humble than their own? They always managed to give me an answer that I could do something about. For example, when I was told that I was called *patrón* because I wore leather shoes, I was able to replace my shoes with a pair of Indian *alpargatas*, footwear with canvas sides and fiber soles.

On another occasion their response was that my poncho was from Otavalo where the Otovalan weavers made a special quality poncho of costly wool whereas the people of Picalquí got their ponchos from the Salcedo weavers, a much cheaper grade of wool, a poor man's garment. I made the switch.

But in spite of my *alpargatas* and rough Salcedo poncho, the moniker *patrón* stuck to me like a leach in a tropical swamp. Nevertheless, I was determined to pursue the matter until I was given a satisfactory answer.

That answer came while building the road to Tabacundo. In the early weeks of that effort—and I had nothing to do with organizing or encouraging it—the Indians had asked me to hold the palms of my hands up so I could see the difference between my rather uncalloused hands and theirs. Alfonso Chorlango held one of my hands and laid his heavily calloused palm on mine and rubbed it. Then he asked me to rub my hands against his. "Your hand is soft as a baby's. That's why we call you *patrón*, understand now?"

Yes, I understood and I was determined to finish the building of the road with hands like theirs. This meant throughout the coming weeks, sores and blisters, bandaged palms and painful nights.

It was the custom for the women to bring chicha to the road gang in the late afternoons. For the men who were tired and had empty stomachs, the chicha quickly induced lightheartedness and lively conversations. By the time the chicha had been consumed, the workers were barely able to gather up their tools and head for home. I thought to myself, "This may be my last chance to learn the uninhibited truth about *patrón*."

I called to Vicente Cuzco one day on the road, "Let me see your hands." He pushed back his poncho and held them out. I turned my palms up and held them beside his. "Now, Don Vicente, look at my hands. How in the name of the most holy santito can you still call me *patrón?*"

Vicente smiled and put his arm around my neck. He did not want to embarrass me in front of the others, so he put his mouth to my ear to share a confidence that he felt must have escaped my notice. "*Don Guillermo*, we call you *patrón* because you were not born of an Indian mother. You understand now?"

A month after the completion of the road, a notice was sent to Picalquí announcing that the mayor of Tabacundo would be visiting the new road. The band that had played for Mariano's funeral was hired again and a table was set up in the road and loaded with food and drinks. Finally, Picalquí, that forgotten, subservient Indian community was to be honored and recognized. On the appointed day a truckload of Tabacundo officials, their friends, and families came to cut the ribbon and open the new road. They likewise devoured the food and drinks. At the end of the festivities, the mayor read a press release and handed to the community a certificate "Class C" from the Department of Public Works in the capital. The folks from Picalquí were cautiously proud of their new status.

Two weeks later an official letter arrived upgrading Picalquí from *predio rústico* to *predio urbano*, a fifty percent increase in taxes. José Chuncho's dream of a snake collecting taxes at a toll booth had become a reality.

Anybody Here

Speak English?

By September 1955 almost three years had passed since we had entered Ecuador and learned from the drivers license examiner that in this nation there were no gentlemen drivers. If they considered me to be one, now with our departure, the number was regrettably back to zero. We had discussed our findings at Picalquí with the United Andean missionaries and made our recommendations about the big farm to the mission executives. As a result, Presbyterian leader, John Coventry Smith, asked if we would be willing to help the mission in Cameroun, West Africa. Africa had not been in our thoughts but after prayer and reflection, we decided to accept. In the meanwhile Dr. Eugene Nida had proposed that we attempt an ethnolinguistic survey of the Miskito (not Mosquito, although they were there too) coast of Honduras and Nicaragua

Governments, educators, linguists and missionaries have argued for a very long time about the demise of tribal languages when these are in competition with each other and with national or colonial languages. A methodology that could show which languages were gaining ground and which were losing and the dynamics of the process would greatly assist the Bible Societies and others in planning translation and publication programs and policies. The Miskito coast of the two central American republics was selected as a complex area with English and Spanish in competition with several Indian languages, the principal one being Miskito. To our knowledge such a study had never been undertaken and we were not yet certain how we would go about it. These were some of the thoughts going through our minds as the little MAF (Mission Aviation Fellowship) plane dipped sharply and glided down to the airstrip at Brus Lagoon, Honduras.

The Reverend and Mrs. Werner Marx of the Moravian mission were expecting us and welcomed us to their home. They made themselves available to assist us, gave us the use of their office and urged the Miskito Indian churches, schools and homes to cooperate in the survey. No one could have been more helpful.

Evangelization of the Miskito people was begun in Nicaragua in 1849 by the General Mission Board of the Moravian Church, Herrnhut, Germany. In 1914 the conditions of the first world war compelled the German mission to transfer its work to the American Moravian Church, Bethlehem, Pennsylvania. The work in Honduras was begun by a Miskito pastor from Nicaragua and only later did missionaries enter that area. At the time of our visit, there were four American missionary families, twelve native pastors and twenty-three helpers. Dedicated Moravian missionaries had translated and written more Miskito literature than existed in any other American Indian language, with the possible exception of Cherokee.

Our first task was to select ten survey areas or population centers and then devise a questionnaire which would give us significant information regarding an individual's ability to understand, speak, read and write Miskito, English or Spanish. Marie taught a bilingual helper who worked with her interviewing all the adults of Brus Lagoon, more than two hundred individuals. During the four weeks of the survey in Brus Lagoon, I did similar interviews in nine outlying areas, some along the Caribbean coast and others in the jungle interior.

Some villages could be reached along rivers by dugouts but others more distant required the service of MAF. Pilots of these planes were accustomed to land on rocky river beds that made the light plane hop and skip before bouncing to a halt. At Cocobila and Huampusirpi we took off on a stony river bed where the little bird jumped, danced, bucked, and finally leaped into the air with a forest wall dead ahead. I could see we were at full throttle as the trees were racing toward us. The pilot, Paul Weir, waited until the very last moment to gain maximum speed then pulled down the wing flaps and we sprang upward as he banked the plane and put one wing through a nitch in the trees and we climbed out to safety. Only then did I open my eyes and hear him remark, "Sorry, Reyburn, but that's the only way I know to get out of that place."

In Nicaragua we were able to find capable Spanish, English and Miskito-speaking assistants and did two thousand interviews, the majority from the costal towns of Bluefields and Puerto Cabezas but also from the mining center at Bonanza and for a hundred miles by motor boat up the Coco river that forms the border between the two nations.

Armed with a massive amount of documentation, we had to decide how to handle the data in order to make use of our findings. Today, this could be done conveniently with computers, but in those days computers were unknown. In Mexico City we met our colleague, Dr. Bill Wonderly, who suggested we transfer the information to punched cards, which we did during the following weeks. The punched cards would travel with us to France and the final draft of the survey report would be written in Paris, *Problems and Procedures in Ethnolinguistic Surveys, An Outline Based on a Pilot Study in a Multilingual Area.*

Before leaving for Paris for French studies, we visited our families in Colorado and North Carolina. Annie's grandmothers, who had waited three years to see her, were less than jubilant that their dear grandchild insisted on speaking only in Spanish.

FRANCE
AND
AFRICA

France

January 1956 we sailed out of New York Harbor on the SS United States. It was a rough Atlantic crossing that brought us to Le Havre in one of the coldest winters on record. In New York we had acquired a set of language learning records that promised we would be speaking fluent Parisian French the moment we stepped on to French soil. *Voulez-vous aller avec moi au cinema ce soir?* "Would you like to go to the cinema with me this evening?" The fact that such questions were hardly appropriate addressed to strangers, did not distract us from our goal. However, we were soon to learn that it was nearly impossible to converse with Parisians, who were too cold and too busy to waste time trying to understand foreigners—even if it was an invitation to the cinema.

European and American students normally enrolled at the *Alliance Française* and followed a prescribed course of grammar, composition and conversation. This school granted diplomas showing that the student had passed a certain number of courses. We had no interest in the diploma, which was often necessary for those who would eventually be involved in teaching and school administration. Instead of enrolling at the *Alliance*, we arranged for one of its teachers, Monsieur Charles Bouton, to give us private lessons with emphasis on conversation. Accordingly, we met at his apartment for two hours five mornings each week, after taking Annie to a day care provider.

During this time we lived in a suburb of Paris called Bois

Colombe that was reached from the Gare San Lazare. There we occupied the upstairs apartment in the home of Monsieur and Madame Beck who eventually invited us for tea and a chat. It was on this occasion that we learned something about Parisians. The Becks had no idea who lived on either side of them, although they had lived in the same house for more than twenty years. We were discouraged by the fact that people in Paris had no time to talk with us, but it may have been that we were not very interesting to listen to.

This may be seen, for example, in the way in which Spanish often got in the way of my speaking French. Sometimes a Spanish and French word were so similar that the Spanish word would cause me to derail and run along on the Spanish track. Take this example, *Je voudrais deux billets deuxième classe.* "I would like two second class tickets." When I thought French *billets* "tickets," Spanish *billetes* might leap into the sentence and the rest of the sentence and more would end up in Spanish. Eventually I learned to practice *code switching* but that was still some time off. I usually knew when I had jumped language tracks because the French listener would suddenly become squint-eyed, thrust his face forward, and then shrug a shoulder. The first time this happened at a ticket window, I turned to Marie and remarked that I had said it very clearly, why can't this person understand? Her reply: "You're right; it was clear . . . clear Spanish!"

When we learned of the presence of a French Protestant church near Bois Colombe, we thought this might be the appropriate place to make friends, invite someone over for coffee and a chat. The church was cold as a freezer and many had their coat collars turned up around their ears. No one shook hands or introduced themselves. Perhaps the place would be friendlier in the spring; maybe so, but we didn't stay to find out.

With the coming of spring we felt we should get out of Paris and try to find someplace where people would not be so harassed by busyness and might even find chatting with foreigners to be entertaining. We explained our decision to the Reverend Camille

Chazeaud, the Presbyterian overseer in Paris, and he seemed to understand our concern to get out of the faceless city. We took the train south for approximately two hundred and fifty kilometers to a small town recommended by our instructor. In Sancergue we found a friendly *pension de famille* across a quiet street from a large park where people sat on benches and seemed to enjoy being alive. It could have been, *sans montagnes*, a town in Ecuador, and we soon felt at home.

Our final attack on learning and using French took us to eastern France near Colmar. Having no contacts there, we telephoned the Lutheran pastor in the village of Etobon and asked if he could help us find accommodation in his parish. He asked us to come to the village by bus where he met us and took us to his house. Pastor Schiller and his wife invited us to remain with them, and for the first time we were made part of a French family, an ideal solution that we had hoped for since getting off the boat in Le Havre.

During World War II Etobon had been occupied by German troops until the allied invasion. We were told that a German officer had spent so much time trying to tie a stolen chair to his motorcycle that he ended up being shot. I wrote in my notes "Be prepared to cut your losses and move on." A memorial in the village listed the names of all the boys and men of Etobon killed by the Germans. As we visited many homes with the pastor, the absence of men in the village was tragically felt.

Again we were grateful for the kindness shown to us by the pastor and his parish and, when we departed, we felt better equipped to move on to West Africa.

The General Mangin

The summer flush of July in Marseille contrasted sharply with the freezing January that had greeted us at Le Havre, and the accommodations aboard the General Mangin were incomparably superior to the cramped and stuffy room below decks on the Atlantic crossing. The French cuisine awakened the appetite and every table was provisioned with three choices of wine. The sea along the west coast of Africa was glassy calm and the sunsets beyond the flaming clouds a picture of peace.

But peace it was not. It was 1956 and France, haunted by the loss of Indochina in 1954, was scrambling to hold on to her African colonies. Algeria, where less than ten percent of the population were French settlers, could look for little if anything from France for its ten million people. The Fourth Republic would be overthrown and General Charles de Gaulle returned to power. Cries for national independence were being heard around the world. Morocco and Tunisia pulled out of the French Union, as did Guinea which proclaimed complete independence and no association with France.

France, which tried unsuccessfully to recolonize Indochina after WWII, had consistently denied autonomous development for its colonies. Colonial people were to be assimilated into French culture, language, political systems and education. Her policy was designed to train an elite core to think and act as good Frenchmen.

Since ancient times imperialist powers have used conquered people to carry out their expansionist policies. In the era of modern colonization Britain, Belgium, Holland and France have trained and incorporated into their armies men from the colonies. For example, France used African colonial troops to fight the Vietminh in an effort to impose French colonial rule upon Asian people who were determined to rule themselves. It became abundantly clear to African soldiers fighting in Indochina that helping the French hold to her Asian colonies was dead wrong and that they needed to go home and win their own freedom.

This was the message conveyed to me by African soldiers on the General Mangin who had been discharged from the French army and were being repatriated to such places as Senegal, Guinea, Ivory Coast, Togo, Dahomey and Cameroun. Every soldier I conversed with was determined to see his country gain its freedom from France and to develop its own political independence, with an economic and educational system based on the realities of the African context.

Little did they or the rest of us realize that the United States would soon rush into the vortex left by the departing French, and become engaged in the longest war in United States history. By the end of that war 57,000 U.S. troops would die and more than 300,000 would be wounded. These figures are small compared to the losses sustained by the South Vietnamese, the Viet Cong and the North Vietnamese.

Talking with soldiers who read their French Bibles, I saw how they read them, as certainly they should, through African eyes. The story of Moses liberating the Hebrews from Egyptian oppression was a favorite. One corporal showed me the outlines of a dozen sermons he said he would preach when he got home: "My village people need to see that they can be liberated." Another passage that was often quoted was John 8:36 *Si donc le Fils vous rend libres, vous serez réellement libres.* "If the Son therefore shall make you free, ye shall be free indeed." The Bible for these men was a call to liberation and they scoured its pages underlining passages that inspired their newly found spirit of independence.

These earnest soldiers, so full of hopes for independence, would return home to find in many places, an active *maquisard* or underground movement already in place. Whole villages would be attacked and massacred because they refused to join the rebellion. The colonial administration built fortifications to protect villagers from night raids. In the cities, sidewalk cafés were strafed by machine gun fire, grenades lobbed into cinemas, and daylight raids carried out in open markets.

However, France was able to bring nearly all its African colonies into the French Union and to select a cadre of African bureaucrats who in a short while became a new salaried elite in African society. Within four years of our arrival in Cameroun, independence was granted to nearly all France's African colonies. Bit by bit these new African nations would be caught up in the cold war struggle between America and the Soviet Union. They became skillful in playing the one off against the other and were denounced by each side as corrupt.

Our ship was right on schedule as we docked at port after port. Then while in the open sea between Abidjan and Cotonou a crewman, who must have been working his broom more than his brain, fell overboard. Fortunately, this happened in the daylight and we all ran to the decks while the siren screeched. The ship made a great circle, returning to where the sailor's head could be seen bobbing in the wake, and fished him out. My memory of falling out of the dugout in the Puyo river in Ecuador was too fresh to leave me indifferent. The man was taken to the doctor's office for examination and when he emerged I was waiting. To my question about the water he replied *C'etait très froid.*

The day before our arrival in Douala, we awoke to find Annie standing naked in the room examining herself. She was covered with chicken pox. To avoid frightening other passengers, we brought her food to the room and kept her out of sight, except to see the doctor who surely reported the case to the captain for the man came to us and growled some unintelligible abuse, almost as if the chicken pox were something we had planned. Wagging his finger in our faces, he told us to keep her out of sight and get her off his ship. I shouted back at him "What do you expect us to do, throw her overboard?" He trundled off still shouting obscenities. Annie was in tears thinking she had committed some outrage that would send the ship to the bottom. Marie, who was five months pregnant with our second daughter, Susie, consoled Annie, assuring her that all would be well, and Annie agreed to keep her face hidden behind her doll until we got past the immigration officer.

From the harbor we bade farewell to the ship then, in anticipation, gazed up to the palm trees along the shore that were waving their fronds in welcome. *Voilà l'Afrique!*

Aloum

Thanks to such magazines as National Geographic and their dedicated film crews, most Americans and Europeans have a view of Africa with great herds of zebra, wildebeest, and impala dashing across endless grasslands chased by hungry hyenas, lions or wild dogs. Exciting and picturesque as these images are, they hardly represent the vast variety of the African continent. In the same way it would be unfair to describe a forested area of West Africa as being the quintessence of the real Africa.

The trip by road from the town of Ebolowa, Cameroun, to the village of Aloum, where we lived while immersing ourselves in the Bulu language, can be two quite different journeys depending upon the season. There are two: rainy and dry.

In the dry season the laterite road surface, a rusty red, is ground to powder and strewn by passing vehicles over the luxuriant vegetation. The road is a narrow ribbon threading its way through a deep forest that extends endlessly from the roadsides. From the air a car rumbling over the dry season road appears to spew rose colored clouds on a carpet of green.

African huts, banana and cocoa trees, cassava plants are showered with a new coat of dust by each passing car or truck. White sheep and goats that scavenge near the road change in color through the dry season from white to cherry pink, to rouge and finally to copper red. During this season when the taste of dust has lingered long in every mouth, streams, no matter how

small, become communal baths, and soap lathered bodies wave
to passing vehicles that are laying down yet another coat of red.

Then, as if loosed by an infuriated nature, the skies darken
and the rains begin, at first a breeze and then a light sprinkle
that bubbles the dust. The great forest trees begin to sway under
the force of tropical winds. The sky is ripped by lightning flashes
and the deluge descends. Animals scramble for shelter and in
the embrace of a single night the dry season's dust and drab are
washed away.

The powdering of plants gives way to a sparkling freshness
revealing myriad hues of green. Massive banana leaves that hung
depressed now extend themselves and serve as umbrellas for
troops of rain-soaked goats. Morning sun warms the palm thatch
roofs that send steam drifting upward. The planted gardens, warm
and damp, awaken to a new growing season. Black legs and feet
that have walked the dusty roads are now washed and glisten
with oil.

The road from Ebolowa to Aloum continues on to the coast.
Across it are numerous streams and small wooden bridges that
rattle with the crossing of each vehicle. The houses, like the
bridges, are all built on the same pattern—mud and wattle. The
banana and cocoa trees and the cassava plants that grow near
each cluster of huts are, like cornfields in Iowa, endlessly the
same.

The miracle of the West African forest people is that they
have existed there for millennia without dependence on roads
and vehicles. Iron instruments such as axes and hoes have been
forged locally or bartered for and it is only in recent times that
dependence on cash crops and town markets with European goods
has developed. In economic terms the import of European goods
and the export of raw materials has been at the very heart of
colonization.

Cameroun had been a German colony until after WWI when
it was divided into British and French mandates of the League of

Nations. The French area was administered as a colony with French language and culture intensively pursued until January 1, 1960, when it gained its independence and became the Republic of Cameroun. October 1, 1961, the Federal Republic of Cameroun was created uniting the former English and French colonies. The country stretches more than seven hundred miles from the rain forest in the south through the rolling grassland to the hot, dry deserts of the north.

Cameroun, covering an area the size of California but with a population equivalent to that of Los Angeles, is the home of some two hundred and sixty different languges and the greatest concentration of ethnic and linguistic diversity in Africa. Little wonder that Marie and I greeted the invitation to work in such a seething linguistic cauldron with enormous pleasure.

Just as the nation is a veritable patchwork quilt of languages, so most villages have people, who in addition to speaking the local language, may speak several other languages as well. In the case of Aloum everyone speaks Bulu, and in addition German, Pidgin English, Spanish, French and Ewondo, a closely related Bantu tongue, could be heard. There were a few elderly people who had been trained by the Germans and, although the Germans disappeared forty years earlier, these aging folks delighted in remembering their school days and the symbol of their youth was the German language. People who had worked in large towns, particularly along the coast, had acquired Pidgin—a much simplified form of English—and when they learned that we were not French, they delighted in showering us with that half-intelligible tongue. I found this language fascinating and had to study it seriously to understand it. Some of the Aloumians had worked in Spanish Guinea (Equatorial Guinea) lying just south of Bululand and they were often happy to converse with us in Spanish. Then everyone who had attended the local school had learned French. This meant, at the time of our stay, nearly all the males under thirty were fluent in French, that is, French spoken in the African forests. Still there was another means of communication—the Bulu drum language. Although only a few men knew how to send drum signals, all the adults and most of the young people understood these messages. In a land with no telephones, receiving and sending drummed messages was frequently vitally important.

It is easy to see, therefore, that living in a Bulu village to learn the African language, the main medium of the Presbyterian church in the rain forest, we had to face the fact that multilingualism was an aspect of village life and we had to adjust to it. As we went about our language learning, we gradually learned which person would likely use which language with us. If we did not exercise some discipline by insisting they speak to us in Bulu, our Bulu studies could easily have been wrecked. Unlike Paris and Bois Colombe where we could find nearly no one to speak with us in French, Aloum was the opposite. Often the problem was how to arrange private and uninterrupted time for study. We found this could be done best, but by no means ideally, when most of the people were out working in their forest gardens in the early morning hours.

Another problem for us was how to identify people by households because they came and went so freely from each other's houses. In order to know which children belonged to which mother and who the father of the family was—there was no polygamy—we asked all the members of a household to stand in front of their house and have their family picture taken. In this way we were able to learn who was who and to which household each belonged.

Presbyterian missionary Mary Hunter had suggested Aloum to us and spoke with the people on our behalf. The chief gave us the small house that belonged to a local man who worked in Yaoundé, the capital. This was a concrete block house with metal roof and was divided into three rooms: kitchen, sitting room and bedroom. Although with no toilet or running water, it was the only house in Aloum with a cement floor and, compared with our thatched hut in Picalquí, it was an imposing mansion.

Aloum lay in a forest clearing a few minutes walk from the main road, some twenty huts that formed a rectangle with a single oblong hut, the men's club house, at the center. Aloum was a quiet gardening community where each weekday began with the public reading of the Bible and the singing of hymns, a Christian ceremony known throughout Bululand as *Filia*.

The males of Aloum were descendanats of a single clan. The married women, by rules of marriage, came from a clan other than that of the husband. This means that the men, their sons and unmarried daughters belonged to the same clan while the wives and mothers were foreigners in their husband's village. In case of divorce a woman could be sent back to her father's clan but would be required to leave her children with her husband, for they belonged, by right of bride payment, to their father's clan.

The advantage of tackling the language in a village is that one learns the culture, or at least aspects of it, along with the language, something that is not possible for those who study in a town or on a mission station. However, it is only fair to say that without adequate linguistic and anthropological training, the young missionary plunged from the outset into tribal life ran the risk of severe culture shock.

To live successfully in Aloum we had to observe and adjust our behavior daily. Marie, who was nearly six months pregnant, found the village women to be solicitous of her condition and therefore would often stop at our house, not just to inquire how she felt, but to feel her belly and breasts thus assuring themselves that mother and baby were developing well.

The men's club house, a mud and thatch hut with walls open from about three feet to the eaves, was the nerve center of the village. Here the men gathered to discuss affairs that impinged on the life of the community. This was the place where marriages were arranged, where communal work projects were planned. The club house, also called palaver house, was the local court where complaints were heard, legal affairs adjudicated. It was the seat of education for young boys, the oral archive of tribal memories where voices in the night told and retold the traditions of the past. And most of all, it was off-limits to women.

The people of Aloum were gentle teachers. They instructed me to stay away from the village spring because it was thought that an expectant father drawing water would cause the spring to go dry. On Sundays men who owned a pair of shoes carried them as far as the stream where they sat down and washed their feet, put on their clean shoes and went on to church. At first, I ignorantly walked all the way to church with my shoes on and it was pointed out to me that anyone who owned a pair of shoes should wear them only after crossing the stream so that they would be clean on entering the sanctuary.

We did not realize at the beginning how our hosts understood our guest status. For example, when we walked out to the main road and visited other people, we learned that the Aloumians expected a full accounting of our absence. Where had we been? Who had we talked with? Had anyone given us food? What did people tell us? Eventually we became resentful of being interrogated and it caused a strain in our relation with the people of Aloum.

Our hosts felt themselves responsible for our food and when we returned one day from visiting outside the village, someone saw that I was carrying two eggs. It was generally believed by the Bulu people that foreigners are egg-hungry people and there is nothing an African can give a white person that will make him happier than a few eggs. The local people used eggs only to raise chicks and did not eat them. While passing a man's hut that day we were urged to stop and rest. His place was clean and comfortably furnished with two cane chairs and a coffee table. We sat and made conversation with the man until we were ready to move on. At that point our host went to an ancient phonograph, reached his arm to the elbow inside the speaker and carefully extracted two brown eggs which he then laid gently in Marie's open hands. When we were again on the road and in a sunlit clearing, we examined the eggs by holding them to the light in our cupped hands. They were as opaque as the African forest on a moonless night.

There are many things about African languages that make them difficult for Americans and Europeans to learn, one thing being too often attitudes of cultural superiority. However, there are also linguistic factors; for example, one characteristic of Bantu languages is that all nouns belong to a particular class and each class has its own classifiers expressed in such things as numerals, adjectives, personal pronouns, etc. For example, if we say "I have one man," the numeral one is *wua*, but in "one body" one is *jia*, in "one nose" one becomes *da*, in "one hair" one is *ji*, in "one tongue" one is *vi*. Some Bantu languages have fourteen or more such noun classes.

Pidgin English appears to have developed in West Africa and the Caribbean as well as in the southeastern United States and evolved in connection with the slave trade in the seventeenth and eighteenth centuries. A pidginized form of a language develops when native people learn parts of the foreigner's language and the foreigner speaks back to the people, not in the standard form of his language, but in the way the native speaker is transforming it. When we first heard Pidgin spoken in Aloum, it struck us as broken English pronounced like an African language and being a mixture of English and African vocabulary strung together in unfamiliar syntactic patterns. Consider the following sentences:

Di man wana mek pria "The man wants to say a prayer;" *Pikin fo nyi go fo sikol fo chiaf* "His children (English 'pickaniny' from Portuguese *pequenino* 'little') go to school at twelve (noon);" *Mai fada yi go fo tison an mebe yi kombak for eben tam* "My father he goes to town (station) and maybe he will come back in the evening time;" *Yi de fo woman hand o fo man hand* "He is on the left side (woman hand) or on the right side (man hand); *Yu sabe u said ma dok yi de?* "You know (Portuguese *saber*) whose side (where) my dog is?"

Today the entire New Testament has been translated into Cameroun Pidgin and the reader of English can sense the flavor of Pidgin's expression in a few verses from Mark 1:9-11.

(9) *I bi bi fo dat tam* "In those days" *Jesus bi kam fo Nazaret weh i bi fo Galile* "Jesus came from Nazareth of Galilee" *an John bi baptas yi fo Jordan wata* "and was baptized by John in the Jordan." (10) *Jos as yi bi komot fo di wata* "And when he came up out of the water" *wantam, yi bi si hawe di heven dem di opun* "immediately he saw the heavens opened" *an di Spirit fo God di kam daun fo yi lek som dov* "and the Spirit of God descending upon him like a dove." (11) *An som vos bi komot fo heven* "And a voice came from heaven" *Yu bi ma pikin weh mi a lekam plenti* "You are my beloved Son" *Mi a di glad fo yu plenti* "with you I am well pleased." (Me, I am glad for you plenty.)

Today there are nearly half a million people in Cameroun for whom this is the language of their everyday working lives, and for many young people in cities it has become their mother tongue. Although Pidgin may strike speakers of standard English as drollish, it is the language of the heart for many West Africans. In it they make love, dream, and confide their innermost secrets to each other and to God.

Elephant

Perhaps the most difficult cultural baggage for Westerners to discard when living in the African context is their concept of private property. In order to obtain meat for the people of Aloum—they were providing us with vegetables from their gardens—I shot birds and monkeys. Although the Aloumians had sheep, goats, ducks and chickens, they did not use them for food but as payment or exchange in marriages. As their sons took brides, these animals were transferred to the family of the bride. On the other hand, when one of their own daughters went off into marriage, animals were added to the stock of Aloum. In this way sheep and goats were a major form of wealth that increased and diminished according to the marriage market.

We did not realize that Aloum was about to be blessed with a vast quantity of meat nor did we know that my rifle, in another man's hands, would provide that meat. The subsequent rivalry between villages would hit an all-time high and bring us into conflict with the French colonial administration.

One day while we were busy with a language helper, a messenger came from the chief and summoned me urgently to accompany him. When I reached the palaver house, it seemed that nearly every adult male in Aloum was present. A stranger—at least I had not seen him before—was miming what appeared to be a hunt. He crouched, crawled, rose to his feet, shaded his eyes, sniffed the air, pushed back invisible foliage, looked right and then left and finally raised an imaginary gun and fired.

Slapping his hands, he leaped across the room and began to hack at his victim. He then lifted his hands to his lips and let go a shrill shout that could be heard across the forest. The hunter had just demonstrated his skill in tracking and killing an elephant.

Marie and I knew there were elephants in the forests around Aloum for we had seen how an elephant could smash and destroy an entire field of cassava in a single night, knock down banana trees and crush growing plants under its monstrous feet. A family's entire living could be wiped out in minutes by one or two of these voracious beasts. We had learned to recognize the rumble of an elephant's digestion in the silence of the night.

The chief of Aloum, known as Nkukum Mengele, had invited one of his relatives to kill one of the elephants and, hopefully, the rest would leave the area. The slaying of an elephant would give the people of Aloum an abundance of meat such as they almost never had. The key to this venture was my rifle. Turning to me, the chief quietly said, *Ya, Obam, tame zu ngale jangan.* The people had given me the name *Obam* "hawk" and Marie they called *Nlemeyen* "sweetheart." I understood the words perfectly and, before I realized it, I was on my feet crossing the courtyard toward our hut. But the words *ngale jangan* mean "our rifle," not "your rifle." *Ngal* "rifle" belongs grammatically to that class of nouns that take "j" as a prefix to each of the possessive pronouns. Surely he must have said *ngale joé* "your rifle." But no, he didn't say "your rifle," he very clearly said *jangan* "our." I know because the two vowels of *jangan* are on high tones. OK, so what was "my gun" is now "the people's gun." I recalled stories from the Soviet Union in which owners were evicted from large houses so that the communist party could provide accommodation for numerous families. I had the guilty feeling of being a capitalist pig in this communistic community. Marie was still sitting in front of our place with the language helper when I told her the purpose of my errand.

She reminded me of the young man in the village who had come home from working in the town of Ebolowa where he had earned money and bought a new Raleigh bicycle. At home in Aloum he tried to keep it as his private property, locking it and keeping it inside his hut. But the Aloumians did not accept that it was his and only his. For refusing to share it with his village brothers and fathers, the young man came in from the forest one day to find his shiny new bicycle bashed to pieces and hanging from a tree limb. If it was not *our* bicycle it was *nobody's* bicycle. Without further reflection, I got "our gun" and returned to the palaver house.

Again in the palaver house, I handed over the gun and a clip of five rounds to the visitor, showed him how to load, aim and fire. He learned quickly. I sat down waiting to find out when we would depart for the hunt. Imagine my surprise when I learned that no expectant father goes on a big game hunt. I could not believe what they were telling me. Looking about the room, I could see several men whose wives were pregnant. "*Ya, Mbutu, on ngule ya ke?*" I asked Mbutu if he could go. He shook his head "no." I inquired of one or two others. Their replies were the same and my heart sank, for I had some hunting credentials of my own.

My mother had been raised on a sheep ranch at Virginia Dale, Colorado, rode a horse to a one-room log school and carried a rifle slung on her saddle. It was the job of all the family to protect the sheep from marauding wolves. By the time she was ten she knew how to load and fire a rifle and had saved more than one lamb from a ravenous wolf. When my father died, he had left several rifles which I was to inherit, but hard times in the depression forced mother to sell all but one, and with this one rifle she had taught me to shoot and to hunt.

The mothers of some boys teach them to play the piano and that is fine. Mine taught me to hunt and how to handle a gun and here I was, an ex-marine sharpshooter, in Africa on the eve of a big-game hunt and with a brand-new high-powered rifle, and I was not allowed to go because my wife was pregnant. I felt the victim of a gross injustice and it took the best of Marie's wise counsel to persuade me to play the game by the rules of Aloum.

Ironically, it was the African hunt that eventually would cause me to liberate myself from the gun complex. Several years after the killing of the elephant in Aloum, I was hunting in the far north of Cameroun when, in the company of four Potoko tribesmen, I caught sight of a pair of large Bubale antelope silhouetted behind a scrub brush. It appeared that they had just mated. The larger of the pair stood nearly four feet tall at the withers and weighed well over four hundred pounds. The Bubale is a curious animal and will often stop moving and stand perfectly still, allowing the hunter to aim and fire at his leisure. I dropped to one knee, calmly brought my sight to the heart, counted slowly to three and fired. The big male collapsed without taking a step. The Potokos behind me demanded I shoot the female; however, I paid no attention and began walking toward the slain antelope. The female kept her nose down, breathing heavily against the hide of her fallen mate. As I approached, she left her companion and slowly strode straight toward me, the reproving look in her large dark eyes causing me to halt in my tracks.

I picked up a stone and flung it to make her leave, but she would not retreat. The tribesmen had withdrawn, thinking she was determined to gore me. No more than twenty feet away she stopped, examining me with her unblinking and censorious stare. Never had I felt more like a murderer. Had I not grown up the child of a widow woman? Where for goodness sakes was the peace resolve that so forcefully had awakened me sixteen years earlier in the crumbled debris of Nagasaki? Somehow the gun and the hunt were in contradiction to something alive in my spirit. I ejected the unspent cartridges into the sand and, later, gave the gun to an African friend. I have never hunted again.

Before daybreak, the elephant hunter and three companions silently filed off into the jungle. The people spent the day in hushed anticipation. It was about dusk when the four returned to the village carrying an elephant trunk wrapped in leaves. That night all of Aloum danced to the beat of drums, celebrating the hunter's success. Only one bullet had been fired. According to the hunter, the elephant was asleep on its feet with its great head hanging, and the hunter had to sneak from its tail to its head to get his shot. He said the huge ears never moved and we later learned that the shell burst through the cavernous sinus directly into the brain.

Early the next morning, like a column of army ants, we marched off to bring home the slaughtered beast. We had been underway for nearly three hours when the hunter took the lead, assuring us that we were now near the place of the kill. However, even after spreading out through the forest, we were unable to locate the fallen elephant. People talked about spirits that carry away dead animals in the night. We had all seen the severed trunk, so how could it be that the animal had revived and was stumbling about in the forest? Some of the men climbed trees to get a better look. A feeling of disappointment and chagrin was developing.

Then a shout was heard. When I reached the spot, the beast lay on its right side with its left legs stiff in the air held aloft by the bloated carcass. The sight of this gray mountain of swollen flesh on the green forest floor was spellbinding. Many of the young people had never seen an elephant. They stood about gaping at it as if beholding a creature from an alien world.

A pool of thick blood soaked the earth where the trunk had been hacked off. Flies buzzed everywhere. I was curious to see where the bullet had entered and was about to lift the head by one of the tusks when someone grabbed me and told me it was taboo for me to touch any part of the animal. "You must think of your wife and baby," they reminded me, again.

Chief Mengele organized the first butchering crew, put the people in groups and told me to sit down with the expectant fathers, whom I had now christened *The Untouchables*. One of my fellow outcasts tried to make our banishment rational by saying, "If you touch or eat the meat, the head of your child will become too large to pass through the birth canal." That got a little heavy for my grasp of Bulu and I called a Spanish speaker over to clear some of it up, which he willingly did then added his own "no touch, no eat, have a happy birth" ending. Accepting that I could do little else, I settled down with this select company of exiles to observe the fine art of African butchering.

The first crew of four armed with sharp machetes hacked off the head and rolled it to one side. Climbing aboard the swollen carcass, they made crisscross cuts through the thick wrinkled hide. While one man pulled up on the hide, another cut beneath it taking it off in large squares, which they dumped into piles. It looked to me like great slabs of bacon, but the man beside me said it would be used to make sandal soles.

During the skinning, the carcass was swollen from the gas in the stomach. To reduce the pressure and make it easier to stand on the slippery surface, one of the team thrust his machete into the stomach causing a geyser of half digested grass to spew into the air and emit a shrill whistle. The fermented grass juice was collected into bowls and eaten, having, I was told, a sharp tangy taste. Unlike the forest pygmies, who eat the grass in the intestines down to the point where it becomes manure, these folks stripped the intestines of their contents and left it behind, the only thing in the animal they did not take home.

When the fountain of stomach grass subsided and the hide had been removed from one side, a second team, naked except for loin cloths, mounted the carcass and began cutting out the body parts which were carried to one side and heaped into piles. By the time this team was finished, they were standing knee-deep in blood. Their final act was to turn the elephant over and, as they did, people sitting close by had to scramble back to escape being soaked by the flood of blood. The butchering of the right side was done by the same two teams and continued without a break until the animal had been reconfigured into six or seven great stacks of hide, meat, body parts, bones and intestines.

The chief then appointed one man to take an axe and cut out the tusks from the head and remove the ears, whose skin would be used for drumheads. After the tusks had been removed, most eyes were fixed on the heaps of meat and so I took advantage of the distraction to crawl near the head, lift the axe and split open the big skull. I was then able to see the brain case and how the bullet had entered it. As I crawled back to my place of excommunion, I could feel that my face was flecked with blood. I pulled off my shirt and wiped away the evidence of my misconduct before the banished brotherhood could condemn me. It felt satisfying to have looked into the skull without anyone knowing that I had delighted in breaking their taboo.

With the butchering completed, I was anxious to see how the great gobs of flesh would be distributed. I had by now lost any desire to have a taste after watching and smelling the proceedings for at least three hours. I was soon to learn that a just and equitable distribution of so much protein was complex and difficult beyond my imagination.

It was about two p.m. when the chief and his helpers began to redistribute the elephant into some twenty batches, which, I assumed, represented the twenty households of Aloum. Too much bone in one pile had to be given more meat and too many intestines in another had also to be adjusted. When finally the piles were completed, the chief gave the signal and each household, clothes-hamper size baskets in hand, made a rush to claim their loot. What followed was a show of aggression I had not seen before this day. Women set about shoving, pushing, pulling, hitting, shouting, name calling and cursing. The peaceful shared community life of Aloum that we had enjoyed was in a moment shattered and abandoned. I was pained and disappointed, regretting that I had brought a rifle to Aloum and disrupted its life so brutally. Without our rifle all of this madness would not have happened and I would have remained innocent and ignorant of this dark side of the Aloumians.

By the time the melee was over and some semblance of order had been reestablished, I thought the families would load their baskets and we would start for home. How wrong I was! For the next two hours I witnessed the legal side of these forest people, the way claims and counter claims remain alive and active for generations.

It began with Mvondo, one of the older men, who walked over to the stack of meat guarded by Ewondo and his family. Mvondo raised his hand to silence the crowd. Then he faced Ewondo and spoke, "Ewondo, if your memory serves you as it should, you will recall that my great grandfather Ndubu came to the aid of your grandfather Mfan when he was ready to take his wife, Abang. I invite you to recall on that occasion what Ndubu gave Mfan. Did he not give three goats, a sheep and four ducks so that Mfan could pay the bride price for your grandmother? Since that day long ago you have done nothing to repay the debt. "Now," Mvondo waved a hand to silence the people, "in the presence of all who are witnesses, you can give up your claim to this meat." Mvondo laid his hand on Ewondo's meat pile. "Your debt to my family will be cleared, cancelled this day and will be remembered against you no more."

It was clear, if the historical facts were correct, that Mvondo had a good claim against Ewondo. I thought Ewondo would make a gesture to repay the debt by giving some of his meat to Mvondo and we could at last—I was getting very hungry—load up the baskets and head for home. The sky was also darkening with rain clouds. How simply I thought these good folks could solve their problems. However, far from sharing his meat with Mvondo, Ewondo marched down the line of baskets until he came to Ze's pile and repeated almost the same claim against Ze. Ze, in his turn, made a speech that lasted twice as long as Mvondo's and wove a skein of rhetoric that involved histories reaching back many generations. I got lost in a jungle of Bulu metaphors and kinship terms and someone's French translation got hopelessly bogged down and gave up. Ze seemed to have claims against nearly everyone in the village. Several of the ostracized fathers of future babies, having no meat to defend, had nodded off. I asked Kulu how this endless litigation was going to be resolved. He simply replied, "It takes more time."

And time it took; it could not be rushed, for if there was anything democratic about Aloum, it was the right to speak, but speaking was an art. Unless you possessed that art, you remained silent. Everyone waited until every orator had had his say. It was now getting late and since everyone was indebted to someone, the only solution was to allow the status quo to continue. In spite of all the claims, no one added or lost an ounce of meat, bones, hide or whatever. The massive rhetorical energy had spent itself and, without further squabbles, baskets were loaded and the protein train finally pulled out.

Back in the village, no one would think of refusing to share a cooked elephant meal with his neighbor. The communal sharing of the goods of this life renewed itself and life went on as before.

I thought the matter of the elephant was now history until a few weeks later when the French colonial administrator, Monsieur Chanlais, appeared in Aloum. He sat in his Deux Chevaux surveying the village as part of his administrative domain at an hour in the morning when the people were busy out in their jungle gardens. After dispersing a knot of curious children, he got down, carefully removed a large white handkerchief from his white jacket pocket, dusted himself, folded the cloth and carefully replaced it and then walked briskly toward our house. I went out to greet him.

"*Soyez vous le bienvenu, Monsieur,*" I welcomed him and invited him into our tiny sitting room. I explained that the people of the village were still out in the forest. He bowed somewhat stiffly and shook hands with Marie. He seemed surprised that we had a small daughter. Invited to have a glass of Marie's tropical fruit mixture, he sipped it cautiously examining the glass as if looking for signs of impurities and sniffing the juice each time he brought it near his lips. "I have not had this brand of drink before," he confessed. "Does it not cause some misbehavior in the liver?" I assured him that we drank it often with no ill effects. "But," he hastened to inform me, "you are from the deserts of Amerique where the grape cannot be cultivated, *n'est-ce-pas?* The French stomach is a product of the Mediterranean climate, more humid and, I am certain, more healthy." He pushed his glass aside and did not touch it again.

Glancing out into the village where goats were resting in the shade of the huts, he continued. "I am disturbed, Monsieur, that you should be living in this dirty . . ." He paused searching for a more bureaucratic term "unsanitary village *avec les noirs.* You do not have the natural immunity to protect this small girl from the scourge of diseases that periodically wipe out entire populations." He motioned over his shoulder to the village. I assured him that we boiled our drinking water and had been immunized against a number of diseases. I could see that he was not impressed. His office in Ebolowa was littered with posters warning people of malaria, syphilis and gonorrhea.

He asked to see our residence permit and sat reading it, all the while making a clicking sound in his throat. "So you are assigned to study the Cameroun languages and teach people to read them." The thought of the disease infested village was suddenly replaced by a much more urgent concern. He arose as if speaking to the world at large. "Monsieur Reyburn, do you not understand that the African of tomorrow will forget his primitive patois and join the international community of French speakers, live on a higher plane where the grunts and guttural noises of his native dialect will be replaced by the Parisian tongue?" Chanlais' face grew grim as he continued to voice the ethos of his colonial training. "To teach these children of the forest to read their grammarless dialects is to rob them of the time they could be learning to speak the language of a somewhat higher species of human. It is for them the necessary evolution from the darkness into the light of civilization. Do you fail to understand how the colonial practice has guided them?" Chanlais' enthusiasm moved him closer to me so that I could feel the flecks of his saliva striking me. I stepped backward to avoid the spray. Chanlais was a hawk in pursuit of its prey. However, his steam soon faded and he settled again into his chair. It seemed he was about to disclose the real purpose of his visit.

"*Monsieur, je dois vous demander . . .*" He hesitated and then tried a new tactic. "Has there been some kind of incident in this village?" He again pointed over his shoulder. I could think of no incident and he rephrased his question. "I refer to the killing of elephants."

"*Des éléphants?*" I asked in surprise. "No, I have heard of no one killing elephants."

He leaned closer. "It is reported by reliable sources—you are no doubt aware that we French have our eyes and ears in the forests—that a white man in this very village has been shooting elephants." His index finger was thumping my knee.

"Oh, I think you mean elephant, one elephant, not two or three." I brought my hunting permit. He examined it carefully, the date it was issued, the stamps, and on the back he gazed for a long while at his own signature. Then, he relaxed for the first time since he had entered. A smile crinkled the corners of his eyes. I think he was relieved that he would not, after all, have to arrest this man who had such a nice wife and little daughter, even if he was going to set the colony back years by teaching *les noirs* to read their own babel of dialects.

Officer Chanlais inquired about the elephant's tusks, which I brought to him. He examined them and said, "You know, Monsieur, that you may only keep a tusk that weighs more than ten kilograms. Smaller tusks must be turned into my office." He estimated the weight of one of the tusks in his hands. "These will weigh far less than the required amount so I must ask you to bring them both to Ebolowa."

Bouncing up onto his feet, he thanked Marie for the drink, which he had barely tasted. "I must continue the inspection of my subdivision." We shook hands and when again near his vehicle, he withdrew the folded cloth and wiped his hands and face all the while casting a sour glance around the village. After scattering the children who had been crawling under his vehicle, he mounted his Deux Chevaux, saluted and putt-putted out of Aloum.

Soon after Chanlais departed, the men gathered in the clubhouse and were expecting me when I went in. With one voice they asked, "What did he say? What did he want? Will he be back?" I told them that he had heard a rumor that a white man in Aloum was killing elephants. In the conversation that followed I learned that the neighbors of Aloum had found out about the elephant. But because the Aloumians refused to share their meat with the neighboring villages, the latter had sought revenge by reporting me to the administration. The sin of stinginess was not easily forgiven.

The day before I delivered the two tusks to Chanlais' office, I learned that Wendell Sprague, dentist for the Presbyterian mission, had made a set of dentures for the man. Dr. Sprague suggested he accompany me to hand in the tusks. When I laid the tusks on Chanlais' desk, Sprague took the Frenchman to the window to inspect his handiwork. The dentist knew that the administrator was delighted with his new teeth, and the coincidence of the elephant's teeth and Chanlais' teeth was too good an opportunity to let slip by. When the smiling officer returned to his desk, he handed me one of the tusks. "I know it is a bit small, but it will always be a souvenir of your days in the French colony. I will remember Doctor Sprague for a fine set of teeth and you can remember Cameroun with your elephant tooth." He clasped my hand warmly, *"Cette affaire d'éléphant est finie."*

Susie

As the time grew near for Susie's birth, we packed our belongings, bade the folks in Aloum farewell and returned to Elat station. Like Aloum, Elat lies in the heart of the rain forest, the hub of the Presbyterian mission in Cameroun, the home of a large hospital with numerous outlying wards, printing plant, industrial training school, missionary children's school, several African schools, missionary residences, and the Elat church that had at one time been the largest Presbyterian church in the world.

The hospital at Elat served not only Cameroun but also neighboring countries, and to it Albert Schweitzer of Lambaréné, two hundred miles to the south, had for years been sending complicated surgical cases. His wife, Hélène, came on various occasions for dental work and for rest. It was reassuring for Marie and me to be near expert medical care as we waited Susie's arrival.

Political independence for Cameroun was still nearly three years away. The recently created U.P.C. *(Union des Populations Camerounaises)* political party demanded elections before the granting of independence. Members of this party distrusted the African leaders handpicked by the French to run the country after independence. The French brushed aside their demands and consequently the U.P.C. stepped up its attacks in number and in violence. African chiefs reluctant to join the party were being executed, recalcitrant villages were burned. Although French and Cameroun troops mounted road barriers and put villages behind stockades, the killings continued. In Douala, the port city, and Yaoundé, the capital, sidewalk cafés and stores were attacked. There was no place that Europeans or Africans were safe. Missionary Bernard Kopf had gone into the Douala *Monoprix*, a busy variety store, to purchase school supplies for his mission when the air exploded with the crack of gun fire. Armed men disguised as shoppers sprayed the store with bullets. Merchandise spilled to the floor and when the gunmen sped away, missionary Kopf was among the dead. Upon learning of the death of Pastor Kopf, the raiders sent a letter of regret to his widow.

In such troubled times we were advised to avoid traveling the roads, a warning that reminded us that we had not yet obtained our Cameroun driver's licenses. So, on a hot October morning in the colonial administrative post of Ebolowa, Marie and I handed our applications to the African clerk, who was drumming on his desk and singing. Without missing a beat, he managed to staple them, fling them into the out-basket and yawn. *"Allez d'hors et attendez Monsieur Calloux."* We stepped outside just as examiner Calloux, who came to Ebolowa only on the last Thursday of the month, appeared. He glanced apprehensively at Marie then instructed me to be examined first. We drove about the African town and I executed the maneuvers he ordered. On a clipboard he kept a careful accounting of my responses. I was impressed how business-like the examination was, not at all like the one I had endured in Ecuador.

Back at the office, I climbed down and Marie took my place at the wheel. Just as she was ready to drive away with the examiner at her side, I said to him, "By the way, she is due to give birth today." Calloux's clipboard hit the roof, *"Stop, Madame, cela suffira."* His door flew open and he ejected himself as if he had been sitting on a nest of vipers. With no further questions asked, we both passed with a grade of *supérieur.*

Living in an area where terrorist attacks are common, it is natural to want to be informed. However, we found it was normally easier to learn what was happening in far away Europe and America than in the next town. The French did not want news of local killings to be known as this created fear and chaos and made the U.P.C. sound stronger than it perhaps was. At this particular time in 1956, we were better informed about the uprising in Hungary than about the attacks in Yaoundé. We knew that Soviet troops had entered Hungary in November and that thousands of Hungarians were fleeing the country. And while world events rolled on, the busy medical staff at Elat cared for the sick, operated, and trained their African assistants. After a day of concentrated activity, they gathered on the tennis courts to play.

Susie was late arriving and, when contractions began around 2:00 a.m., we crossed the hospital grounds with the aid of a flashlight. Dr. Frank Newman got out of bed to examine Marie and suggested we spend the rest of the night in the Johnson Pavilion. It was not until 11:00 a.m. that nurse Betty said it was time to get Marie ready for delivery.

Unlike the clinic in Quito, where I was not permitted in the delivery room, this time it was assumed that I would be beside Marie and give whatever help I was instructed to give. I was certain that I would have the stamina and resolution to assist and see my child born. In case of a girl, we had chosen the name Susie. We had not told our friends in Aloum that we had chosen a name, because for them infant mortality was high and naming a child at birth was considered sheer folly.

Betty instructed Marie to push each time she felt a contraction. And said to me, "Here, Bill, stand right here and when Marie pushes, you put your hands here and push." I watched Marie who would nod when it was pushing time and together we would bear down. After some time, streams of sweat were running down Marie's face and neck. Betty gave me a wet wash cloth to wipe her with. It seemed to me that we had been in this push-down mode for a very long while and I was not feeling nearly as certain of my stamina now, and my shirt was soaked.

Then I saw Frank pick up a scalpel and when he made an episiotomy, I saw the tears run down Marie's eyes and she grasped my hand like a vice. My legs were getting numb and rubbery and I found myself saying "never again, never again!" In the midst of Marie's pain and my numbness, I saw Frank slide the tiny body from the birth canal. He laid it over one of his hands and with the other patted its back and a cry rang out. From within her sweat and tears, Marie's lips flashed a smile and my eyes welled up with tears.

Three years would pass before Susie's grandmothers would see her and, in contrast to older sister Annie, we did our best to insure that she would speak to them in American English.

After we returned to Yaoundé, the capital of Cameroun, Susie was four years old and began attending a French-speaking Catholic kindergarten. Annie enrolled in the public school. Wishing to know what Susie was learning from the nuns—we were seated at the breakfast table—I asked her to recite something in French. She obliged instantly by scooting out of her chair and standing stiffly at attention. In staccato syllables she raced through the Lord's Prayer as if her breakfast was threatening to fly away. *Notre Père qui es dans les cieux, que ton nom soit sanctifié. Que ton règne arrive, que ta volonté soit faite . . . Donne-nous aujourd'hui le pain . . . Ne nous soumets pas à la tentacion, mais délivre-nous du Malin asseyez-vous!*" With the last two words, "sit down," uttered each morning by the nun at the end of the prayer, Susie obeyed and dived back into her breakfast. Not wanting to laugh and cause the dear child to think we were mocking her high-speed performance, Marie and I bit our lips to restrain ourselves until we were alone.

With our move to northern Nigeria when she was seven years old, Susie had no further contact with French. A play language they invented and called Chicalacapaca developed between Annie and Susie and they seemed able, with the help of a few gestures, to pass secrets between them and to keep mom and dad in the dark.

Susie converted one of our outbuildings—we occupied a house on what had been a tin miner's compound—into a school room and each afternoon when home from Hillcrest School, she rang her bell (an old iron wheel) and gathered neighborhood Nigerian children for literacy lessons. That sounds far more organized than was the case. She was not interested in pedagogical suggestions from her parents. Her little school gave her an opportunity to be in charge, role-play the disciplinarian—a paddle was clearly displayed on her desk—and she no doubt enjoyed imposing rules on her students—some were considerably older than the teacher. We had no doubt that these unschooled children learned and enjoyed the experience. They continued to come back each day for more.

The reading was in English and the language of instruction was "Susieglish," Susie's own adaptation of English to African sounds. I have stood outside and listened with amazement to the creative manner in which she communicated. Her students mimicked her speech faithfully and somehow they all communicated with a high degree of comprehension. We had no doubt that Susie would grow up, as she certainly did, to work with people with special needs and to teach.

When we left Nigeria for England in 1968, we enrolled Susie in a private school, Michael Hall in East Grinstead. In spite of her ability to acquire an English accent, she was "the Yank," a term which she resented profoundly. At the time of our move to Lebanon in 1972, Susie who had spent a year in Texas with my sister and her family, joined us and enrolled in Beirut University College. After two years, the war in Lebanon forced the college to close and Susie, who had opted for a degree in social work, transferred to Chapman College in Orange, Ca. As she looked back at the beginning of college she says, "I was not really certain what social work was, but it seemed to me that my life in Africa and England had put me on a track where I was at home with all kinds of people and I wanted a profession that would enable me to work with people and their problems."

Following her graduation from Chapman, Susie took a job in Costa Mesa, California, as a social worker at Fairview Developmental Center, a state institution for developmentally disabled people. Her vocation required her to work with people struggling to live with all types of mental and physical impairments. Her many experiences growing up contributed immeasurably to her success. "When I worked with those I was helping, I saw past their deformities and other limitations. I felt a strong need to help them make the most of what life and circumstances had given them. Having grown up in Africa, I was accustomed to seeing people with leprosy, blindness, legless adults propelling themselves along the ground, hunters with bodies bearing the scars of bush fires and the goring horns of animals. We don't live in an ideal world nor do we improve it by fleeing its imperfections."

After fifteen years at Fairview Developmental Center, Susie obtained a masters degree in special education and became the principal of an Advocate School in Banning, California. This is a primary and secondary school for seriously emotionally disturbed students. At the time of this writing she and her husband, Peter Lemieux, are teachers in Camden County in south Georgia. Like Annie, Susie is the mother of two children, daughter Natascha and son Brandon.

Kambélé Station

Kambélé, the hilltop mission station, was an enclave of Americana carefully planned and built by missionary Harris whose sawmill, planing machines and cement mixers roared into action each morning at the wail of a siren. Through the years this desolate promontory east of Batouri, the last colonial outpost in southeastern Cameroun, had grown to become an institution for the glory of God. At the foot of the hill stood the church, the school for evangelists, the African pastor's small house and other tiny houses for servants. Also at this level was the hospital and ward and two-room houses for African nurses. The road to the top wound about leading to large missionary residences and to the school campus with its class rooms and teachers' quarters. Along the roadway ornamental shrubs caught the morning sun and lent the upper echelons of Kambélé a kaleidoscope of colors.

The enterprising spirit of Earl Harris, coupled with the financial backing of several wealthy American churches, transformed this chunk of the colony into a Presbyterian Shangri-la. The missionary residences were equipped with kerosene refrigerators—staggering conundrums to African house boys who knew that a flame is for heating, not converting water into ice. Rainwater was collected from roofs and stored in large underground cisterns then pumped to elevated tanks. Washboys drew water from the cisterns and washed monsieur and madame's laundry on scrub boards. As gardeners, cooks, cleaners, washmen, laborers, child minders, carpenters and clerks, there was work for many. Over the years the trickle down of money from their work at the mission brought some changes: school fees for the children and perhaps a bicycle for papa.

Unlike Aloum and Elat, Kambélé lay in the rolling grasslands interspersed with riverine forests in the lower elevations. Located some four hundred kilometers east of the capital, Yaoundé, the road beyond Kambélé ran eastward to the neighboring colony, Ubangui Chari, later to become The Central African Republic. It was to Kambélé that Marie, Annie, newly-born Susie and I were sent to put the Kako language into written form and to teach the people to read. Compared with our humble abode at Picalquí, Ecuador, and our modest block house in Aloum, our move to Kambélé was a shift to four star accommodations.

It immediately became evident that Kambélé station would become an albatross around my neck if I carried out my work there. The leaders, the missionary pastor, the African pastor and the doctor and their wives carried on their work in Bulu and French. The school for Kako evangelists was taught in Bulu. The church services were conducted in Bulu. This language had become the medium of administration, evangelization and biblical instruction. The gospels had been available since 1896 and the complete Bible since 1940. Therefore, it was only natural that knowing Bulu was the only way for an African to become an evangelist or pastor. Also, because Kambélé had workers from many areas who did not know Kako, Bulu was the language of choice for interethnic communication. Even Annie, building on her language exposure in Aloum, learned to speak Bulu. I would seek out a good Kako language helper and when I was fluent enough to fly on my own, I would look for a village.

The annual mission conference at Elat had appointed Marie *Directrice des Écoles de Kambélé*. This job, plus nurturing Annie and Susie, made it necessary for her to remain at Kambélé while I worked on the Kako language in the villages.

Gwe Nemeno

We seldom knew when someone was at our door. Like Carlos Bawa in Ecuador, our callers would stand silently outside and wait until Marie or I went out. At first, we thought the Africans had been trained this way by missionary Harris, but we soon learned that it was customary. The African school principal, Mbomo, came nearly every morning with some problem to take up with Marie. On this particular morning I stepped outside and was greeted in Kako by a thin young man leaning on a stick. His head turned from side to side as he listened for my response. *Oje miae, mbam,* "Have you awakened, man?" This was the typical morning greeting addressed to another male. As I approached him I noticed he was blind in both eyes.

He laughed and snapped his fingers as he said in Bulu, "My friend, word has come to me in the village that you will write our language." He snapped again and thrust his stick out. "Oh, that is good news." He turned his head as if to listen for a reply. "Isn't it good news?" he shouted. When there was no response, he added, "Well, listen to my lips, where is everybody?" He lifted his stick and began to sing in Kako, waving his arms as if he were directing a chorus. When his song was finished he threw his head back and laughed, "Yes, friend, we'll march through Kakoland and teach them to read this black man's language."

I took my visitor by the hand and led him into the house to a chair. For two weeks since we had arrived in Kambélé, I had prayed to find just such a person as this, and here he was on my doorstep. When he was seated and had carefully explored the chair with his fingers, he said "I am Gwe Nemeno and I am going to teach you to speak."

Only later I learned the story of this man. Gwe Nemeno is not a name; it is a sentence meaning "he will die tomorrow." This sentence was pronounced by the village medicine man when the midwife showed him the new-born child and asked if he could save its life. Although advised not to nurse him, the mother refused to accept the prediction of the elders. She nurtured him and cared for him in spite of threats and abuse. In a society where every male is expected to clear land, hunt and be a warrior, a blind child has no future. It took a miracle to keep this sickly, blind child alive long enough for the clan elders to recognize that the child had an exceptional memory. While still very young he was able to recite nearly all the legends of the tribe, recount long genealogies, tell stories that even the acknowledged storytellers could not compete with. Although not allowed to enroll in the local school, he sat beyond the walls and learned French as well as the history, geography, arithmetic and poetry taught to the others. When he asked to be enrolled in the evangelist school, he was turned down. Nevertheless, he listened to the sermons and walked miles to other villages where he preached and repreached the sermons to whomever would listen. He listened to the Bulu hymns and gave them Kako lyrics and went about like a traveling troubadour teaching them to children. He could recite long passages from the Bulu gospels and interpret them in Kako. He was known to have corrected pastors in the middle of sermons when they gave a wrong wording or a wrong biblical reference. Gwe Nemeno owned nothing in this world but the ragged T shirt and shorts he wore. He had never seen a golden sunset, the resplendence of a rose, the brilliance of a rainbow, yet in his blindness he was a radiant, joyful, positive personality. I am certain if Mahatma Ghandi had ever met him, he would have said "Now, I have known a Christian."

Though he had never before taught his language to a foreigner,

Gwe Nemeno was from the first day an exceptional language teacher. I probably urged him to respond more quickly than he wanted. If, for example, I asked "How do you say egg?" he would need to reflect, not that he had forgotten how to say "egg," but often he needed to rephrase the question. Did I refer to a chicken or a duck egg, a freshly-laid egg or one that was not fresh, an egg that would produce a chick, or a rotten egg, a white or a brown or a speckled egg? All of these distinctions were essential to saying "egg" in his language. The very thought of eating an egg was revolting to him, although he had heard that white people ate them. He didn't know that white people could fry or boil them, but thought they ate them raw.

Being a singer he had a finely-tuned sense of pitch and insisted I put the correct tones on vowels. For example, the word *djo* with high tone means "honey bee," with rising tone it means "bitter," and with falling tone means "to vomit." His method for teaching me tone was to whistle. He would say, "Let's review; the word is *djo*." Then he would give me three whistled tones and ask me to identify each. Later I gave him a mouth harp which he learned to play and he used it sometimes for tone exercises, but I preferred his whistling.

I soon learned that Kako was not a typical Bantu language with complex noun classes as was Bulu. This made it easier to acquire, but it was clearly a Bantu type of language structure and a comparison of Kako vocabulary with that of Bulu and other Bantu languages showed that it was genetically related to Bantu languages.

Kako exhibited the same consonants as Bulu with two striking differences: it had a voiced bilabial b, as in "boy," but with ingressive pharynx air. That is, the lips are together and the vocal chords vibrating but when the lips part, the voice box is pulled down and the air enters the mouth. We wrote this particular b with two b's, hence *bo* "they" but *bbo* "hand." D also has an implosive counterpart that we wrote as dd and so *doukou* "cold," but *ddoukou* "stream."

Gwe Nemeno used his snapping fingers or his guide-stick to stop me if I failed to give these consonants their correct pronunciation. As our work progressed and we began to write the words to hymns and to translate the gospels, this man's uncanny hearing was an invaluable asset. A Kako translator would read aloud his draft, which I had already checked for faithfulness to the original, in the hearing of Gwe whose fingers would snap and halt the reading when he detected an unnatural or meaningless phrase.

It is probably impossible to say whether or not Gwe as a sighted person would have been as language sensitive as he was. However that may be, certainly his attention to sounds in the African bush was imperative for his survival and his keen sense of language and meaning made a profound contribution to the work we undertook in the Kako language.

Lolo Village

The ageing Renault bus sat beside the market in Batouri waiting for passengers to climb aboard. Departure time would arrive whenever the driver was satisfied there were enough passengers to make the run to the border profitable. He dozed while his *moto-boy* loaded onto the roof baskets of chickens, fruits and vegetables, an occasional mattress roll and an assortment of boxes and suitcases. When the bus was full or he failed to drum up any more business, moto-boy climbed aboard and collected fares, charging according to the destination. Collecting fares was a tricky task because passengers would often say they were going to a nearby village, but when it was reached, would change their minds and refuse to pay an additional fare. Arguing over fares could hold up the bus, sometimes for hours. Gwe and I were headed for his village, Lolo.

When *moto-boy* had stuffed all the cash into his shirt, he took up his position on the step beyond the open door and the departure dialogue began.

> Driver: *Moto-boy*
> Moto-boy: *eee* "yes"
> Driver: *Petrol fo tank he de?* "Is there gasoline in the tank?"
> Moto-boy: *eee*
> Driver: *Briz fo fut he de?* "Is there air (breeze) in the tires?"

Moto-boy: *eee*

Driver: *Ol cago fo up he de?* "Is all the cargo loaded on
   top?"

Moto-boy: *eee*

Driver: *Wata fo moto he de?* "Does the engine have water?"

Moto-boy: *eee*

Driver: *Ol pipi done pay moni?* "Has everybody paid
   their money?"

Moto-boy: *eee*

Driver: *Insaid shat Ol moni de?* "Is all the money inside
   the shirt?"

Moto-boy: *eee*

It appears that all is clear for takeoff. Driver turns the ignition
key but the starter fails, as it has done for days. Turning to face
the passengers, he points at them with his lower lip: *Hea me, ol
pipi go down pus em!* "Listen, everybody get out and push!"

The bus empties slowly and moto-boy, now nested on the
roof among the baggage, a black miniature General Patton
protruding from the turret of his tank, shouts and waves his troops
forward. After a sluggish spurt of effort, the old Renault bus bucks
and coughs, trembles then clatters into fiery motion while
passengers scamper through a cloud of exhaust and pile back
in. The only ones who did not get out to push were Gwe Nemeno
and two mothers with babes at the breast. Most of the pushing
was done by women—the men considering such work for
women—something akin to pounding grain in a mortar.

I sat down by Gwe whose head rotated, listening for voices
he recognized. "Ah, Mbonjiko, what brings your black skin to
Batouri?" A voice three rows behind calls back "Gwe Nemeno,
are you awake? I came to see my mother's brother and collect a
little money."

"Did you have success?"

"No, but he gave me a pair of chickens and a duck."

"Ah, cousin of my heart, we will eat again"

We bounced and shook over the rutted road as village after village flew past. When a stop was necessary, moto-boy rapped on the roof with a piece of pipe. The length of our stops, like the train from Ciudad Juárez to Mexico City, depended on the friends, relatives and needs of the driver. In any event, little time was lost because passengers debussed quickly and got busy selling, bartering and trading with the locals.

It was nearly noon when I led Gwe by the hand and we planted our feet on the soil of Lolo, his native village. As the Renault headed on down the dusty road, Gwe shouted in Kako "Is there anybody awake in Lolo? Your own infant son has come home to you." The only response was the bleat of a goat resting in the shade of the eaves of the men's club house. Gwe replied, "Thank you, friend. I know the fathers of Lolo would not go to their gardens without leaving a watchman." We entered the club house where the ashes from last night's fire were cold and the silence of the normally boisterous village was ominous.

Lolo, unlike Aloum, was built alongside the road, a row of tottering huts on either side, where its inhabitants breathed and ate the dry season dust. There were 220 souls in Lolo, when everyone was home, counting men, women, children and infants. Nearly a third of the adult men had more than one wife while two-thirds had only one. The village boasted a school with twenty-five children attending, when not required in their parents' gardens, and a single male teacher who was from another Kako village to the east. There was a resident evangelist and a small thatched church where on rainy days goats and chickens sought refuge from the lashing torrents and thunder that smote the place.

The food staple of Lolo was manioc or cassava root. This nutritious root starch was eaten with cooked vegetables, usually okra, or preferably with a meat sauce when available. The cassava root is soaked in water to remove the poison, cut and dried, pounded into flour and boiled. The finished product is a sticky dough-like mass eaten with the fingers. Every meal in Lolo ends by licking the fingers. Every woman had a manioc garden and the men, encouraged by the French administration, grew cocoa or coffee in the shaded areas of the forest glades.

Contrary to the mission's crusade against the evils of polygamy, I found in Lolo and other Kako villages that most of the women preferred the polygamous family life. A woman with co-wives has more freedom than her monogamous sisters and unlike the latter she is not required to serve her husband full-time. When she is not on duty, she is often free to take her produce to market, sell it and buy things for herself and her children. The mothers in the one-man-one-wife families gave birth more often and so were tied to more family responsibilities. While the mission preached a message of freedom in Christ and condemnation of polygamy, the women found this to be highly questionable. Freedom was more likely to be found by being a member of a team of wives. In short, polygamy meant less births, less work, more freedom to look after one's own needs. In the long run the mission would win, not because it was morally right but because the economy would make polygamy too expensive.

Christianity, represented by an itinerating African pastor and the local evangelist, revealed the bureaucracy and colonial mentality of the mission. Candidates for church membership would be advised that they would be examined by the pastor and, if found fit, would be given a certificate, a proud possession that would give a woman a legitimate role in life. The people of Lolo seemed to need an official paper of some kind. Only women in monogamous marriages were considered suitable to belong to the mission. Attired in the only dresses they owned, the women would not go to their gardens on this special day but would await the arrival of pastor Mvondo who alone held the keys to open or shut for them the gates to the Kingdom. Dressed in khaki shirt and shorts with white stockings and polished shoes, the pastor, from a down-country tribe, had the commanding air of a French colonial officer.

The women candidates, anxious to obtain the coveted certificate that none of them could read, stood about waiting for their names to be called. The evangelist led them one by one into the church where they stood before pastor Mvondo ensconced behind a wobbly table. He directed his questions in Bulu to the evangelist.

"What's her name?"

"She is Makate."

"I don't find such a name in your ledger."

"Maybe I forgot to write it."

"How can you be so careless? How am I supposed to trust anything you do here?"

The gaggle of women beyond the church wall speaking in Kako defended the evangelist, but the Reverend Mvondo did not understand them. He shouted over the wall for them to be silent. He then addressed his question to a nervous Makate. "Explain your belief in God." Makate looked to the evangelist for a translation then replied "God is three: father, son and . . ." She scratched her head trying to recall the third person then glanced over the wall looking to her sisters for help. The pastor slammed his fist on the table. "You see, you are not teaching these people. What do you do with your time?" He did not wait for the evangelist to reply but put another question to Makate.

"How was Jesus Christ put to death?"

Makate wiped the sweat from her face and replied "soja."

"What about the soldier?" inquired her interrogator.

Makate looked toward the evangelist, "Soja stick him with spear."

Mvondo was not happy with a response that did not say clearly, "hung on a cross." Outside Gwe was listening. He leaned over the wall and said, "Makate has spoken straight words." He and the evangelist launched into a long conversation about women not having a chance to go to school. Pastor Mvondo's eyelids grew heavy. Raising his voice to awaken the pastor, the evangelist asked if he should call the next candidate. Mvondo yawned and asked the evangelist how much Makate had paid on her pledge. The evangelist did not know, but Makate knew. She raised her arm and extended three fingers as a sign of swearing the truth by the father, son and the holy spirit. "Fifteen francs." Mvondo objected that this was a paltry sum and not acceptable. Makate may not have been at home in theological abstractions but she was lucid, assertive and loud in bargaining and defending herself. "I paid five francs when I sold a gourd of palm wine in Batouri." Mvondo was enraged that a candidate for the mission should be trafficking in alcohol and, after a temperance lecture, was ready to send her away. Makate, who had not understood, did not ask for a translation. She would not be interrupted. "And then seven francs when I took a chicken to market at Mbombol and three more francs when I sold a basket I made during the dry season. That is fifteen francs, Misyur Pastur, and I want my certificate," she exclaimed, leaning on the table and shaking her finger in her inquisitor's face. Outside, Makate's cheering section was urging her on. Mvondo, who had heard the Bulu translation, was now on his feet looking at his wrist watch. The day would soon be spent if Makate's sisters were all like her. Mvondo was ready to retreat. He ordered the evangelist to bring in the next two. As Makate danced triumphantly toward her sisters, they shouted, danced, clapped their hands and ululated so vociferously, the evangelist had to beg them to be silent.

As I witnessed this miscarriage of Christ's compassion for the least of these, I could not but feel that it would have to be the courageous women of the Lolo road who would show the way. Gwe Nemeno's comment echoed the voice of the ancient prophet Jeremiah, "These are the mothers of Lolo and if the pastor turns their hearts away from Christ, they will be eating sour berries and their children will end up with a foul taste in their mouths."

God, Space and Sputnik

The elders of Lolo delighted in explaining to me their views of marriage and family life, circumcision rituals, the hunt, the powers of native medicines, and genealogies. Their personal names were often associated with events that occurred near the time of their births. Some were happy occasions such as house building, a big wedding or killing an elephant. Some recalled a time of tragedy such as Gwe Nemeno "die tomorrow." Men who had joined the church always acquired a biblical name such as Pierre, Jean, Paul to add to their Kako name. Polygamous men were not eligible to be church members but in some cases these men had given their senior wives to the church and were certain that the Christian God would not fail to reward them for such generous acts.

God in the Kako language is *Ndjambie* which means spider. Although there are many kinds of spiders such as Black Widow, Jumping Spider and Water Spider each with its distinctive name, *Ndjambie* is a generic term and denotes a space spider busily weaving webs in the heavens to prevent the heavenly bodies such as stars and moon from crashing through the web and falling to earth. Even so, the frequent sight of a shooting star is believed to be the result of a tear in the web allowing a star to plummet earthward.

In no sense is *Ndjambie* a personal God who might intercede on someone's behalf. Neither is he a creator God for he has had nothing to do with the creation of the heavenly bodies he attends to. His role is that of sustainer, keeping the heavens in order and preventing celestial chaos. It must be remembered that in the African night where no city lights obscure the view, the starry skies are a brilliant dome of gem-like luminosity.

It was into these peaceful heavens managed by *Ndjambie's* busy spinnerets that the Russians on October 4, 1957 launched the first artificial satellite, known to the world as Sputnik I. A month later on November 3 Sputnik II carried the dog Laika into space and on January 31, 1958 the United States launched Explorer I. The night sky over Lolo became the scene of a silent light moving in a straight line, disappearing and then reappearing.

With the help of articles appearing in Time Magazine, I attempted to interpret and demonstrate the mechanics of putting a satellite into orbit around the earth. The main problem I ran into was the persistent belief that the earth was flat and that the speed of 27,000 kilometers per hour made absolutely no sense to people who had never travelled a hundred kilometers and who had no watches or clocks to know how long an hour was. However, they were intrigued by the launch rocket which I described as a gun larger than their tallest trees. What a superb weapon to shoot an elephant! They argued that although the satellite box may be able to fly high in the air, it could never break through the web from the outside. They insisted that a satellite box shot up from the big gun would be as helpless as a fly caught in the spider's web. It would just hang there until *Ndjambie* cut it loose and let it fall back to the ground. They were particularly moved to think that a Russian dog would die of starvation in the web as there was nothing there to hunt and they thought ill of the dog's owner for letting it fly in the box.

Explaining these new lights in the sky seemed at first of little value but over the ensuing weeks as they talked among themselves, some of the more venturesome minds suggested that perhaps the ancestors did not pass on the heavenly web story in its most original and authentic form. There may have been openings in the web which allowed for satellite boxes to enter and to exit. Some of the more heretical even suggested that perhaps there never was a web; perhaps something else held the stars in place. Kako agnosticism seemed to be growing nightly. But the problem preventing them from becoming space believers seemed to be related to gravity. The idea that the earth exerts a pulling force on objects was clear enough when a mango falls from a tree to the ground, but to say that the same gravity enables the satellite box to orbit the earth was stretching the point a bit. Even the most heretical were not ready to give up the flat earth theory.

In his 1961 single orbit of the earth, cosmonaut Yuri Gagarin is reported to have said that he did not see God in space. But there is little doubt that the Russians caused the men of Lolo to have another look at their God. Certainly some were now questioning a metaphor that had been accepted for countless generations. Like Gagarin, they may not have seen God, but they were becoming sceptics of sacred tradition, and for some the old *Ndjambie* was about to be cast down from his starry web.

Bushfire

The rainy season in 1958, as compared in memory with other years, was excessive and unabated and consequently the great stretches of savanna grass had grown higher and more abundant than in years past, reaching a height of about ten feet. When the grasslands were open, after being burned, the people of Lolo had easy access to the streams and the forest glades. As the grass grew, the paths across the savannas were cut off making it nearly impossible to reach villages that lay at great distances from the main road. The coming of the dry season brought a halt to the ever-expanding grassy plains and the blazing sun dried the fibers of the massive plants, preparing them for the annual burning.

The grasslands were burned to open the vast expanses for easier communication as well as to hunt the antelope, warthog and bushcow. The people of Lolo had little access to protein and counted heavily on the bushfires as a means of securing meat which, when it was abundant, would be preserved by smoking and drying. It sometimes happened that the dry grasslands would be struck by lightning and burn out of control with no opportunity to hunt.

After the decision had been made to burn the bush, the hunters of Lolo had to undergo special preparations, all intended to give them success. Instruments such as bows, arrows and spears and knives had to be anointed with special medicines to give them accuracy. For three days prior to the hunt, hunters were required to abstain from certain foods, clean and sweep their compounds, remove all bones and animal parts from earlier hunts and most of all to practice sexual abstinence. Animals, it was believed, could at a great distance pick up the scent of anyone who had been intimate with a woman. It was the woman's sexual odor that was detected, particularly by the warthog.

The elephant hunt in Aloum had taught me to leave my rifle in Kambélé and never to even mention that tale to the hunters of Lolo. When the day for the bushfire arrived—all the taboos observed, the medicines applied—I was given a spear with a sharp metal point honed by a neighboring blacksmith. Most of the hunters carried a bow with five or six arrows in a monkey skin quiver. They wore only loincloths and sandals made of hippo hide.

We left the sleeping village before daybreak and made our way in a long single file, every hunter carrying hot embers from a fire that had been burning since midnight. It was still early when we reached a designated point where the two lead hunters separated and half of the troop followed one and half strung out behind the other. The two columns then moved forward making a great circle until the two lead men met. They were the first to set fire to the grass. Then, when the next hunters in line saw the smoke, they lit their fires. In an orderly manner the fires were lit on each side of the circle until the last two where the circle closed.

In principle, the fire would burn toward the center of the ring and the game, finding no safe escape, would be forced to attempt to break through the flames. In principle and often in practice, the escaping animals would be blinded by smoke and fire and would be wounded or killed by the waiting hunters' spears and arrows.

As I lit my fire, I could see little in any direction except the sky overhead. I was not at all certain that the fire would burn away from me and move toward the center of the ring. Watching anxiously as the blackened shreds were driven into the sky by the leaping flames, I could hear the crackling of the fire to my right and left and wondered if it was racing in my direction. If it were burning down on me, where would I go in this wall of towering grass? I pushed back to escape the searing heat before me and could see hawks soaring overhead in the rising blur of smoke and flying ash. Any moment the wind could change direction and the predator could become the prey. The grass burned ahead of me and I moved forward on the hot blistering and clumped earth, the burning shreds of grass falling back to the ground, burning my hands and face.

Then I saw the wall of fire leap forward fanned by a gust of wind. This meant that the firewall on the other side of the circle was being blown back upon those hunters. I tried to listen for their shouts but the raging fireball so near engulfed all sight and sound.

As I made my way forward over the scorched earth, I could faintly make out the other hunters to my right and left. By now the wind at our backs was driving the galloping flames straight to the far side. There the hunters, we later learned, were forced to retreat until they came to a stream where they flung themselves in and saved their lives.

The sun was low in the west when we stumbled back into Lolo. Women and children watched us pass looking for the animals we did not bear. No, not a bushcow, not a warthog, not an antelope, not even a rat. We were vanquished troops that had trekked across hell: bodies burned, hair singed, blistered and battered.

Into the men's clubhouse we limped and dropped exhausted. Never have I heard Africans so silent. Finally, one hunter managed to pull a coal from the fire and light his pipe. Then he looked at me and said:

"*Boui* (white man), you've told us about God and we have listened. But there is one thing you didn't tell us."

"What's that?" I inquired.

"You didn't tell us that God doesn't have a stomach, for if he did have, he wouldn't have let us come home without even a rat to eat."

Incest, Sex and Adultery

The conclusion of **Cherokee Wedding** in this book recounts the story of our marriage and the distasteful conviction of a Lolo elder that "white men marry just like fish." As the people of Lolo educated me in the ways of Kako kinship and society, I came more and more to sense the great gulf that separated us. This was painful for me because in so many ways we shared the same needs, the same basic humanity. Being a parent I knew how a mother felt when her child would not stop crying, but when she brought the child to me and said to the fear-filled infant, "If you don't stop crying that white man will eat you," I was being used as a bogeyman and the mother seemed unaware, in spite of my protestations, how offensive this was to me and how destructive of interracial relations it was for her child's future.

Kako kinship and social behavior are based on the patriclan. Everyone belongs to their father's clan, provided the brideprice has been paid, for it is this payment that establishes a father's right to claim his children as his own. Since a man cannot marry a woman belonging to his clan, every child is related, but in a different way, to father's clan and to mother's clan. All the women of father's clan are either "mothers" or "sisters" and the same is true for the females of mother's clan. Accordingly, any sexual deed or thought regarding any of the girls or women in father's or mother's clan is incestuous and considered to be the most grievous sin. Upon reading in Genesis 19 that Lot—although soundly drunk—slept with his two daughters and made them pregnant, the Kako were astounded beyond belief that the two offspring, Moab and Benammi, lived to become ancestors of many people. According to Kako belief incestuous relations result in death for both the offspring and the parents.

Although the rules covering incest are strictly drawn and include people who would not be included in European society, the Kako term for "wife" and reciprocally "husband" contrasts with that used by Europeans. For example, all the wives of a man's older brothers are addressed as "my wives" whereas the wives of a man's younger brothers are called, as in English, "sisters-in-law." The reason for this usage is that a man stands to inherit his older brother's wives but never the wives of his younger brothers. That would be incest.

For the most part a man treats the people of his mother's clan with respect and often with a degree of formality. However, there is one person in mother's family with whom a man has a very special relationship. This is mother's brother who is called *Koko* and who addresses his sister's sons as *Taa*. As in the case of the wives of older brothers, a man calls *Koko's* wife "my wife." Furthermore, the Kako rules of kinship and social conduct allow *Taa* to have sexual access to uncle *Koko's* wife or wives without it being considered in any way as wrong, incestuous or deviant. *Koko* does not have reciprocal rights with *Taa's* wife or wives. Moreover, *Taa* is permitted by custom to take a chicken or duck from *Koko's* place without asking permission. However, *Taa* is obligated to give uncle *Koko* the entire front quarter of any animal he kills in the hunt.

Another male-female relationship and one that causes some stress among the Kako is that called *wandja*. If a man is able to have sex with another man's wife, without the husband knowing it, the wife is thereafter called *wandja-mbe* "my mistress" and her husband is addressed as *ko-mbe* "my comrade." The price for successfully seducing another man's wife is a small payment of a few francs paid to the husband. The successful seducer is expected to give gifts to his *wandja* and the Kako women generally found it desirable to be the *wandja* of many men and so to receive many gifts. Having *wandja* is not considered wrong. It is an act between two consenting adults, although it is usually done without the husband's knowledge.

In 1957-59, the years spent among the Kako, Aids was not yet known. However, syphilis and gonorrhea were widespread and sexual practices of the people were putting them at greater and greater risk The number of syphilitic babies born was rising rapidly. It is not surprising, therefore, that Christian teaching was becoming viewed as a way to preserve the family and to avoid the rapid spread of sexually transmitted diseases.

Outside the clan restrictions, the permissive sexual practices were related to the desire to accumulate material goods. There was no clear idea or vocabulary to express the idea of adultery. However, there were three sins recognized and condemned by all the people: incest, stinginess and theft.

Say It from the Heart

As the preparation and production of literacy materials became the focus of our work, I needed to spend more time at Kambélé and less time in the villages. With the help of the village leaders, we selected three teams: one for translation, one for preparing hymns and one for literacy. The translators, working from the French and Bulu scriptures, produced drafts of Mark's gospel. I served as consultant, examining their work regarding faithfulness to the meaning of the Greek text. Gwe Nemeno, who listened to the reading of the Kako drafts, served as the stylist. His sharp ears caught anything that was not idiomatic Kako and when he slapped the table top or thumped his cane on the floor, the translators would stop and revise the wording until it received the approval of Gwe's critical ears.

When not required with the translators, Gwe was singing his way through the Bulu hymnal, fitting Kako lyrics to the Bulu tunes. Two secretaries worked at well-worn upright typewriters putting words to paper. The final draft of the Kako hymnal was prepared by Marie and the literacy booklets when completed were sent to the mission press at Elat for printing.

Because we had adapted the Kako writing system to French, anyone knowing how to read French could read Kako with little difficulty. Likewise, those who could read Bulu found the reading of Kako easy to master. This meant that most of our efforts were focused on illiterate villagers who had some motivation for learning to read. As in many initial literacy programs, the main criticism was "What is there in Kako for me to read if I do become literate?" The main motivation for reading on the part of the Christians was to be able to read the Bible. And since it would be a long while before there would be a Kako Bible, many people refused to invest the effort just to be literate in a bookless language. Nevertheless, many villagers responded well and in many places those who could read taught those who could not.

To encourage reading we produced a newsletter, a single mimeographed sheet that carried news and announcements of events in Kakoland. These sheets often contained proverbial sayings or short folktales, thus providing readers with entertainment. These were well received and wherever we went, people asked for them.

During the preparation phase of the literacy booklets and newsletter, I was continuously learning new aspects of the language, sometimes through my mistakes. For example, wanting to encourage readers to make the effort to study, I used the expression "Lift up your hearts," which sounded like good biblical advice. I learned, however, that this expression means "Be conceited."

Kako and other languages of the area are rich in heart metaphors and these often have meanings that are quite different from the same expressions in English. *A big heart* does not denote generosity, but rather "deceit." *A long heart* describes a person who is "patient and slow to anger." By contrast, "one who is quick to anger" is described as having *a short heart*. *A thick heart* expresses "trust and confidence" and *a hard heart* refers to "courage." A person having *a fragile heart* is one who is "easily angered" and *a weak heart* means "to be nauseated." *A light-hearted person* is "one who cannot keep a secret" and *a hot heart* is "one who is extremely busy."

A dog heart refers to a "glutton" and *a leopard heart* to "one who is cruel." A person with *a mouse heart* is "frivolous" and *a woman's heart* is "one who lacks intelligence." *A bird heart* describes a person who is "easily upset" and *a chicken heart* is "one who is timid."

If you *hang up your heart* you are "nervous and anxious" and to *have the heart on one's back"* is "to faint." To have *the heart in the water* is to be "forgetful." To "*lower the heart,"* the opposite of *lift up the heart,* means to be "humble." One who *ties up the heart* "withholds confidence" and to *squeeze the heart* is to be "surprised." A person who is "repentant" has *turned over the heart.*

To have *one heart* is to be "agreed or in union with others." To doubt is to be *without thought in the heart.* To comfort someone is to *cause the heart to rest.* Wisdom is said to be *heart thinking.*

The translation committee was busy at work one day when Edward Cozzens, founder of the Industrial School in Elat, visited Kambélé before returning to America for retirement. Mr. Cozzens, who had reached the age of sixty-five having spent some forty years in Cameroun, stopped to speak with the translators and to encourage them in their work They listened intently as he described to them some of the changes he had seen throughout his life. He told them how his first students could not read and had never before used a plane or a saw, but that over the years they had learned to make fine furniture that was sought after by visitors from France and America. When finally he shook their hands and left, I had the feeling that these men had not focused on the content of his talk, but that something about Mr. Cozzens had, nevertheless, grasped their attention. They were whispering and showing gestures of surprise and wide-eyed wonder. Then one of the team asked,

"How old did that white man say he was?"

"Sixty-five years," I replied.

There was again a silence and I could not resist asking,

"What is it that is eating your hearts?"

After another pause, one of the men answered,

"Our hearts tremble when we try to imagine how much food a man his age has eaten."

God Hears

In **Incest, Sex and Adultery** in this book, the sense of *belonging* in Kako society was explained as being gender related. Every son belongs to his father's lineage, as indeed do daughters, but marriage requires daughters to leave the paternal home and live with the husband in his patriclan. Consequently, married females in a village are outsiders—strangers in the male world of the husband.

By strict rules of exogamy, males must seek their mates from outside both their father's and mother's clans. Marriage or sex with any female in those two clans is incest and stringently prohibited. When asked if they knew anyone who had violated these taboos, people always responded, "People who did that would be dead and no one would again utter their names."

A man's sons will remain, ideally, in their father's village after marriage, but his daughters will raise their children in their husbands' villages and the children will belong to the husbands' clan. In the event of a husband's death, the wife will not be free to take her children if she goes away into another marriage. If the dead husband has no older brothers to inherit her, another male in her husband's clan may marry her but if not, she may be exchanged for cash or kind to another village but her children will remain in their dead father's clan and village.

It follows that a woman's life is often fragile and insecure, threatened frequently by loss and a nagging awareness of social and psychic dislocation. Because a woman's value is judged by her ability to bear offspring, she is not considered of much worth to her husband's people until she has given birth several times. True, she may gain a degree of acceptance through planting, harvesting, fishing, cooking and caring for her husband's needs, but if she fails to have children, she has little or no status. Furthermore, she may be a second or third wife in a polygamous family and therefore subject to the authority of the first wife, who in Kako is called *Nya Tou* "Woman of the House." A second or third wife who becomes pregnant may, like the expectant Hagar in the story in Genesis 16, flaunt her conception before *Nya Tou* and so create serious tensions in the family.

After seeing examples of conflicts in polygamous families in Lolo, I decided to relate the Abraham, Sarah and Hagar story to a group of women. Perhaps they would discover in it something of value for their own lives. I knew I would get instant feedback because the Kako were not accustomed to sit passively and listen quietly to a story. They were in the habit of interjecting their comments freely at any point and did not hesitate to object or disagree with the speaker. Sometimes it was necessary to wait until the hub bub of comments had subsided before continuing.

On this particular night, I explained to Gwe that I wanted to tell the Abraham story to the women and asked him to make certain that some of the women were from polygamous families. For some time I had been concerned that perhaps the Kako's *Ndjambie*, that strange cosmic spider, would not serve to express the idea of a Supreme Being and that perhaps they should use the Bulu cognate term *Zambe* that had none of the spiderish features of *Ndjambie*. Gwe's reaction had always been, "*Ndjambie* is *our* word and *Ndjambie* changes as we learn new things that he has done."

Gwe said that he knew about Abraham who had a wife named Sarah, but had not heard of a woman called Hagar and knew nothing of her son, Ishmael. Hence, I read the story to him from the Bulu Bible. He listened carefully, showing that he understood by making clicking noises in his throat. When the reading was finished, he snapped his fingers and said, "It needs to be sung!" I was not certain what he meant, but I would find out a few nights later.

When some ten or more women were gathered around Mekate's fire, some crouched on their haunches and some resting on tiny stools, and Gwe half hidden in the shadows, I began, as the Kako often do, "My mouth has three words for your ears: There was once a big rich man named Abram who had enough sheep and goats to fill two whole villages. He had only one wife and her name was Sara."

—That many sheep and goats to buy wives and only one wife?—

"Well, Sara couldn't have children. They laid down together but she never got a belly (pregnant)."

—A sigh of pain—

"But Sara had a work-girl from another tribe and she being *Nya Tou* told her work-girl to go lie down with Abram, the rich man."

—Clicks of agreement—

"So, work-girl named Hagar got a belly

—Yes, yes, yes, Hagar got a belly—

"Well, what do you think? Hagar lifted up her heart (became proud) and turned her head away from Sara."

—Oh, Oh, Oh, Hagar makes trouble for *Nya Tou*. Sara's head will get hot—

"Yes, Sara's head got hot and she made Hagar work harder and harder. Sara had a leopard's heart (was cruel) toward Hagar and so one night Hagar ran away from the rich man's camp."

—Yi, yi yi, Hagar running to the bush with a belly—

"After going a long way, Hagar got thirsty and knelt down by a spring to drink when she heard the voice of *Ndjambie* speaking to her.

—Silence—

"Where you going, Hagar?" Hagar answered, "I am running away from *Nya Tou*; she has a leopard's heart."

—Go back home, Hagar, take care of your belly—
"*Ndjambie* told her just that. You will have a male child
and you must name him *Ndjambie-hears-you* (Ishmael)."
—Oh, Makate, Nzili, Abula, does *Ndjambie* have ears
to hear? Before anyone could respond, the voice of
Gwe spoke out from the shadows "Mothers, put your
ears on his words. You are hearing something new
tonight."
"*Ndjambie* has heard your cries, Hagar."
—Silence again—
"Then Hagar asked herself, 'Have I seen *Ndjambie* and I
am still alive and well?' "Hagar named that spring
Ndjambie is one who sees me."
—Did you hear this, *Ndjambie* hears the cries of a
second wife, goes to the bush to find a second wife,
hears and sees work-girl with a belly. Oh, sisters, did
we ever think such a thing of *Ndjambie*?—

A few nights later, Gwe suggested we walk to a neighboring village where we would find another group of women waiting to hear *The Hagar Story*. When we found the women, Gwe sat before them with a drum between his knees and began the story. As he spoke and drummed the women got on their feet and began to dance in a circle. It was the same story but what had been in Lolo a teacher giving a lesson became under Gwe's inspiration a drama with rhythm, dance and songs.

Once through the story with Gwe, the women danced while one woman called out the story as the rest swayed and fluttered, shuffled and shook to the pulsation of Gwe's drum. At intervals Gwe would sing out:

Did you hear the good news?
Did you hear the good news?

The women would repeat his words and the dance continued.

Ndjambie followed work-girl to the spring
There tired and thirsty she sat down
Ndjambie said, I heard you cry
Yes, *Ndjambie* heard her cry
Did you hear the news of Hagar?
He told me to name my baby *Ndjambie-hears*
Does *Ndjambie* hear?
Oh, yes, he hears
Does he only hear *Nya Tou*?
No, No, he hears the cries of work-girl
Who is *Ndjambie*?
One who sees and hears
Yes, sing out the good news
Ndjambie sees and hears

Before long the men had formed another dance group and were following Gwe's rhythms and songs.

The full moon was high in the western sky when at last Gwe and I walked the road back to Lolo. As I lay down to sleep that night, I realized more than I had ever before that a person like Gwe, one who knows the communication patterns among his people is vastly more effective than an outsider such as I. This had been verified in nearly every aspect of our work together. At best I could be his seed-man, a resource for him. This lesson was to be of incomparable value in the years ahead as we trained native speakers to translate into their own languages.

Gwe's performace sent my mind traveling back to Guam and Mama Agancho, who thirteen years earlier had led her neighbors dancing and singing the story of *The Lost Coin* in Luke's gospel. There was no question about it, the outsider may have the words but does not have the music, meaning the insider's knowledge and experience of what is meaningful and appropriate and how to relate these to the people's thoughts and emotions.

Overboard, Almost

During the years 1957-59, in addition to work in Kako, I guided several young Camerounians interested in analyzing and writing their languages. These included Meka, Mbobo, Bangando, Kozime, Bizom, Ngoumba and Bafia. Together we compiled legends, anecdotes, proverbs, and prepared literacy materials and Bible story translations. However, a major problem for the continuation of this work in the smaller languages was the fear on the part of church leaders that it promoted tribalism. *L'Eglise Presbyterienne Camerounaise* had become independent of the mission and held its first General Assembly on 11 December 1957. Personnel and available funds were needed for more immediate needs and, consequently, efforts to promote literacy and translations in the smaller languages received no priority or were downright discouraged. A major concern of church leaders, and understandably so, was to concentrate on efforts to unify the church, embarked as it was like a ship on a sea of linguistic and cultural diversity.

I argued with the leadership that use of the local languages was the most effective means of making the gospel intelligible and that literacy in these languages served as a stepping-stone to acquire the larger languages, including French. I regretted that I did not see this clearly when French administrator Chanlais in Aloum had confronted me. Nevertheless, it became clear that the young church, although encouraged by a few missionaries, would not endorse the work I had been doing. It was heart-rending to me to recognize that the intensive work done among the Kako would simply lapse after our departure.

On the positive side, it had been proposed that we return to Cameroun, after a study leave, to assist Bible translators throughout West Africa, a task that would utilize our Africa experience to the fullest. In the meanwhile, we were making plans that would take us first to Heidelberg, Germany, and then to Princeton. Walter Trobisch, a teacher at Libamba College, helped us with our plans for Germany.

Walter, the author of *I Loved a Girl, Love is a Feeling to be Learned* and other books, had become a close personal friend and colleague. During WWII he had been an infantryman in the German army until wounded in Russia and sent to the rear and eventually to Vienna for convalescence. While there he enrolled in the University for theological studies and, with the benevolent cooperation of a German army doctor, he became, as he sometimes remarked, "the first student on the German G. I. Bill."

When I informed Walter of my desire to spend a semester at the University of Heidelberg, he wrote the Reverend Rudolf Boesinger, pastor of the Lutheran church in Kirchheim, who in turn arranged with one of his parishioners to rent us a small apartment.

Anxious to return to an academic institution and equipped with an armful of German books, on February 28, 1959, we boarded the French liner *Foucauld* in Douala, where the *General Mangin* had deposited us in July 1956. The *Foucauld* was bound for Bordeaux and scheduled to call at French ports on the West African coast. The voyage along the coast was calm and peaceful. Annie was now five and a half and Susie two years and three months old. We had survived pre-independence terrorist attacks, bouts with malaria, worms and assorted ailments and were happy to be heading for Europe and America. The savory French cuisine, superb wines, the swimming pool and deck games put the harshness of the African bush far from our minds.

One evening as we four were strolling along the deck, we

suddenly realized that Susie, who loved to play hide-and-seek with her sister, was no longer with us. Somehow she had instantly disappeared. We retraced our steps, calling to her but hearing no response. While passing a lifeboat, we heard her say, "Annie, come find me." We dropped to our hands and knees and saw the tiny child edging backward toward the side of the ship. The space between the deck and the bottom of the lifeboat was too narrow for even Annie to enter. Fear that she would slip over the edge and fall into the dark sea below paralyzed us. Now, flat on our stomachs and seeing her legs over the side, we knew that the slightest roll of the ship could pitch her into the sea.

Marie, with characteristic presence of mind, asked her calmly, "Susie, did you get your candy yet?" Susie, who would never refuse anything sweet, shook her head No. Marie continued, "Susie, if you don't come and get it, it will all be gone." Annie and I made lip-smacking noises and told her how good these chocolates tasted. I pushed my closed hand toward her as far as I could with the make-believe candy. Our hearts nearly stopped as we waited to see if she would take the bait. Then, she began wriggling toward my hand. The moment she was within reach, I grasped her tiny outreached hand and she cried out in pain as I snatched her away from her hideout.

Back in our cabin, Susie was in tears, convinced that we had gobbled up all that candy. In the meanwhile, I had rushed to the dining room, the bar, and finally to the galley before locating some sweets to dry up our little sailor's tears. From that time forward, when we promenaded on the deck, Susie was kept on a lead.

On to Europe

The Majestic Hotel in Paris was worthy of its name and, although we would only stay one night before moving on to Heidelberg, it was a relief to be off the ship and not worried about Susie slipping down some perilous stairwell. Having explained to Annie that we were meeting friends for dinner in the ground floor dining room, we fed and bathed the girls, dressed them for bed, joined them in their prayers and instructed them to remain in the room. Free at last, we went down and met Dr. Frank and Betty Newman, the ones who had delivered Susie.

We had nearly finished our meal and were enjoying pleasant conversation when my eye detected a child's head at the far end of the room slowly drifting among the tables then stopping occasionally to scrutinize the diners. At first, I thought this wanderer was alone until I caught sight of a second head, one with a thumb stuffed into the mouth and dragging a piece of blanket like a faithful dog on a leash. As the pair moved closer and into an open space, I could see that the seat flap of Susie's pajamas was also dragging, evidence of some emergency that had occurred upstairs.

"Don't look now but some of your relatives may be visiting us soon," I whispered to Marie. The pair of wanderers were now holding hands, Annie the scouting engine coupled to a reluctant caboose.

"Why shouldn't I look?" Marie asked as she turned in her chair just in time to meet Annie's Ah-there-you-are gaze. Susie spat out her thumb, dropped her blanket, raced up and dived into her mother's lap. Pulling up the flap of her pajama seat, Marie was bent over in laughter, "Annie, what happened here?" Annie's nose that was just above table height was sniffing the food. "Oh, she said she wanted to go potty. Can I have some of that?" she added, sticking a finger into my *pot de crème* and licking it.

The following day our train to Heidelberg was met by Pastor Rudolf Boesinger and daughter who took as by taxi to Frau Hauk's house in Kirchheim where she and Mrs. Boesinger were waiting to welcome us with a richly decorated chocolate cake and coffee. From the moment of our arrival until our departure five months later, we have never been received by more gracious and hospitable folk.

Kirchheim, a fifteen-minute streetcar ride from the center of Heidelberg, was, like many German towns, the home of people who spoke a dialect of German that was as different from standard German as Pidgin English is from standard spoken American English. We soon learned that Kirchheimers stuck to their own dialect and did not care too much to converse with foreigners, even other Germans. We found that Germans who were not natives of the town were more likely to make friends with us. The Hauk family, although true Kirchheimers, were exceptions to this rule.

Many Sunday mornings, Pastor Boesinger came to the apartment and accompanied us as we walked to the parish church, where he preached to a congregation of eight hundred souls. He was known by nearly everyone and as he passed along on the sidewalk, he often called out greetings to his parishioners, calling them by name. Particularly unforgettable was our walk to the Easter Sunday service with the pastor waving and calling to people standing at their open bedroom window shutters where the eiderdowns were sunning, *"Guten Morgen, Christus ist Heute auferstanden!"* "Good morning, Christ is risen today!"

At the University of Heidelberg I attended the Old Testament lectures of Gerhard von Rad, delivered in a large auditorium where many in his audience were engineering and science students. I also sat in the missions classes taught by Hans Gensichen, whom I had met earlier in Africa. Walter Trobisch, still in Cameroun, put me in touch with persons who invited me to conferences to speak about the work we had done among the Kako. I prepared a number of lectures and often practiced them on Frau Hauk to make sure I was saying what I meant to say. I was grateful for the time in Germany and for the many friendships made. At the time, I did not know that nine years later I would be asked to leave Africa and to coordinate the translation work of the United Bible Societies from London, a task that would take me often behind the iron curtain and to much of the rest of the world.

David

With the help of colleague Cullen Storey we located an empty old house in Hightstown, New Jersey belonging to the local Methodist church. We were delighted to find ourselves surrounded by Puerto Rican neighbors. When I remarked to Annie, "Too bad you've forgotten your Spanish," she replied, "What Spanish, did I speak Spanish?"

"Ask your grandmothers about that," I replied.

With no one to speak Bulu, her Spanish completely melted away and with German still resounding in her ears, she enrolled in the Hightstown Elementary School for her first and only year in a school in the USA. I registered as a special student at Princeton Seminary. Susie on a little red tricycle became the sidewalk terror of Rogers Street and Marie took care of us all while she awaited the birth of our son, David.

On the night of January 29, 1960, while I was home looking after the two girls, the phone rang and Dr. Rose, Marie's obstetrician who knew we had two daughters, was calling from the Princeton Hospital.

"Mr. Reyburn?"

"Yes, speaking."

"Well, you're **really** a father now."

I became nervous, thinking that Marie had given birth to twins or triplets.

"Congratulations. You've got a beautiful baby boy."

The two perplexed little girls beside me stared at this strange father who laughed with joy while tears streamed down his cheeks. Annie put her arm around my neck to comfort me. "What's wrong, daddy?"

"Nothing at all; you've got a little brother."

David, the only one of our four children born in America and not delivered by a medical missionary had, therefore, the distinction of "being paid for." Eventually, I gave him the doctor's receipt for three hundred dollars, a very modest price compared with the cost of birthing his own three children.

Annie completed the first grade and Susie wore out the tires on her tricycle. After completing Bruce Metzger's courses in New Testament textual criticism, I taught linguistics at the Toronto Institute of Linguistics, then under the direction of Dr. William Smalley. We traveled to Colorado, New Mexico and North Carolina to visit families and then flew to London. In Paris, Air France was unable to confirm our continuing flight to Yaoundé and we were forced to camp in a small hotel near the Gare du Nord for three weeks that seemed like three years. Fortunately, the Wallace Dietrich family, medical missionaries to Cameroun, was in Paris for language study. They relieved our crowded conditions by inviting Annie to stay with them and to attend the local French school with their son, Willy.

Conventional wisdom—it should not be trusted, but tested— has it that many French persons feel themselves superior to their fellow humans, be they foreigners or other Frenchmen. Annie at age seven fully subscribed to this bit of nationalistic discernment when she and Willy Dietrich were chased halfway home from school each day by mean-spirited *gamins français* who shouted abusive language that is not taught in schoolrooms. *"Vous les sales morveux . . . Vous les deux vous êtes plein de totos . . ."*

David was slower than his sisters learning to walk and to speak. We observed him carefully and by age two he was making pencil sketches on paper while lying on his side and with one side of his face against the floor. This peculiar position did not seem to distort his perspective or skew his angles. Beginning at age three his interest was in airplanes and he drew fighter planes firing rockets at each other until the paper was covered. Wherever we went as a family, David was not fully dressed until he had a tiny metal airplane in his hands. While all others were chatting, David was putting his plane through endless dives, loops and barrel rolls, all the while keeping up a soft droning of the engines. We wondered if this little boy would one day become a pilot or an artist. What we did not know was that by the time he would be in college, the personal computer, unknown at the time, would affect his life profoundly.

David was eight years old when we moved from Nigeria to England where he became an avid soccer player. He was twelve when we left England for Lebanon and for the next few years, aside from learning Lebanese Arabic while living in the boys dorm at Brummana High School, he was content to get by with as little effort as possible. Knowing Arabic gave him considerable freedom to explore the places and things that held his interest. The war in Lebanon forced David and his sister to leave their Arab friends and transfer to a sister school in Ackworth, England. They are today, a quarter of a century later, both still in touch by email with some of their Brummana friends.

In 1978 David joined his sister Susie in California and, after a final year of high school, enrolled in an airplane maintenance course connected with Northrop University in Los Angeles. He never worked as a plane mechanic but transferred his credits to the university and graduated with a BS in aviation technology in 1982.

He says, "I started my professional career working for Northrop Corporation as a weight and balance engineer. We called ourselves mass properties engineers to sound important. I was working on the B2 stealth bomber program. Working in that environment exposed me to some very advanced technologies. In particular I was attracted to the rows of designers working on large CAD (computer assisted design) workstations. Their three dimensional displays looked to me like magic and I was immediately hooked. I knew then that this would somehow become part of my future career."

Although David's interests were in science and technology, like his sisters he says that living in Africa, England and Lebanon with so many different types of people made it possible for him to be flexible and adjust easily to changing situations. It is not surprising that David was attracted to a computer programmer at Northrop who was a deaf-mute. "I would give this man Roger, who could only communicate with us in writing, the credit for inspiring me to get into computer related work."

While still with Northrop Corporation, David applied and was accepted as a junior level programmer. He felt his dream had come true and he pursued mathematics courses at night at UCLA. He moved to the Douglas Aircraft Company, and after three years there, David and two friends decided to work on the development of a software package that was needed by engineers and designers working with complex surfaces. He gave up his job at Douglas and concentrated on software that gave CADKEY surface modeling capability. This effort resulted in a software application known now among designers worldwide as FastSURF. "This software is used by designers, machinists and mold-makers to define the complex surface shapes of everything from household appliances to aircraft fuselage panels."

In 1997 the rights to FastSURF were sold to Baystate Technologies, the makers of CADKEY software, and David was employed by that company to continue to upgrade his creation as well as to work on other applications.

David and his wife Tina Walter have two sons, Travis and Andrew, and a daughter, Kate Marie. They make their home in Goshen, Indiana,

Bibles and Beer

For months I had been studying the complexities of West Africa and, now that we were again in Cameroun, I had to decide how I would serve the Bible Societies in my role as Translations Consultant. The geographical area I was to work in—from Senegal in the north to the Congo in the south and from the Atlantic coast to central Africa, an area equivalent to the United States minus Alaska and Hawaii—left me breathless. We had been in many of the coastal cities on our first journey to and from Cameroun, but the interior of West Africa—Mali, Upper Volta (Burkina Faso) Niger, Chad, Nigeria—to name a few were to me *terrae incognitae.*

The number of languages was mind numbing and they were bewildering in their variety of structures. If until this time I had been marching through Babel, I was now to be tottering, slouching and creeping. Of course, I would be called upon to help translators in only a small percentage of these tongues, but that could still mean fifty to a hundred. To make matters more difficult, there were few published helps available, Yaoundé had no public library and there was as yet no university. True, I had file drawers of language notes on languages of south Cameroun, but these were all Bantu type languages and would be of little help in working with Hausa, Igbo, Yoruba, Fulani, Mandingo, Baoule, Moré and many others.

Important for the entire West Africa area was the arrival of political independence. Ghana had become independent in 1957 followed by Guinea in 1958 and many countries like Cameroun received their independence in 1960 while we were in America. The main exception was Liberia, independent since 1847. Although political independence from the colonial powers was in many ways a blessing and liberation, it often meant that utilities, always in short supply, were reduced, transportation was often less dependable and few of the new African nations had embassies or consular services in other African countries.

I became particularly aware of the difficulties in obtaining visas required for travel from Cameroun to, for example, Upper Volta, Mali, Ghana, Ivory Coast. However, when confronted by obstacles the determined person accepts them as challenges and works to overcome them. Frenchman Jean Keller, missionary statesman, was just such a person and his guidance was sought by anyone who faced administrative hurdles. I once accompanied this mustached giant of a man to make a request from a high official in Yaoundé. After listening to Keller's request in strict logical and legal terms with a summary of the advantages to be gained by all concerned, the African official pushed his pad and pencil across the desk to Jean Keller saying, "You write it; I sign it."

Monsieur Keller's advice on traveling to countries that had no embassy in Yaoundé or Douala was to send a letter to the immigration department of the country to be visited, then wait at least two to three weeks for the letter to reach its destination. Upon arrival at the airport, present a copy of the letter and hope for the best.

As the wheels of the Air France plane touched the runway in Ouagadougou, I could see Keller shrug his gallic shoulders and say, *Oui, c'est tout ce qu'on peut faire*, "Yes, that is all one can do." In the airport I handed my passport to the control officer who began flipping through the pages. "Sir. There is no visa, but I have a letter addressed to your government."

The man pushed the letter aside and slapped the closed passport on his desktop. Then wild-eyed and furious, he ordered me to leave the arrival hall and to get back on the plane, which was bound for Bamako, Mali, and Paris. He called a security guard who took me by the arm and led me to the next room where passengers were standing about waiting for the flight to be called. I nodded my thanks to the guard and melted into the crowd all the while keeping an eye on him until I saw him leave.

When the passengers began to file out to the waiting plane, I slipped quietly into the men's room, closed the door and waited until I heard the roar of the plane die away. Certain that I could not be forced to get back on the plane, I reappeared in the passport office prepared to be berated, barked at and bitten by this uniformed watchdog, zealous to preserve the letter of the law. He saw me, then covered his face with his hands, hoping, I am sure, that I was only a bad memory that would fade away. I was not good at disappearing, although he never bothered to inquire how I had vanished in the departure hall. While he fumed and fussed, I brought Jean Keller's image before me and asked, *Mon cher, qu'est-ce-que je dois faire maintenant?* "Use your letter," he seemed to reply.

"Sir," I said in my calm and friendly voice, "this letter is at the immigration office. They know it is not possible to get a visa in Yaoundé and if I fail to show up in the city, they will begin to investigate, starting right here." I tapped his desktop. The man took my passport and disappeared for twenty minutes. When he returned he asked if I knew anyone in the city. I showed him several names and addresses of people who had requested me to come. In the end I was ordered to present myself at the immigration office at eight sharp (it did not open until nine). I collected my baggage and went to my friends' place. The next day the visa was stamped into my passport and, as Monsieur Chanlais, the administrator who allowed me to keep the elephant's tusk, would have said, *"Cette affaire du visa est finie."*

The work of the Bible Societies in West Africa had been, with the exception of Liberia, under the direction of the British and Foreign Bible Society in London. I was now working for the British,

American and, most recently, the Dutch. The Netherlands Bible Society had made arrangements in 1959 for the Dutch to take responsibility for the translation, production and distribution of Scriptures in Cameroun and Gabon and had sent Ype Schaaf as its representative. Schaaf, a native of Friesland who had been ordained in 1959 as a minister in the Netherlands Reformed Church, was an enterprising and energetic organizer. He spent four years in Cameroun establishing the work of the Bible Society and founding a publishing house for French-speaking Africa. We shared offices in the same building on a busy Yaoundé street and made several long trips together.

On one occasion when I needed to confer with the Bamoun translators, we drove the Bible Society car, a French Domaine, to Douala and then north to the city of Foumban. The Bamoun had, under the direction of their Sultan Njoya, invented a script to write their language. Although many documents were produced, it never became popular like the Cherokee syllabary in America. I was thrilled to think of visiting this historic place. However, the excitement nearly drained away when we had an emergency stop due to an overheated engine. I called Schaaf to the rear of the car where oil and water were running from the exhaust pipe. My colleague, who was more at home on a bicycle among the polders of Leeuwarden than in a steaming car in the hills of Cameroun, lit up a cigarette. This always seemed to relax him.

"What have we got here?" he inquired.

"We've got a crack in the block," I replied.

"How do we fix it?"

"We can't."

We waited for the cooking engine to cool and I saw Schaaf and his motor boy, Jean, pulling boxes of Bibles from the back of the car. One box labeled Heineken Export clinked cheerily as Schaaf broke it open and began uncapping the bottles. "Mister William, keep in mind this is a *voiture française* and no doubt has an appetite for Chablis but it will have to recognize that it is now under Dutch command . . . Jean, give the poor beast a drink of Holland's best."

Jean looked perplexed. Was his boss talking about the car or me? He handed me two open bottles. "Why not? There is probably not a river within miles," I thought as I began to pour in bottle after bottle of the golden suds. When the radiator was reasonably full, I screwed on the cap and we jumped in and raced for Foumban before the injured animal could spew up its innards. At the top of a long hill facing the town, the engine was again in crisis. Like a puffing locomotive, steam was again shooting from beneath the hood, and Pastor Schaaf's brake foot slapped metal against the floorboards. We were perched atop the long slope, half concealed in a cloud of yeasty aromatic steam, and now with no brakes. The safest thing to do was to run it into the hillside and jump out. That suggestion did not strike Schaaf as good stewardship of his patron's funds. So we moved to plan B: Jean and I would sit on the front bumper, our backs against the steaming grill and our feet pushing against the roadbed, restraining, in some small measure, the forward motion of the wild and dying critter. Schaaf was at the wheel waving to the pedestrians who, like the children of Hamelin behind the Pied Piper, had picked up the scent of this rolling brewery and were running alongside. Many of those who came for the beer left with a Bible. When we pushed the moribund vehicle into a mechanic's garage, Schaaf remarked, "Well, Mister William, I think we have found a new way to advertise the Bible."

Maria

The year 1962 marked ten years since Marie and I had sailed for Ecuador. It seemed like a long journey from Quechua (Ecuador), Toba (Argentina), Miskito (Honduras and Nicaragua), French (Paris), Bulu (Aloum) and Kako (Kambélé), German (Heidelberg). Since 1960 I had been traveling throughout West Africa including North Cameroun, responding to requests from Bible translators for help in analyzing and writing unwritten languages, giving guidance in translation and literacy. There seemed to be no end to the problems of communication and, although I could have kept a dozen linguists busy, there was as yet no one ready to join me. The frequent month-long absences from my family made me consider resigning and returning to the US or, if we were to remain in Africa—something we very much desired to do—we could join one of the missions and concentrate on one or two languages in depth. However, if truth be told, the pilgrimage of the past ten years had internationalized us perhaps to the point of no return.

Because Marie and I had been drawn to each other by a shared value in cross-cultural communication, and had lived with Cherokee Indians, South American Latinos and Indians, West Africans, French, Germans, Dutch and other Europeans, it would require a reversal of our dispositions now to identify ourselves with any one nationality or religious persuasion. Part of this ecumenicity had been conscious and part unconscious. If, in fact, we had abandoned or lost certain features of our backgrounds, we had at the same time been challenged and enriched in the process. Marching through Babel with a closed mind would be no journey at all, but with a critical and open mind it meant an opportunity that could and should result in a conscience-changing pilgrimage.

Reading and discussion had, since Marie and I first met, been an integral part of our union. We shall always remain grateful to our colleagues in the American Bible Society for encouraging us to buy books that would contribute to our lives and thought. When we went to Ecuador in 1952, we had one small orange crate of books; they covered no more than a foot or two on a book shelf. Through the years books and journals increased until they eventually became the largest part of our household equipment.

1962 saw the publication of Rachel Carson's landmark volume *Silent Spring,* Betty Friedan's *The Feminine Mystique,* and James Baldwin's *The Fire Next Time.* This was the decade of political assassinations in America: John F. Kennedy, Malcom X, Martin Luther King and Robert F. Kennedy. Bob Dylan was singing *The Times They Are a-Changin'.*

The Reyburn household was also changing. Marie went back to the Presbyterian Hospital in Elat for the birth of Maria, our fourth child and second to be born in Cameroun. She had timed her journey to Elat almost with precision. She checked into the Johnson Pavilion where Susie had been born six years earlier, had an evening meal with Swiss agriculturalist, René Ryter and wife, nurse Rose, and Maria was born the following afternoon, February 21.

Late afternoon at the hospital, when busy days of surgery, rounds of the wards, teaching African assistants are over, means gathering on the tennis courts for a game of doubles or singles, depending on how many hospital staff show up to play. Busy doctors and nurses always have to play hoping no emergency will interrupt their games. Being called away in a close match is frustrating but common. Dr. Frank Newman signalled his opponent to hold his serve while he walked to the fence and heard Rose

Ryter tell him that Marie Reyburn's baby was not going to wait until the end of his game.

In the delivery room Frank, still dripping with sweat, calmly scrubbed and prepared for the delivery. Back in Yaoundé I was caring for David and Susie. Annie, who had transferred to the missionary childrens' school at Elat, was the first of the children to see this new little sister. René Ryter sent me a message through a truck driver, far more reliable than the telephone in those days. Marie said the birth of Maria Jeannette was the easiest of her four birthings.

As our four children grew, I observed them closely, wondering who, if anyone, would have their dad's love of language. Annie by age nine had had more natural child language experience than most: English, Spanish, Quechua, French, German and Bulu. Susie had a knack at imitating and could amuse the family with any number of English accents. David's gifts were in visual art and at age three could draw pictures and designs with three dimensional depth that neither his mother nor I could do. But of the four it was this last one who had the love of language in her heart.

At age four during an early morning walk Maria confided to me that words are not just sounds; "My words have colors." When asked to explain how words could have colors, especially since there are thousands of words and relatively few colors, she explained that many words have the same color and gave examples. "There are all kinds of houses with different colors but the word *house* is white. *Tree* is a yellow word and *hill* is green." Since I had not read of this kind of color association nor had I heard anyone speak of it, I asked Maria to tell me the colors of many nouns, verbs, and modifiers. Prepositions and conjunctions did not seem to suggest colors to her. To make certain that she was not inventing a word game, I later went over each of the words she had identified with a particular color and found that she recalled them exactly as she had given them to me. Two weeks later I gave her the same list in different order and she gave me a hundred percent consistent responses. I was amazed.

I later learned there are people called synesthetes—said to be as few as ten people in a million—for whom sounds conjure up such sensations as taste or color. It was quite clear that Maria enjoyed the color of words and it seemed to give her linguistic experience a texture that none of the rest of us had.

When we moved from Africa to England, Maria was six years old and she, like her siblings, entered an English school, adapted to British English outside the home, but spoke a slightly modified American English in the home. In Lebanon at age ten she and David, then twelve years old, lived in school dormitories where they learned spoken Lebanese Arabic.

By the time Maria was in college, Marie and I were living in Costa Rica and Maria came to spend a summer working in a Spanish-speaking day-care center where her school Spanish blossomed into fluent and idiomatic usage. Having read and heard of our experiences among the Quechua, she elected to fill the requirements in a sociology course by living with a Quechua family in the high Andes of Ecuador, a community called Cochapamba in the province of Chimborazo. One of Maria's daily chores for her hosts, the Chorlongo family, was to take the family cow from its pen and lead it to the bottom of a steep ravine to be watered. One cold and wet day the rains had made the narrow trail slippery and in order to get up out of the ravine, Maria clutched the cow's tail with both hands as she and the cow struggled up the slope. Just when she thought they were about to reach the top, the cow let go a hot bath of liquid manure that caught Maria full in the face. When we next saw our cow-girl daughter she was covered from neck to ankles with flea bites, having slept on a pile of straw in Señora Chorlongo's kitchen hut with a chirping brood of guinea pigs.

After graduation from college, Maria spent seven years working in the Sandinista's Nicaragua—part of the time as a stringer for CBS. When she returned to the US, she obtained a master's degree in TESOL and linguistics then went to Egypt to teach English at Cairo University, using her free time to study

Arabic. Today she is again in Nicaragua, the wife of Francisco Guadamuz and mother of Anya who she is preparing to be bilingual in Spanish and English.

Looking back at her childhood, Maria says, "When I started school in England, I knew I was different but was not sure what the nature of the difference was. Only much later did it come into focus. I was the youngest of four children and had the advantage of learning from my older siblings. I had seen through the eyes of a child the devastation of the civil war in Nigeria, our neighbors being massacred. Yet, the Nigerians I knew were kind and particularly good to children. I heard the Hausa language spoken and many dialects of English. I learned to respect differences in life style and to be grateful. God was the source of all goodness. Having lived in different countries gave me a curiosity about cultures and people and I found that I was, perhaps even from childhood, an internationalist."

The Hollowed Bible

of Edouard Ewutu

The Bible and holy writ in general have served many purposes, not all for the spiritual edification of the reader. For example, During WWII, and perhaps at other times of shortages, the fine quality India paper in Bibles has been used for cigarette paper, and many a smoker has puffed his or her way from Genesis to Malachi before the paper crisis has been relieved.

Sometimes the would-be reader has been drawn to the Bible through negative publicity received from secular or even religious authorities. This was the case of Simón Izarra, whom I knew as a translator of the Ayacucho Quechua Bible in Peru. Simón explained how he obtained and read bits of the Bible for the first time while a primary school student in Huanta, Peru. One of his classmates was clandestinely reading a Bible concealed behind a large geography text. Unknown to the student, Padre Ramírez, teacher of religion, tiptoed down the aisle and snatched the Bible, tore it to pieces and flung it portion by portion into the wastebasket while shouting, "I've warned you before that I will not tolerate anyone reading a protestant book in my class." Ramírez had confiscated students' books and magazines before, but today his acerbity reached new heights as he raged nearly out of control.

"What," thought Simón and his classmates, "could be so

vile in that book as to cause Ramírez to shake with emotion? The religious instruction he gave was so dull we always thought he would put himself to sleep at his desk. We were frightened to see his face so red and the veins in his neck balloon up like ropes. What was it about this book that sent his blood boiling?"

When the bell rang, Simón's class left the room quietly behind Ramírez and waited in the hall for him to disappear. No sooner had he rounded the corner than half a dozen inquisitive boys charged back into the classroom and raced for the trashcan. Simón said that he only recovered a handful of torn pages but "that was enough to introduce me to the Good News." It was certainly not good news to professor Ramírez, who a few years later blew his brains out. Later Simón obtained a whole Bible; his life was changed and, after finishing university in Lima, he became a member of the team of Ayacucho translators.

In Latin America I have watched *curanderos* give scraps of the Bible to sick people to be eaten. No doubt if the sick believed in the cure, they were often made well. Muslims in West Africa also believe in the holiness of the words of the Qur'an. I have sat with young boys under the instruction of a *malam* watching them learn to write in Arabic with chalk on their slates the words *Bismi allahi alrahani alrahmin* "In the name of Allah the Beneficent, the Merciful," the first line in the opening surah of the Qur'an. When the writing has been inspected and corrected by the instructor, the students' slates are washed clean. However, the water that removes these sacred words does not fall to the ground, but is caught in a bowl and drunk, not entirely unlike the Christian priest who must himself drink the leftover wine in the chalice that has been consecrated in the Eucharist.

As suggested at the beginning where smokers roll cigarettes with fine Bible paper, the Bible is used for more than cures and charms. The improper use of the Bible can also land a person in jail. This was the experience of young Edouard Ewutu whom I met in a Yaoundé prison. Walking to and from my office, I would pass through a wooded lot where a jailhouse stood and where prisoners would frequently call to passers-by asking for food, cigarettes or anything that came to their minds. Perhaps because I often carried a book, one prisoner called for me to come closer where he could speak with me through the barred window; he begged me to bring him a French Bible. The following day when I delivered the Bible to the jailer and told him it was for Ewutu—he had given me his full name—the jailer refused to accept it. When I asked why he refused, the jailor asked if I knew the reason Ewutu was in his jailhouse. He then brought the young African to the front cell and ordered him to confess his story.

Edouard, according to his own account, went about town wearing a clerical collar and with a Bible piously tucked under his arm. He told how he practiced his artifice before a mirror until he was certain that shopkeepers would be convinced that this priestly appearing person would require no monitoring as he moved about among the merchandise. What the shop owners did not know was that the Bible under his arm had the center of all the pages cut out, leaving only the red edges and the covers uncut. Ewutu could deftly slip a watch, ring or other small items into the hollowed book, bow graciously to the owner and depart.

Ewutu's Bible served him well and his shoplifting prospered. Before too long, he obtained a larger Bible, one that could be made to accommodate still grander blessings. But Yaoundé is not a large city and the storeowners and their clerks became suspicious of this man of the cloth who only came to peer and never to purchase. During one of his smiling departures, an armed guard stopped the reverend and ordered him to open his book. At first Ewutu refused but when the guard rammed his gun into Ewutu's chest, the Bible dropped to the floor spilling its loot. With the guard in hot pursuit, Ewutu was tackled on the street and turned over to the police. His hollowed Bible was used as evidence in his trial. Further, the room where he lived turned out to be a thief's den from which he carried on a brisk trade in stolen goods. The judge gave him a two-year sentence.

Ewutu's jailor handed me back the Bible I had brought, "You

Translators School

By 1963 it became evident that we needed to conduct training courses for Bible translators, three-and four-week sessions that were given the high sounding name of translators institutes. In the early years, and particularly in the interior of West Africa, most of the translators were missionaries who were sometimes accompanied by their African helpers. In some cases these helpers were domestic servants who played no real role in the translation process. The instruction was provided by Bible Society staff who came from Europe and America and the participants were exclusively protestants until the Second Vatican Council beginning in 1962. The first of these courses was held in the town of Bobo Dioulassou, Upper Volta, now called Burkina Faso.

Howard and Anne Beardslee, then of the Christian and Missionary Alliance mission, managed, under great difficulties, to obtain the use of a school room and find accommodations and meals for some thirty people. The history of missions in West Africa reveals how the older mainline churches had established their work along the coast and only later did the younger and more conservative groups begin work in the interior. Since most of these newer missions were American, instruction could be given in English with the missionary translators passing on something of what they had learned to their African helpers. These missions are geared principally to evangelization and are only minimally involved in promoting hospitals, clinics and schools. In fact, most do not see their task as founding churches but rather winning individual converts. They are often very protective of their geographical area and seek to maintain the doctrinal purity of their converts by avoiding contacts with Roman Catholics and often other protestant organizations.

At the Bobo institute, as it became known, E.A. Nida taught the theory and practice of translation, Robert Bratcher handled New Testament text and exegesis, André Wilson from the University of Ghana and I lectured on linguistics and cultural aspects of translation. No doubt Bratcher had the most delicate task of all, explaining numerous examples like the King James version of Roman 8.28 "And we know that all things work together for good to them that love God . . ." that are not based on the best Greek manuscripts. People who had all their lives memorized this version were not comfortable when told that in many passages the text of the King James Bible did not reflect the best attested manuscript evidence. Nearly all the participants had studied in Bible colleges where text critical studies are not included in the curriculum. At Bobo some were upset and ready to leave, some realized there was a whole field of study they had not been aware of, and one couple, convinced that they needed to make a new start, resigned from their mission and returned to America for further training.

Because accommodations were very limited in Bobo, arrangements were made for Bratcher and me to be housed in the one hotel in town. This was *Le Buffet*, which in French refers to a dining room or restaurant in a railway station and, in this case, one that had rooms on the second floor overlooking a large chicken pen where, we soon learned, a great proud rooster began to chant his *coquerico* each morning long before dawn. The effect of being awakened between three and four a.m. meant that by the time our neighborly bird had exhausted himself, we fell asleep and barely managed to arouse ourselves for breakfast and the eight o'clock class.

About midway through the first week of this daily torture, I approached the owner and proposed that for Sunday lunch he serve *un bon dîner à la coque*. He reflected for only a moment.

"You have a rooster to cook?"

"No, but you have."

"What? Cook my *coque*? Never have I heard such a ridiculous suggestion. I am offended."

"I'll buy him; you cook him."

"*Monsieur*, this discussion is finished. *Mon Dieu!*" He slapped his bald head as if awakening himself from a bad dream. "Cook my chanticleer, *jamais, jamais!*"

Fellow traveler Bratcher and I had nowhere else to go. We buried our heads under our pillows until the Bobo course was finished, then we left for home, Bratcher to Long Island and I back to Yaoundé.

The second translators institute in West Africa took place in July-August, 1963, in the heart of the south Cameroun forest at Libamba college, a secondary school of the Cameroun Presbyterian church. This three-week course brought together some seventy translators, a majority Africans but also many missionaries. Both French and English were used in instruction. Participants arriving in Douala on the coast or Yaoundé in the interior took the train to Makak station where we met them and brought them by truck to the jungle campus. Due to the mountain of preparatory work to be done, we had to begin six months in advance.

The college students were on vacation and since it was the custom for them to supply their own mattresses, towels, pillows and sheets, they took them home at the end of the school year. We had either to purchase or make seventy mattresses and find bedding and towels. We had to organize a kitchen crew of cooks, helpers, dishwashers, lay in a huge amount of food, arrange for daily shipments of fresh vegetables from the Yaoundé markets, plant a large garden, buy chickens, goats and a cow, and make everything ripe and ready when needed. To successfully put together an undertaking of this magnitude and complexity would frighten a seasoned quartermaster sergeant. I knew only one person who'had the organizational and managerial skills to make it all work: Marie Reyburn.

As Marie began to put together her plans, she contacted agricultural missionary, Wade Reeves, who in turn planned and planted a large vegetable garden timed to be in full production for the conference. He bought the animals, fattened them and at the appropriate time butchered and delivered them to the kitchen. A team of Africans set about cutting grass while others cut and sewed burlap bags that were stuffed and made into mattresses. Marie had the job of making up daily menus with recipes for 50 persons, and she scoured the country to borrow all kinds of cooking equipment and what could not be borrowed was purchased. At the end of the conference she would organize a sale of bedding, kitchen equipment, and countless other items. She enlisted her friends, who in some cases gave up their vacations, to be part of this international and ecumenical effort.

As the opening day approached, I worried that some missionary ladies would be a bit shocked upon seeing their student dormitory accommodations. I needed a scheme to lift up their hearts. How could I do this? The answer came while I was talking to one of the village chiefs living between the college and the Makak station. The chief loved the idea of being an actor in my drama. A hastily prepared sign in French and English placed at the entrance to his village read "Welcome translators to your new home." While the passengers got down from the truck and gazed about the helter-skelter village where chickens, ducks, goats and naked children ran about, a large cane chair was brought for the chief. A praise singer intoned blessings and praises for the great one as the latter strode from his hut and took his seat. He addressed himself to the visitors in broken French and proper Pidgin English:

"My dear travelers. I welcome you to this your home

for the next three weeks. The hearts of my wives and children are filled with joy to know that you have come so far to be part of our family." The African guests were not quite sure how to take this reception and the missionaries, who no longer gazed at the untidy village, were clearly disturbed. The chief continued along the lines I had prompted him. "We have buckets so you can draw water from the spring to wash your feet. We will keep our dogs tied when you are here and I suggest you not go outside in the night, however, because at this season of the year we have a problem with poisonous snakes."

Some of our women guests were beginning to pale and one whispered to me, asking what time the next train left for Douala. I took this as a sign that it was now safe to move on to the campus. I thanked the chief for his kind reception, assuring him that we would be back plenty early to get inside before snake time. With the reception speech completed, we bounced over the dusty road to the college where all our guests were moderately happy with their rustic but clean accommodations. "I didn't really think you were going to dump us in that dingy village" opined one missionary lady, "but I must say this old dorm looks pretty nice now."

Although some thirty African languages were represented among the translators, the problem of tribalism came not from the Africans but from the Euro-Americans. The English had to have early morning tea and could not carry on at all without their afternoon spot of tea. Marie, having not yet lived among the British, had failed to take this into consideration. The French and Swiss were upset if they could not get a glass of wine with their evening meal. The Germans and Dutch felt the day was nearly a total loss if they did not have a smoke and a beer. In Holland cigar smoking was the badge of fundamentalists, cigarettes were for conservatives and liberals identified themselves with the pipe. And the Americans? Well, many of these brethren had long ago decided that Euopeans were unregenerate and to be avoided.

With all their newfound knowledge packed in their suitcases, we put everyone back on the train and, after Marie's big sale, Libamba college became again a quiet spot in the heart of the African forest.

Travel Risks

After the conclusion of the translators' training course at Libamba College in Cameroun, it was decided that the Reyburn family should move to Nigeria and so we settled in the northern town of Jos where there was a fine missionary school for children. I began an intensive routine of travel that took me throughout Nigeria and the rest of West Africa.

Nigeria, a country of some three hundred languages, has three major languages whose speakers run into the millions: Yoruba in the West, Igbo in the East and Hausa in the North. Hausa, in addition to being the native language of the largest group in the country, is also the second language of many smaller northern tribes. Most native speakers of Hausa are Muslims as are the tribal people, but due to the influence of western missions there are also many Christians. English is spoken by most people who have been educated in government and mission schools.

When I look back on my travels in Africa, I am amazed that more air and ground accidents did not happen. I know of only two colleagues, both Nigerians, who were killed in a crash of a Kenya Airways jet taking off from Abidjan in 1999. Although I had been badly frightened taking off in a boulder strewn river bed in Honduras, as told in **Anyone Here Speak English ?**, most of my flying in Africa was on scheduled commercial planes that fortunately seemed to develop mechanical problems on the ground rather than in the air.

Nigerian Airways seemed plagued with problems and passengers were often unsure of their flight until they actually reached their destination. While waiting for a scheduled flight from Jos to Kano to make an internatioinal connection, we saw the plane approach Jos, circle and then depart. Passengers were unable to learn from the ground crew why the plane had not landed. However, there was no choice but to drive the six hours to Kano. When we reached Kano and found the pilots in the hotel dining room, they said they had radioed the Jos tower asking if it was clear to land—cows often wandered on to the runway— and the reply from the tower was "decide for yourself." That was enough to bypass Jos.

I once boarded a Nigerian Airways plane in Lagos and it seemed we were cleared for take-off when the pilot shut down the engines and came into the passenger section announcing that we were overloaded and would Mr. Oladupo please leave the plane. After half an hour in rising temperatures another appeal was made to passenger Oladupo. Still later an official car pulled up alongside the plane and passenger Oladupo was again invited to deplane and be taken in the car to a hotel. No one moved and it was not certain to the other passengers if there was such a person on board. After more than an hour on the steaming runway, two Englishmen volunteered to stay behind. Finally, soaked in our sweat, the engines started and we took off. Was there ever a Mr. Oladupo? Who knows?

On another flight from Jos to Lagos in a Fokker Friendship, I noticed we were circling over what appeared to be a cow pasture. I could see no runway and there was no explanation given why we should be preparing to land in this odd place. When the plane finally bounced to a halt, the copilot opened the door and stepped out. We could see he was asking directions from a goat herdsman who pointed in one direction and then in another. After what must have been a-not-too-informative consultation, our lost copilot got back in, pulled the door shut and, without a word of explanation, reentered the cockpit. We again bounced along the field, turned around and roared back along the field getting into the air just before a woods took shape before us. I asked the stewardess what that was all about. She shrugged and asked me,

"Sir, would you like tea or coffee?"

"Coffee, please"

"Sorry, no coffee."

Sometimes it is better not to have strong preferences, but I do think all on board were interested in safely reaching their destination.

The Air Congo plane from Kinshasa to Luluaburg was battling fierce head winds. The Belgium pilot tried to escape these currents by gaining altitude. The big four engine plane seemed to drop like a stone, strike bottom and begin to lift again. Nearly everyone was sick from the violent pitching and many were vomiting. The pilots brought the plane to the lowest elevation possible but the rain was so heavy we could not see out the windows. Every now and then tree tops came into view, sickeningly close. The pilot, his shirt soaked and sticking to his skin, rushed from the cockpit to the toilet. He too was sick and his face pale and drained. When we reached the Luluaburg runway, the plane had to make three attempts before successfully setting the big bird down in the driving rain. When the engines were cut off, no one rushed to get off. We were frightened stiff and unable to move.

On a flight from Accra to Lagos I was the only passenger. The Nigerian Airways stewardess sat across the aisle and we chatted until she pulled her wig over her eyes and went to sleep. I read. As we approached Lagos, the fasten-seat-belts sign came on. I noticed my fellow pasenger was not buckled in so I reached across the aisle and woke her up.

"We're landing, Miss," I said

Pushing her wig out of her eyes she seemed dazed for a moment then leaped from her seat and announced over the intercom, "Please return to your seats, extinguish all cigarettes, place your seatbacks in the upright position and fasten all seat belts."

"But I've done all that," I said

"Sir, I'm talking to all the passengers, not just to you."

Air travel memories were not always in the air. I found that going and coming through Lagos and Kano airports were often memorable occasions. While departing from Lagos one time, the Nigerian customs officer lectured me on the serious consequences of departing the country carrying Nigerian currency. I assured the good man that I was aware of the currency regulations and that I had no Nigerian money at all. I offered him my billfold for his inspection. Nevertheless, a few minutes later in the departure hall, the same official appeared at my side and whispered how much he would give me for each Nigerian pound I was carrying. I never knew if he was dishonestly trying to earn some money or if he was determined to catch me breaking the currency laws. Perhaps both.

One of the most common tricks I encountered traveling by air throughout West Africa was the invitation to act as someone's delivery agent. The typical ploy was for a well-dressed African woman to approach me while I was waiting for my flight. From her bag she would remove a neatly wrapped package, usually about the size of a cigar box, sealed with layers of tape. "Sir, are you going to Abidjan?"

"Perhaps."

"I'm sorry to bother you, but my brother is in the hospital there and requires urgently this medicine. Could you take it?" Then follow details about the person who will meet me at the airport. The package must not be given to anyone else.

"Yes, I'd be glad to help your sick brother."

There is a sigh of relief. "Oh, I was just certain you were that kind of gentleman." She then pushes the package toward me. I hand her a pocket knife and ask her to open it. I hear a rush of reasons why that must not be done.

"Sorry, Miss, if you can't open it, I can't carry it."

The nattily dressed lady returns her package to her bag and without an *au revoir* walks away. It is evident that the chances of her being honest are nil. Either the package is illicit—gems or drugs—or it is a sting operation to put me behind bars.

British Airways flights from London to Kano brought both Nigerians and British, many of whom had been working the tin mines of the North for years. British women often wore hats and frequently their newly acquired *chapeaux* were decorated with colorful ornaments. On one occasion the customs officer asked the lady ahead of me to hand him her hat.

"What on earth for, do you think I am hiding something in it?" she asked.

The man insisted and when finally he had her hat in his hands, he explained,

"Don't you know that it is against the law to bring fruit into Nigeria?" The lady was flummoxed.

"I don't have any fruit," she protested. "Of course, I know it's against the law."

"Oh yes you do," replied the customs clerk holding up the hat adorned with a small cluster of glass grapes. The hat's owner watched with disbelief as the man took a pair of pliers and smashed each of the glass grapes then handed back the hat. By this time the woman was shouting abuse and calling the customs officer "a silly ape."

Nigerian customs officers, in spite of their official scowl, could often be humored. Once when Marie and I were departing from Kano, a rotund customs man stopped us and explained in the most serious tone that the removal of archeological artifacts from the country was a criminal offense.

"Sir," he adressed me, "are you taking any archeological objects out of Nigeria?"

"Only one."

"Only one?" The man was visibly disturbed. "Where is it?"
"Following me," I said lowering my voice.

The man's eyes bulged as he looked at Marie. "Oh please go, madam." He produced a large handerchief from his pocket and covered his embarrassed laughter.

In 1965 the United Bible Societies held a translators insitute at the university of Ghana. Our children were on vacation from school and so we decided to make it a family trip. In Nigeria we drove on the left as in all countries colonized by the British. This is very natural and easy when the steering wheel is on the right side. Our road trip went very smoothly until we got to Dahomey (Benin), a former French colony. Here we had to switch to driving on the right. But we soon became hungry and stopped for lunch. Back again in the car—old habits do not die easily—we continued on our way. I remarked to Marie and the children how friendly the people of Cotonou were, nearly everyone along the street was waving friendly greetings to us.

"Try driving on the other side of the road," Marie suggested. When I got the car on the left side, everyone seemed to lose interest in us.

African airlines seemed to be as expert in losing passengers' baggage as most others. I had thought it was the fault of the airlines until I met Eugene and Althea Nida at the Accra airport. When the baggage had been brought into the airport and the Nidas identified their bags, a man in uniform set them aside while the Nidas checked on their continuing flight. After a few minutes, I looked to see if our man in uniform was still guarding their bags. What a shock, both man and bags had disappeared. I raced outside the airport just in time to see the Nidas' luggage being put into a pick-up that was departing. Running alongside, I was able to snatch out the two suitcases while the driver looked back to see his loot was being looted then sped up and disappeared. Since this incident I have not been so anxious to blame the airlines for lost luggage.

To end on a positive note, I will describe an incident that happened in 1966 when the Volkswagen bug I was driving broke down in Igbo country in Eastern Nigeria. I had gone to the area to meet with Igbo translators and while passing a few huts in the late afternoon in an isolated area, the car lost power, sputtered and died. When it refused to start again, I checked the engine and could find nothing on the exterior to be out of place. There was no sign of life in the nearby huts but I crossed the road and went to the one house whose door stood open and called. A girl about seven years of age with an infant tied to her back appeared around the corner. She said nothing but departed and later returned with a man I took to be her father.

"My car is broken," I explained. "How far to the nearest garage?"

"Garage here," the man replied and pointed to a large oak. "You got tools?"

"Yes, a few," but I wondered what on earth this man would want with tools.

He motioned for me to steer to his tree while he pushed.

"I don't think it will start by pushing." However, once under the big oak, the man went inside his hut and from beneath a bed fished out a chain and pulley. In a minute he had the rear of the car dangling two feet off the ground. After examining from underneath, he crawled out saying he had to go to Enugu to get parts. I gave him money and he stopped the next bus and climbed aboard. Would I ever see him again? I certainly hoped so.

It was some time after dark when his wife came out and handed me a bowl of spicy soup with two hard boiled eggs. Immediately I began to feel that this tasty soup was evidence of this family's integrity. Around ten o'clock at night the dark was illumined by the lights of a bus and my oak tree mechanic arrived with the parts wrapped in a newspaper. He handed me the bill of sale and the exact change minus the round-trip bus fare. My flashlight was nearly dead or he would have tried to repair the car immediately. I lowered the rear end to the ground and stretched across the seat, fighting a losing battle with mosquitoes until daylight.

About nine o'clock in the morning he scraped the last nut out of the dirt then told me to start the engine. It purred like a kitten. We settled the bill and I drove away. On my return a few days later, I stopped at his house with gifts for his family. It is not surprising that I had a deep sympathy for his people when later that year the massacre of thirty thousand Igbos burst upon Northern Nigeria.

Blessed are the Peacemakers

When the civil war in Nigeria began in 1966, it had been eighteen years since I had stumbled into the Guatemalan revolution, and the start of the independence wars in Cameroun was now ten years behind us. Nevertheless, it seemed we were fated to be caught up in political strife and, after the riots in Nigeria, the worst still lay ahead in the Middle East. But more on that later.

In January 1966, six years after Nigeria received its independence from Britain, a group of Igbo army officers overthrew the federal government and the three regional governments. Prime Minister Balewa, a Hausa man from the North was murdered, as were the prime ministers of the northern and western regions. General Johnson Aguiyi-Ironsi, commander of the Nigerian army, took control of the central government and appointed many Igbos as his advisers. In May the federal system of government was abolished and most northerners feared the Igbos would take control of the entire country. In July a group of army officers from the North revolted against the central government and murdered General Aguiyi-Ironsi. The army chief of staff, Major Yakubu Gowon, a northern Christian, became head of the new military government. Colonel Ojukwu, the military governor of the eastern region, refused to accept Gowon as head of state and subsequently broke from the federal government and declared his part of Nigeria as the independent republic of

Biafra. From January until September, 1966, the country was experiencing the aftershocks of the original coup.

The Igbos living in the North were numerous and industrious. They were the craftsmen, clerks, teachers, business operators, police, administrators, and entrepreneurs. Whether you wanted a skilled carpenter, plumber, electrician, surveyor, mechanic or lawyer, chances were you would be dealing with an Igbo. Most of the cars in Jos were driven by Igbos and most of the better houses in the town were owned by them.

The area of Jos where we lived, Dogon Dutse, was occupied by African and British tin miners. Whether owned by Africans or foreigners, most equipment was operated by Igbos and repaired by Igbos who lived at the miners' compounds.

Following the army coup, we heard rumors of Igbos being attacked and killed but did not know of this happening in Jos. Some Igbos anticipated the riots and therefore returned to the eastern region. However, the majority had jobs and property in the North and refused to leave until it was too late.

On the morning of September 28 the dam of pent-up hatred broke. Mobs of northerners—Hausas and tribesmen—armed with clubs and machetes poured into the streets and began to attack and slaughter Igbo men, women and children. Breaking into hospitals and operating rooms they dragged the sick from their beds. Shops, houses, offices were pillaged and their inhabitants murdered. Marauding mobs were often followed by swarms of women and children looting and carting off clothing, sewing machines, bicycles, furniture and anything else they could carry away.

Some Igbos attempted to flee by car but were stopped at road barricades, dragged from their vehicles and hacked to death. During the first two hellish days we could not be certain if the killing would be limited to the Igbos or if it would extend to the Europeans and Americans. Many Igbos sought protection from the police but the police had lost control of law enforcement. Complete anarchy ruled and the dead and dying lay helpless in the streets. Maria, age four, crawled into her mother's lap and innocently asked, "Mommy, are they going to kill us today?"

On the second day a gang came to our house demanding that I turn over to them any Igbo workers. We had never had Igbos living on our property and our servant, Musa, a northerner, tried to convince them of the truth. When they insisted, I invited them to select one of their number to come in and search our house. However, being a mob they were leaderless and did not enter the house. Among them was one man who clutched a Bible in one hand and a club in the other. I asked him if he was converting his victims before bashing in their brains. He surprised me when he replied: "God told Joshua to ambush the city of Ai and Israel killed them all until no one was left and Israel took away all the spoil and hanged the king . . . Joshua chapter 8." I felt like vomiting and told the mob to clear out. They left and went to our neighbors, Mr. and Mrs. Garth Andrews. In the meanwhile the Andrews had left their house and reached us by a back trail. We heard doors being battered down and screams. The looters carried away the property of the dead. Andrews asked me to go to his place and tell him what had happened. I found the bodies of his workers and their families scattered about the property, their heads crushed and their throats cut.

Returning to our place, I crossed a small field where only minutes before the mob had carried off the plundered property. My heart was racing. How was it possible that I had not been able to do something to save my neighbors from such a grisly death? As I walked along I reached down and snatched up a piece of paper that had fallen from the looters, a page torn from a child's copybook. I didn't notice what was written on it until I neared our driveway. Then I saw that a child had printed on this torn sheet the words from Matthew chapter 5 "*Blessed are the merciful: for they shall obtain mercy. Blessed are the pure in heart: for they shall see God. Blessed are the peacemakers: for they shall be called . . . .*" It was as if some child, now dead, had written these words just for me, for someone who needed strength and the courage to act compassionately.

When my eyes landed on *peacemakers*, I was jolted as if I had taken hold of a high voltage wire. At first, I did not really understand the powerful effect of these words. For certain, I was not being a peacemaker, for to be that required far more courage than I could find. I was concerned only about my family, keeping them safe and protected, out of the way of this dreadful vengeance that was cutting off the lives of people all around us.

It was not until I had reached our house and had time to reflect on the massacres I had just witnessed that the internal turmoil in my heart began to subside. Twenty years had passed since that conscience changing day in a bombed out church in Nagasaki. It was there that I had caught a vision of a world reduced to nuclear rubble and had dedicated myself to the Christ of peace who said to his followers in his final days, *"Peace I leave with you; my peace I give to you . . . . Do not let your hearts be troubled, and do not let them be afraid."* The truth was that my heart was badly troubled and, indeed, I was afraid.

The scrap of paper bearing the words from Matthew 5 did make a difference. No doubt I had read these words in a number of languages and many times, but now in the torment of death and destruction they seemed to have leaped up from the ground at me. To the looters who had grabbed and fled, a child's copybook had no value, part of a paper trail scattered across a field like the wake of a parting ship.

Thirty-four years have passed since that fateful day and I have guarded that precious piece of paper as one of my most valued possessions. It came to me unexpectedly in my hour of need and has challenged and inspired me to be true to my calling.

The next morning, Marie and I loaded the car with blankets, food and first aid supplies and drove to the police barracks. There we found nearly two thousand people in need of help. Trucks, buses and cars were being enlisted to run a convoy to the East. Slowly the police were reestablishing order. A curfew went into effect from seven p.m. to seven a.m. with orders to shoot anyone found on the streets. The three days and nights of terror were coming to an end.

Many Igbos told us how their Hausa and other northern neighbors, instead of joining the mobs, took them in to their houses and saved their lives. Near our house lived Jock Campbell, a Scot and retired miner. Jock could only get about on crutches. When the mobs came to his house demanding that he hand over his Igbo cook, Jock planted himself in front of his door and told them they could only have his cook if they killed him first. The crowd left and came back several times and each time Jock stood his ground. The fearlessness of this nearly helpless old man unhinged this calloused mob. After the slayings ceased, Jock's cook managed to return to the East and Jock, worn and weakened, was forced to go into a mission hospital where the staff made every effort to convert the man and prepare him for his heavenly home. Jock would have none of it. He resisted their efforts to save his soul as resolutely as he denied the mobs a chance to get at his cook, and when Jock died in hospital, the mission refused to bury him.

When word of Jock's demise reached the Reverend Chuck Bremmer of the Lutheran mission, Bremmer was in bed with hepatitis. Nevertheless, he managed to get out of bed and to give Jock a Christian burial. It was later learned that Jock had left a will. His house and more than a hundred and sixty thousand dollars were waiting for his faithful cook when he returned to Jos. Today a plaque in Jock's memory can be found in the graveyard of the Anglican church, put there in loving memory by his Igbo cook.

Hausa

The Hausa language fascinated me, probably because it is spoken over such a vast area and by millions of people. Hausa traders can be found in any coastal city in West Africa and in the interior from Congo north to Algeria. The language is most commonly written in Roman script, as in English, but with special marks for consonants not found in English. Moreover, Hausa is also written in Arabic script called Aljemi characters. The language has borrowed heavily from Arabic, particularly in the domain of religious vocabulary. I knew as soon as I began to study Hausa that one day I would have to learn Arabic, a wish that began to be fulfilled in Lebanon in 1972.

Studying Hausa was not like the language experience in Bulu and Kako. In these it was the whole village (Aloum and Lolo) that were the teachers and the language was learned in the cultural context—hunting, gardening, house building, men's club house, and church. By contrast my study of Hausa was not in a Hausa village but was done with an informant-teacher who came to our place several times a week. I would gather linguistic texts, file words and phrases on cards—the computer was not yet known—and organize my own language lessons. In this method the informant soon learns the procedure and is able to play the language game according to the rules of the learner. We became quite proficient in the use of substitution frames, simple narratives and in question and answer exercises. However, as soon as the linguist is confronted by real life conversations, he often finds himself in deep water. People everywhere enliven their speech with metaphors and idioms and if you don't get a good dose of them, you just don't get it. Please recall my experience as a boy in **Hairs in the Soup.**

My Hausa helper was Malam Zengina, a faithful Muslim about fifty years of age who pedalled about Jos selling flowers. Malam, from Arabic *mu'allim*, means teacher or master of a trade. He spoke excellent English and was literate in English and in both Roman and Arabic forms of written Hausa. In his cap, gown, and sandals he stood over six feet tall and when it was time to pray he took his kettle from his bicycle, filled it and performed his ablutions, unrolled his prayer mat to the north-east—direction of Mecca—and recited his prayers. When he finished we resumed our work.

It was most often the midday (zuhur) prayer because we began our work around 10 a.m. Malam Zengina never felt it necessary to excuse himself to go pray. He just stood up and walked out of the room. Because prayers must be said in Arabic, he explained that he had learned them as a child in a Hausa Quranic school. We often discussed prayer and he claimed that everything—trees, houses, plants and animals—feels the impact of prayer. To demonstrate what he meant, he took me to his walled compound and showed me the plants that grew near his house where he said his early morning, evening and nighttime prayers. In this sacred place where bougainvillea blossomed in abundance and fragrant frangipani sweetened the air, there grew a variety of roses, poinsettia, carnations, amaryllis, gardenias, begonias, and Michaelmas daisies. Their leaves were brilliantly green, the stems strong and the colors vivid and rich. Zengina said that a sick plant could be placed in his prayer ground and in a few weeks it would be transformed into a healthy plant. Of course, he did not deny that he fed and watered his plants, but he said the evidence was clear, "My plants join me in prayers and Allah blesses them with life."

At this time I had not yet read *The Secret Life of Plants* by

Tompkins and Byrd and Malam Zengina did not need scientific proof to know that plants participate with humans in the spiritual life. When I read to him Matthew 6.28 *"Consider the lilies of the field how they grow, they neither toil nor spin, yet I tell you even Solomon in all his glory was not clothed like one of these,"* he asked, "Is that from *l'ingil,* the gospel?" He asked me to read it again slowly. As I did I could see his lips moving. Several weeks later he quoted it and added "Isa ibn Maryam, he is called in the Qur'an, Jesus son of Mary." He went on: "While still a baby he made a clay bird fly, healed the blind and cured a leper."

During the time I had for Hausa studies (1964-67) I was becoming aware that African languages shared many things in common. Kako and Hausa had similar plosive consonant stops. All the West African languages I had worked with were tone languages, that is, each vowel has one of several pitch levels. Many of the languages had both long and short vowels. Moreover, many of these languages expressed certain ideas in similar ways. For example, in Hausa the verb to eat is *ci, Ya ci abinci* "He ate food," but to eat may also be used in an extended sense to mean dull. *Wukan nan ba ta ci* "This knife is not sharp," literally "does not eat." The same verb may express "to injure" *Kayan nan ya ci kaina* "This load has hurt (eaten) my head." *Wuta tona ci* "The fire is burning (eating)."

In a number of West African languages the verb "to drink" expresses the idea of experiencing something. "He drank trouble" means he had trouble. "He drank blame" means he was blamed for something. Similarly the verb "to die" indicates something broken. "His car is dead" means his car won't run. "His bicycle tire died" means his bicycle tire went flat. Many emotional and physical states are said "to take hold" of a person. "Hunger has hold of me" means I am hungry. "Fear has hold of him" means he is afraid.

Because I had worked in some forty languages and because I was involved in translation of the Bible, I was greatly interested in language universals and in semantics, the way meaning is encoded in words, phrases, sentences, and longer discourses. Two books appeared in 1964 that were seminal and contributed to my understanding of the function of language: *Aspects of the Theory of Syntax* by Noam Chomsky and *Toward a Science of Translating* by Eugene Nida. I had received the manuscript of the Nida book two years prior to its publication and had used it effectively in teaching semantic concepts to translators. Furthermore, Nida's treatment of linguistic, referential and emotive meaning provided a useful framework for describing these kinds of meaning.

It had become evident in my study of languages that they all expressed subject-predicate constructions, that is, the speaker chooses a subject and then says something about it, for example, "My brother was killed by a bush cow." Also, everywhere one finds a contrast between words that signal objects and those that signal events. These are traditionally called nouns and verbs. All languages are capable of qualifying objects as in "big house" or "old dog." Events are everywhere also qualified, for example, "He runs fast" or "She eats slowly." These qualifications or abstractions may not be what we call adjectives and adverbs but may have the form of static verbs, particles or verb affixes. Nevertheless, as I applied this information to languages as different as Cherokee and Quechua, Toba and Bulu, Kako and Hausa, it was clear that they all displayed at the simplest structural level the basic function classes of objects, events, abstracts (abstractions of objects, events and other abstracts) and relationals. Because each language exhibits so much in form and meaning that is peculiar or distinctive, it is liberating to discover that at their deep structures they are so much alike. This is a bit analogous to the discovery of DNA fingerprinting made many years later.

The town of Jos, elevation about 4,500 feet, lies on the Jos plateau surrounded by hills. The rainy season from April to October is sometimes excessive and the harmattan, a dust-bearing wind that blows down from the Sahara during November-December, cuts off the sun and leaves a residue of dust over everything. During this season the temperature may drop to fifty degrees Fahrenheit, ten degrees Celsius.

Our five years in Jos, aside from the political tragedy, was a happy time. Annie, Susie and David progressed well in the Hillcrest school. Maria who began kindergarten at age four did not attend Hillcrest before our departure. The Plateau Club swimming pool gave Marie the opportunity to teach Susie, David and Maria to swim and all the children became excellent swimmers. Susie developed a superb style of the crawl that won her several awards. Marie, who had played tennis in high-school and college, taught Annie and teamed up with her to win several mother-daughter competitions.

Marie also built a tennis court on our property by enlisting the help of neighboring miners and their crews. To provide a hard clay surface, we broke down a huge termite mound, sifted the dirt and spread it on the court. The termites were most obliging because as soon as we would haul away half of their ten-foot high castle, they would build it back up. The termite dirt when dampened and rolled made an excellent surface that gave the ball a fast bounce.

One night as Marie and I drove home from visiting friends, our lights focused on a man standing in the main street of town and waving for us to stop. The streets were deserted and I slowed down to get a better look. He was clearly anxious but showed no sign of drunkenness so I stopped. He pointed down a darkened alleyway and said, "Please, sir, my wife is having a baby there." I turned to Marie, "What do you think?" I asked. Marie's advice was never impetuous. "Turn the car so we can see what's there," she suggested. I backed up and turned the car toward the alley where a half block away we could see someone lying on the ground. "You think it's a trap?" I asked. "Certainly not, let's get down there," Marie urged.

I opened the back door and told the man to get in and we drove through the ominous alley until we were close and could see the baby lying on its mother, the placenta still connecting the two of them. We opened the tailgate and laid the mother and baby inside and the husband climbed in beside them. We then drove quickly to the government hospital and in less than a minute two nurses came with scissors and string. There in the back of the car they tied and cut the cord. Two men came with a stretcher and carried the mother in. Before following them, the father came to me and expressed his thanks and asked for my name. Two weeks later the same young father appeared at our door to announce that his son, William, "blessed by the God of all mercies is doing fine and drinking his milk like a young calf."

We attended St. Pirans Anglican church where Marie taught the children's class on Friday afternoons and I served on the parish council. Also serving on the council was Peter Gowon, elder brother of Major Yakubu Gowon, Nigeria's head of state. Peter worked for the local telephone company as a repairman and, like Malam Zengina, pedalled his bicycle about town to repair phones, lines and switches.

Yakubu Gowon, in an attempt to establish more regional autonomy, divided the nation into twelve states. Eastern Nigeria was to be broken up into three states but this was unacceptable to Colonel Ojukwu who on May 30, 1967 declared the entire Eastern Region the independent republic of Biafra. The following month civil war broke out.

The Nigeria we had come to in 1963 no longer existed. The many abandoned Igbo houses with smashed windows and doors, walls spray painted *Igbo go hom* were a constant reminder of the death and destruction visited upon Jos for three days and nights. The constant threat of insecurity and of an unsure future affected everyone, but I still had trips to make to the Congo.

Diamonds for Ramadan

During the years 1960-67 I made numerous tips to Zaire (Republic of Congo) to assist translators and was always enlightened, if not entertained, by the Congolese experience. There are few places in the world where good impulses and tragic consequences seem to go hand-in-hand more completely than in Zaire

Belgium granted independence to its colony on June 30, 1960. Immediately, fighting broke out, many people were killed and Belgium officers and government servants fled for home. The general elections held a month before independence gave seats in the national legislature to nine parties and none received a majority. In a compromise move the two main opposing leaders, Kasavubu and Lumumba, became president and prime minister respectively. Within days of independence the copper rich province of Katanga (Shaba) seceded and in August the diamond-producing province of Kasai declared itself independent. The following year, Lumumba was murdered and fighting intensified between the rival groups.

Fighting continued for five years with UN troops involved as well as white mercenaries. In 1964 Moïse Tshombe, who had led the secession in Katanga, became prime minister of a reunited nation. Tshombe managed to lead a loose coalition that soon fell apart and the Congolese army stepped in and took control. Thus began the long and corrupt reign of General Joseph Désiré Mobutu, who africanized his name in 1972 to Mobutu Sese Seko.

The government, in fact, required all Congolese who had European names to drop them and take African names.

The idea of one man one vote had not been particularly appealing to the Congolese, not because each wanted to vote several times, but rather because voters learned that it is dangerous to vote for a candidate who loses an election. In Luluaburg (Katanga) I saw people who had been tortured for voting for a losing candidate. As one man put it, "If they would just tell us who is going to win, we would be happy to vote for the winner. It is not democratic to keep people in the dark and them punish them for making the wrong choice."

In the southeastern province of Shaba, I learned one of the most effective lessons about Christian missions. There a Belgian anthropologist was recording legends of the Luba people, a very large and powerful tribe whose language had become the lingua franca of the mining areas. The chief had appointed informants who were well versed in the oral literature of the people and who also happened to be Methodist elders. The anthropologist recorded the stories as told but objected that his raconteurs too frequently added a Christian moral to the traditional tales. For example, a tale of the struggle between a turtle and a rabbit might end "and so you see the turtle learned that it does not pay to be greedy but it is better, as Jesus said, to sell whatever you have and give it to the poor." A story about a fox that steals from a lion might end "so you see this story tells us to be helpful, for freely you have received so freely give to others." When the anthropologist found that he was unable to prevent his storytellers from drawing their biblical morals, he went to the chief and voiced his complaint.

The chief listened carefully while the Belgian unloaded his concerns. He then replied, "Young man, if your father had come to collect stories from my father, my father's wives would have cooked him and they would have had a feast. Now think about that. Where would you be today?" The anthropologist went back humbly and gratefully to his storytellers.

The fast of Ramadan, the ninth month of the Islamic year, is a fast that begins at sunrise and continues until sundown. Observing this fast is the fourth pillar of Islam. It had become quite familiar to me living in northern Nigeria; however, in Kasai province where there were few Muslims, it was little known. The fast begins upon the first sighting of the new moon. According to the Qur'an, the nighttime is for feasting and continues until one can distinguish in the early dawn between a white and a black thread. From that moment until the following sundown there is sexual abstinence and fasting, even the swallowing of one's spittle is prohibited. If the sky is cloudy so that the new moon is not visible, the fast begins thirty days from the beginning of the previous month.

It was common practice for Air Congo planes to carry bananas, oranges, pineapples, and even smoked meat and stock fish for its passengers, but for the first time in Kasai province I saw three Muslims trying to convince a ticket agent that a live goat had to accompany them. After much argument, the three were told to stand aside until the agent could confer with the pilot. From what I could hear, the goat in question—really a small kid—was from a special breed and was being taken as a Ramadan gift from a high dignitary in Uganda to a great chief in Senegal. The trio offered to pay several fares to get their mascot on board with them and no doubt a pile of cash eventually opened the portals and allowed them, sweating and rumpled in their robes, to cradle their precious cargo and occupy their seats.

Interested to see what would transpire when we landed in Kinshasa, I hung about to watch and listen. The three men and goat were called to the side by two uniformed customs officers and while one began to question the men, the second officer took the young kid to the side and slit its throat. The three owners looked with shock upon their darling as it kicked and jerked in a pool of blood. With another deft stroke of his knife, the officer removed the stomach and intestines and in another moment was holding a handful of rough diamonds.

As I watched the trio being led away to a waiting police van, I thought of a 45-carat diamond in the Smithsonian Institute. That one bears the name "The Hope Diamond." I guess this little goat was bearing "The Hopeless Diamonds."

Out of Africa

In 1939 a conference in Holland attended by Bible Society representatives from England, Scotland, the Netherlands, Norway, France and America agreed to form a Council of Bible Societies. However, WWII caused these plans to be postponed and they were not again taken up until 1946. At that time Norwegian Bishop Berggrav stated, "We have lost the basis of life, and we have to find again the fundamental law of God in the Bible. The Bible is the only place where we can find it." Bishop Berggrav became the first president of the newly created United Bible Societies and Dr. John R. Temple its first secretary with headquarters in London and a branch office in Geneva. Following Dr. Temple's death in Hong Kong in November 1948, Olivier Béguin of Switzerland was appointed to replace him and served in that capacity from 1949 until his death in 1972.

As a translations consultant in West Africa I had experienced from the beginning the conflict in methods and orientation between the British and Foreign Bible Society and that of the American Bible Society, represented by Eugene Nida. The former concentrated their work on manuscript examination in London and correspondence with missionary translators. The Nida approach called for working with translators on the field and providing guidance and training long before a manuscript would . be developed. The BFBS approach was becoming less and less realistic simply because translation work was becoming the work of mother tongue translators, and missionaries needed to serve national translators as resource persons as the missionaries were often better equipped to be exegetical helpers. However, in some cases missionary translators were convinced that God had bestowed upon them the gifts of language and translation and to ask them to take on a supporting role was to deny their heavenly calling. There was, furthermore, the fact that once a translation is printed it often becomes "holy writ" and the people will not allow changes to be made, even when the translator recognizes that corrections are necessary.

The strain of working under conflicting directions while attempting to accomplish the aim of providing intelligible Scriptures for all readers was for me frustrating and discouraging. The only way ahead was for the European and American Bible Societies to work as the United Bible Societies and to develop agreed procedures that would apply on a world-wide basis.

From about 1960 when we returned to West Africa from our leave in America, a vast array of helps for translators was envisioned some of which would take nearly fifty years to complete. The publication in 1961 of *A Translator's Handbook on Mark* by Bratcher and Nida was the first of its kind in the New Testament commentary series. The list of helps is far too large to mention here but I cannot omit the *UBS Greek New Testament* and *The Hebrew Old Testament Text Project.* As a result of the effort to provide translators with adequate published helps, there is now available a large body of scholarly books that are indispensable to guide translators.

A second factor that made it necessary to shift the focus to the language projects in the countries where these were spoken was the Second Vatican Council (1962-65). It was at this important event that it was decided to set aside Latin and to use the vernacular, the language of the people, in the Eucharist. This decision gave local languages a status they had never before enjoyed in the Roman Catholic church. One of the results of Vatican II was the creation of a department of Common Bible Work in the Secretariat for Promoting Christian Unity. In 1968 the UBS and the Vatican drew up a set of guidelines called *Guiding Principles for Interconfessional Cooperation in Translating the Bible*. The purpose of this document was to produce editions of the Scriptures that would be acceptable to the entire Christian community. These guidelines, slightly revised and reissued in 1987, made clear that complete Bibles bearing the imprimatur of Roman Catholic authorities would contain the deuterocanonical (apocrypha) texts placed in a separate section before the New Testament. Beginning in the early 60's and continuing to the present, interconfessional translations of the Scriptures have met with outstanding success. In West Africa I often worked with committees made up of Baptist, Presbyterian, Pentecostal and Roman Catholic members. In these situations where Christian scholars are seeking to represent the best of scholarly judgment rather than being spokesmen for their denominations, the interconfessional nature of their work is carried out in the best tradition of Christian unity.

By 1967 the translation services of consultants like myself were being shifted from the British, Dutch, German and American Bible Societies to the United Bible Societies. This move was liberating for me because I was no longer representing an American or Dutch Society but was acting on behalf of an international fellowship.

In 1968, after being based for five years in northern Nigeria, I received word requesting that I prayerfully consider accepting the job of UBS translations coordinator. This post had been filled for two years by an English colleague, Wesley Culshaw, but Culshaw, nearing retirement, suffered a heart attack and would not be able to return to the work.

Marie and I thought long and hard about this invitation which would mean moving to England, uprooting the children—Annie now fifteen, Susie twelve, David eight and Maria six. I would be required to travel to the ends of the earth, be away from my family for weeks at a time. I had little idea how radical the change would be. When finally we agreed to move, Marie was forty-three and I was forty-six.

When we departed Nigeria in June 1968 there was a wave of global student protests in such disparate places as Paris, Mexico City, Tokyo, and New York City. At the Miss America pageant in Atlantic City objects of female oppression—brassieres, high-heeled shoes, and copies of *Playboy* magazine were being tossed into the "freedom trash can." Hippies were celebrating a Summer of Love. Black Power was replacing nonviolence as a slogan of civil rights and a hundred cities in America were burning.

We had lived outside the US for sixteen years and knew, whether in Europe or America, we were entering a new age. Were we prepared for what lay ahead? And how was the sexual revolution going to affect our children? Living in the restrictive confines of Latin America and Africa, I had thought of myself as politically and socially liberal. In Europe, where young people were throwing off traditional restraints, I found myself shifting more to the center. Where would we end up?

EUROPE

The Eternal City

The UBS recognized that our move from Africa to England was a major transition for the family and so agreed that Marie and I should make an exploratory trip before our final move. Consequently, on March 9, 1968, we placed Susie and David in school dormitories and settled Maria with friends. Annie was uncertain if she should pursue her schooling in America—she had had only the first grade in a US school while we were on leave in 1959-60—or make the move to England. She was to accompany Marie and me to England and then go on to North Carolina where she would be with Marie's brother and family for the remainder of the school year. With the three younger children happily settled for the next several weeks, Marie, Annie and I drove six hours to Kano and on March 10th we flew to London. Two days later we put Annie on a plane to New York where colleague Robert Bratcher met her and sent her on to North Carolina.

This first visit to England was filled with new experiences and the sound of a familiar but different English. We rode the trains from Brighton to Edinburgh and visited the Peter Woods family, who had been our neighbors in Jos. In Easington, Yorkshire, we attended the Anglican Sunday service with the Woods family, where eleven persons were in attendance, four in the choir and seven in the congregation. The temptation to fall asleep was easily dispelled by the frigid indoor temperature. In Edinburgh we were guests of the Reverend and Mrs. Hamish Alexander of the Bible Society of Scotland. Our bodies, so accustomed to the warmth of Nigeria, did not adjust quickly to the cold and we had to wear heavy socks in bed to keep our feet warm.

The Flying Scotsman was a comfortable, heated train that brought us back to King's Cross, London. We made a whirlwind visit to Westminster Abbey, the House of Parliament, took a boat to the London Tower, walked by Scotland Yard, No. 10 Downing Street, through St. James' Park to Buckingham Palace, through Hyde Park along the Serpentine to the Albert Memorial, the Science Museum and the Natural History Museum. We still had energy to attend the Royal Philharmonic at the Royal Albert Hall.

Through the kindness of the Reverend Wilfred Bradnock of the BFBS, we were able to obtain a house to rent in Amersham, Buckinghamshire, forty-five minutes from Marylebone station in London. The owners of the house, a semi-retired couple, were leaving England to teach at the University of Zaria, Nigeria. The arrangement worked out well and we moved in for a year just after they departed. The owner's parting instruction to me was, "Just don't asphalt the place over." He was under the impression that Americans preferred asphalt to green grass.

Having found a place to live and having learned how to travel into the city and to my workplace, and knowing where the children would attend school, we felt our journey to England had accomplished its purpose and so were ready to leave. Because a triennial workshop for translations personnel was to be held in Spain in 1969, we were asked to go to Madrid and begin making arrangements with the Secretary, Dr. José Flores. After completing plans for the next year, we were off to Italy.

We had met Father Walter Abbott, S.J. in Africa not long after he had been appointed to the Department of Common Bible Work in the Vatican's Secretariat for Promoting Christian Unity. Walter had sent us a warm invitation to visit Rome and to be his guests for a tour of the Vatican. As we would be working closely together in the coming years, I felt this would be a splendid opportunity for us to become more personally acquainted. I was particularly glad that Marie was with me because her insights into this all-male world of the Vatican would be of special value.

My first shock in Rome was the terrifying speed of the traffic outside the Colosseum; perhaps more threatening to the pedestrian than what went on inside the place in ancient times. Vatican City is not nearly as large as I had imagined. In fact, it covers an area of approximately one hundred acres, almost like a small Midwestern college campus. The dome of Saint Peter's Church dominates the skyline very much as does Saint Paul's in London. Our gracious host had rented a small Fiat so that he could give us his special tour of the Vatican City as well as Rome.

Upon entering Vatican City a sign reads *Stato della Città del Vaticano*, "The State of Vatican City." Once you enter this place, you are no longer on Italian soil. Since the signing of the Lateran Treaty in 1929, the Vatican area has been an independent sovereign state over which the Pope—"Holy Father" is the term of reference used by those who work there—has absolute power.

As we moved quietly along the streets—even the traffic here seems polite and subdued in these stately precincts—Walter pointed out the Vatican Palace with its more than a thousand rooms and apartments, the museum, archives, and library. The Vatican, he explained, issues its own postage stamps, coins and even automobile license plates. Walter was particularly pleased to explain how the Vatican bank reports to no one but the Holy Father. When I remarked that there seemed to be a preponderance of shiny new cars, he explained that every Cardinal in the church receives from the Pope a new Mercedez-Benz. When we crawled out of Walter's diminutive Fiat, I commented that perhaps Jesus would have felt more at home in a Fiat. Walter winked and opened the door for us to enter the Secretariat.

Here we met Dutch Cardinal Wilebrands, Walter's boss, from who we learned that Vatican conferences are conducted not in Latin, as I had assumed, but in a more ecumenical tongue—English. Further along on our tour we had opportunity to chat with the director of the Pontifical Biblical Institute and the Father

General of the Jesuit order. Walter led us through the Vatican Museum, showed us famous manuscripts in the Vatican Library, and then took us to the Sistine Chapel, where the ceiling and rear wall are covered by the paintings of Michelangelo. Inside Saint Peter's Church, we visited the crypt beneath the altar and then many other places in Rome itself.

After a delicious Italian dinner, it was getting late, but Walter wanted us to see where he lived. The building had been the palatial home of a Polish Duke but now belonged to the Jesuits. Walter shared it with a small number of Jesuit intellectuals working in the Vatican. He took us to the top of a broad and winding staircase, where we gazed down upon great chandeliers illuminating in resplendence the rose marble floor far below and the statuary that stood like silent sentinels. It was a stunning sight of pure opulence.

Outside we bade each other good-night and Marie and I returned to our hotel, foot-sore and fatigued from a never-to-be-forgotten day. As our taxi raced through the broad boulevards, I noticed Marie was humming a tune.

"What's that you're singing?" I asked.

"Don't you remember that hymn the people of Appalachia like to sing?"

"Sing it for me."

Marie began to sing softly, *"I'm satisfied with just a cottage below. A little silver and a little gold: But in that city where the ransomed will shine, I want a gold one that's silver lined."*

I joined her on the chorus *"I've got a mansion over the hill-top. In that bright land where we'll never grow old. And some day yonder we will never more wander but walk on streets that are purest gold . . . I'm just a pilgrim in search of a city. I want a mansion, a harp and a crown."*

At the hotel room Marie kicked off her shoes and I rubbed her tired feet. "Bill, think about this: It's only been two thousand

years since Saint Peter was here and now it's *The Eternal City.*
Funny how time gets converted into eternity. You know, I think
Christianity, be it the Vatican variety or the Appalachian kind,
has so materialized the message of Christ that there is no spirit
left. I really have no interest in living in a gold house or walking
on gold streets."

"Well, those are metaphors, a manner of speaking," I replied.
Marie yawned, "Yaaa, manner of sleeping . . . ."
"Good-night, Marie."
"Uh-huh . . . ."

A Good Night's Sleep

During our home leave in the summer of 1968 while Marie and our children were enjoying their visit with Marie's family in North Carolina and before our move to England, I had to return to Europe to participate in a translators' institute held in Halle, East Germany. This three-week course was the first in Europe which translators from communist Czechoslovakia had been able to attend. The reforms brought about by Alexander Dubchek, the party leader, included increased freedom of the press and easier access to non-communist countries. Accordingly, three Slovak and three Czech pastors were able to obtain visas and the course was making steady headway until three days before it was due to end. Russian and other east European tanks rolled into Prague. Our work came to a halt and we stayed awake at night while our colleagues from the East tried in vain to telephone their families.

The Dubchek reforms were a temptation for other communist nations to follow, and the leaders of the Soviet Union feared that such freedoms would lead to the weakening of communist control. Soviet troops were allowed to remain but Dubchek, under Soviet pressure, was replaced by the less liberal Gustáv Husák. Discouraged and saddened by these events, our Czechoslovakian colleagues returned to their families.

In my role of UBS Translations Coordinator, I traveled to East Europe and the Soviet Union a number of times. The purpose of these trips was usually to make preparations for holding translators' seminars, contacting church officials, lecturing and recruiting translators. My Swiss colleague, Olivier Béguin, in London, knew both western and eastern Europe well and was able to advise me where to go, what not to take with me, and particularly what not to say.

At the end of WWII Berlin was divided into French, British, American and Soviet sectors. The Soviet sector was East Berlin and the other three sectors made up West Berlin. I often flew from London to Templehoff Airport in the American sector of West Berlin.

West Berlin had been rebuilt, a modern booming economy where chemicals, food and machinery were manufactured. West Berlin had a lively cultural life with more than a hundred public libraries, an opera, theatrical groups and a symphony orchestra known throughout the world. Its nightlife was similar to that of Broadway in New York City and its electric signs blazed through the night and crowds of Berliners and foreigners paraded the streets in endless revelry. On my first night there, a gigantic flashing neon sign on my hotel on the busy Bismarkstrasse forced me to cover my head with my pillow. The endless screech of tires, the blaring of horns and the din of voices from the street below made me wish I were sleeping again in any of the dozen peaceful places we had passed our nights in Africa.

In the morning I would have gladly gone back to bed but I had a rendezvous in East Berlin. Sleepy or not, I had to take a taxi to Checkpoint Charlie, a guarded opening in the Berlin wall on Friedrichstrasse. While Khrushchev threatened and made demands on the western powers, more than a thousand East Germans were fleeing daily to West Berlin. In August of 1961 East German police began to build a wall sealing off the border. Angry Berliners gave it the name *Schandmauer* "Wall of Shame."

Eventually I got used to passing through Checkpoint Charlie but it was always something that seemed to have been created by mad men, the stuff of nightmares. The moment the taxi let me out by the wall, I saw gun barrels aimed straight at me. Armed guards with guard dogs were patrolling the area. Clearly, I was made to feel like a convicted criminal. I eventually learned to look straight ahead and tell myself this was only a game people play. Inside the guard house I handed over my passport, the guards looked me up and down as if I were a suspicious piece of baggage. Whatever is carried is opened and every article taken out and laid on a counter. A tube of toothpaste may be squeezed empty and for certain Time magazine confiscated. My Greek New Testament was always flipped open and looked at upside down before being thrown back into the suitcase. I must admit how much I was tempted to crack a joke to see if these dreadfully sour faces could smile, but felt it wiser to say nothing, as Olivier had advised.

With my passport finally stamped, I made my way outside where stepping into the city of East Berlin was a step back to 1945. The contrast between the glitter and shine of West Berlin and the drab grayness of East Berlin was a shock. As arranged, I spotted a man in an overcoat reading a copy of *The Bible Translator* with its bright blue cover. "*Guten Morgen, Ich bin Reyburn.*" My contact extended his hand, clicked his heels and bobbed his head. Some things never change. As we walked together, he noticed that I was eyeing the buildings that had not been repaired since the end of the war. "*Bruder Reyburn*, we have a saying here. `If you win second prize in the lottery, you get a Mercedes Benz. If you win first prize, you get a sack of cement.'"

Most of the vehicles on the streets were military trucks and a few polluting East German mini cars. But I learned that the traffic ceases at night. The city becomes eerily silent and is a splendid place to sleep. I arranged on my future trips to Berlin to pass the nights here.

Getting a good night's sleep became a major problem as I traveled about the world. I once flew into Nairobi in the same plane as a Ghanaian school master, Mr. Kwalla, whom I had known in Accra. As we left the plane Mr. Kwalla was paged and a limousine bearing the Ghanaian ambassador picked us up and took us to the embassy for lunch and then delivered us to our hotel. The ambassador had been one of Mr. Kwalla's students and this relationship is not soon forgotten among Africans. Mr. Kwalla and I shared the same room but his snoring turned out to be so loud I barely slept a wink for the three nights we were together.

When a person travels a great deal and sleeps in a different bed nearly every night, eventually the back begins to ache and it is necessary to devise ways to keep from falling apart. To this end I carried a rope in my suitcase and used it doing stretch exercises, often before going to bed. However, I learned that it was prudent always to test the mattress. To do this I let my full weight drop on to the bed. If the mattress remained firm, I was safe. If it bounced or sagged, there was only one thing to do: pull the mattress off the bed and put it on the floor. However, before doing this, it was advisable to look under the bed where, as it often happened, dirt had accumulated for so long that it was taking on a menacing shape.

At a small hotel in Istanbul, I had gone through my three-step procedure and concluded the flaccid pad had to go to the floor. However, the room being too narow for both bed and pad, I removed the pad and stood the bed on end. This maneuver revealed several years of unswept floor, beer cans, chicken bones, condoms and a woman's bra. I called the desk and asked that a broom be brought to the room, probably the first occasion room service had received such an order. At any rate, a clerk came to the open door, looked in and saw no bed. He scratched and blinked.

"Oh no! People sometime is steal towel or sheet, but no people is steal bed."

"No, no, here's the bed." I pointed to it.

"Oh, mister, you sleeps stand up like dat?" His eyes were wide with disbelief.

I took the broom from him and began sweeping. The clerk brought a box and we filled it with the under-the-bed goodies.

In the morning when I checked out, the clerk raced up to the room to see if I had collapsed the bed and perhaps stuffed it into my suitcase. He was smiling contentedly when he returned.

"All right, you sleeped good, no? You come back again to Healthful Home Hotel?"

Traveling with Dutchman Jan de Waard and German Rudolf Kassuhlke in north Cameroun, we arrived late one night at a mission and were offered beds in a newly constructed hospital that had not yet become operational. The three of us went to bed and sometime in the night de Waard and I were awakened by the thunderous snores of Kassuhlke. Since the hospital beds had wheels, de Waard and I rolled our steam whistling companion out of the room and shut him up in another room down the hall. We both returned to bed and were sleeping soundly until the clamorous Mr. K. awoke and found himself alone, whereupon he rolled his bed back into our room and fell again into a booming slumber. Again we quietly banished our colleague to a remote corner of the hospital where he managed to remain until morning and as a result all got a pretty good night's sleep.

Armenia and Mittens

The Reyburn family adapted to English life. The children did well in school and in sports. Maria, like her mother and older sisters, was becoming a superb swimmer. David was active in Cubs and played on several football (soccer) teams. Marie, who had been a Sunday school teacher at Saint Pirans Anglican Church in Jos, was welcomed as a teacher in the Anglican Sunday school in Beaconsfield, where we were now living. She also served as Baloo in a local Cub Scout pack as well as book reviews editor for the journal *Practical Anthropology*.

My adaptation to British life was knowing how to reach Heathrow airport. My prolonged absences from home caught up with me when I attended a neighborhood Christmas party with Marie. "Oh, you mean there really is a mister Reyburn?" It was painful for me to be absent from my family so much but I determined to get the organizational aspect of my job accomplished so that we could return to Africa or perhaps move on to Asia by 1972. As it turned out, we left England for Beirut in September 1972, a story that waits to be told.

Winters in England are frequently cold and wet but often with little or no snow. Having been raised in the mountains of Colorado where winter sports are enjoyed by so many, I was anxious that my children have the opportunity at least once to play in the snow. During December 1969 while in Amsterdam, I heard on the news that the British Isles would be covered with half a foot of snow. Searching the shops in the city, I found a fine sled, bought it and had it loaded with my suitcase on the London bound flight. At Heathrow I watched as suitcases slid on to the revolving carousel. Finally, I spied my own case sliding down the ramp and not far behind, the sled. It shot across the smooth metal surface, hit the ridge and leapt on to the baggage room floor. Having landed on its runners, it zipped like an arrow across the floor with me in hot pursuit. Fearing that the steering bar may have broken, I picked it up gently and examined it. It was still in first class shape.

For the next four days, as long as the snow lasted, I became the frazzled horse at the end of a rope pulling David and Maria everywhere they wanted to go. After this I failed to become so enthusiastic about weather forecasts predicting snow.

The snows in England had barely melted when I was off again to the land of blizzards and flurry—Russia. I had boarded an Aeroflot flight in London on which there were no more than fifteen passengers. The seats had a minimum of padding and frequent strolls in the aisles relieved the discomfort of sitting. Most of central Europe was covered with snow but nothing compared to the depth of it surrounding the frozen white Moscow airport. My destination was Yerevan, the capital of Armenia, or as it was then called The Armenian Soviet Socialist Republic.

I had been invited by the head of the Armenian Apostolic (Orthodox) Church, Vasken I, Catholicos of all Armenia, to meet with the translators of a new version of the Bible being done in the Holy See of Echmiadzin. I would have to overnight in Moscow before making a connecting flight the following morning.

Because the shipment of religious books often resulted in their being confiscated, I had been asked to bring Greek New Testaments for the Echmiadzin theological seminary. I had been warned to make each book appear to be different from the others to avoid the appearance of importing a number of the same book. To this end I had put paper covers each with a different color on each book. The Moscow customs officer emptied my suitcase and laid the books in one pile and my clothes and toilet articles in another. He then pointed to the books that took up more space than my personal effects and made some comment or question in Russian. I shrugged and replied that I liked books. He too shrugged then turned away while I dumped the books and my things back into the suitcase.

The Intourist desk was my next stop where I showed my passport and ticket and where I received a stamped card with a number and was directed to a taxi that plied through the snowy streets to the Metropol hotel on Sverdlov Square. Children were riding their sleds down the slopes beneath the Kremlin wall and I made a note in my diary so I would not forget to tell David and Maria.

Fresh snow fell in the night and my taxi to the airport in the early dawn slipped and spun about. My driver spoke German and when I asked if people in Moscow didn't use chains, he pointed to his neck and replied *Ya, Ya, zu viel,* "Yes, too much." I wasn't sure if this was humor, satire or just misunderstanding. Outside the airport in the bitter cold, I was accompanied across the snow-packed runway to my plane, where I handed my ticket to a stewardess of Amazonian stature who led me to my seat. Another passenger was already in the seat and a brisk but brief conversation ensued. The man in the seat looked away in disgust, whereupon the stewardess grasped his overcoat lapels, hoisted him out of the seat and motioned for me to sit. I obediently occupied the warm seat and in another minute we were racing into the wintry wind and climbing into the soviet dawn.

Armenia lies approximately a thousand miles southeast of Moscow and between the Black and Caspian Seas. The land is a mountainous plateau where ranges and gorges extend from the Caucasus Mountains southwest into Turkey. On the day I flew into Yerevan, snow-capped Mount Ararat in Turkey was radiant in the morning sun.

It was a thrill for me to visit this ancient land, which at the end of the third century was the first nation to accept Christianity as a state religion. Mesrob Mashtotz, who had invented an alphabet for the language, translated the Bible in the fifth century. The ancient language continues to be the liturgical language of the Armenian Church, which has one Holy See in Echmiadzin and one in Antelias, Lebanon. The unity of the Church, however, resides in the spiritual primacy of Echmiadzin. The modern language is recognized as having an eastern and a western dialect, the former being that spoken by the people of Armenia. Although the vast majority of Armenians belong to the Orthodox Church, there also exists an Armenian Catholic Church united with Rome and a Protestant Church known as the Union of Armenian Evangelical Churches in the Near East.

In Echmiadzin I was graciously received by Catholicos Vasken I who gave generously of his time to acquaint me with the Armenian Church, its history and its people. The Catholicosat, or headquarters, is housed in a palace, which had been confiscated during WWII by the Soviet army and used as a barracks. It was not returned to the Church until 1956 when Premier Bulganin was in power. Vasken I was raised in Rumania and educated in Armenian and French. His widowed mother joined us each day for lunch. I was given a tour of the palace, the museum, the Cathedral and the printing plant. The latter was particularly important to me because the UBS was supplying paper that was hauled by trucks from Norway to Armenia. In order for the Echmiadzin press to print church literature, a portion of its output was required to be literature for the Soviet State.

Near the Cathedral was the theological seminary where I was invited to lecture on Bible translation. I spoke in English and the director of the seminary interpreted. I noticed one young man who seemed to catch immediately what I was saying without having to wait for the translation. I interrupted myself to say to him, "You seem to understand English very well." He replied, "I should. I'm from Detroit." He had been consecrated to the ministry by his church and sent to Armenia to study.

Following my lecture, the director showed me about the small seminary and at one point stopped and pointed to a desk. "Could you perhaps guess who was once a student sitting at that desk?" I could not. "That," he said, "is the seat once occupied by young Anastas Mikoyan, former president of the Soviet Union." The director added, "Mikoyan admits that perhaps he did not learn all the lessons he was supposed to learn." The director then reeled off a long list of the names of Armenian scientists, philanthropists, and literary figures.

In spite of being wined and dined, entertained and indoctrinated, I managed to have time to examine the work of the translators and to give them helpful suggestions for their continuing efforts and at the end of my five-day visit, I returned to Moscow where the snow was still falling and children were still riding their sleds on the slopes.

When I boarded a British Airways flight bound for London, I was surprised to see two armed Russian police standing beside my seat. I nearly wondered aloud, "Oh, boy, what have I done now?" But then I reasoned that if they were going to arrest me, why wait until I am on the plane? I laid my coat in the overhead compartment and motioned for a policeman to step aside so I could take my seat. Once seated, I began to comprehend a bit of what was going on. Seated in my row and next to the window was a young man whose head had been shaved. He sat rigidly at attention and did not look to the right or to the left. He was dressed in a rough woolen uniform that was far too large for his slender frame. The policemen did not leave their positions until our departure had been announced and we were told to fasten our seat belts. My seat companion, more a shabby manikin than a person, did not peer out the window as we took off and circled over Moscow before heading toward the west.

Later, I was lost in my reading when the captain announced, "We are now leaving Soviet air space and flying over Poland. From the right side of the plane you will soon be able to see the city of Warsaw." The wax figure by the window suddenly leaped to his feet, threw his hands in the air and vaulted over me into the aisle. I was startled to see that he had come to life. "I'm free, free, free. At last I'm free!" he shouted as passengers stretched their necks to see what all the commotion was about. A stewardess rushed down the aisle and told him to return to his seat. I stood to give him room to pass but he collapsed in the middle seat and with tears streaming down his sallow cheeks he put his arms around me and with his face buried in my chest he sobbed uncontrollably. When at last he was no longer shaking, I gave him my handkerchief and asked if he would like to tell me what had happened. Here is his story.

Five years earlier he had been picked up by Soviet police while waiting for a connecting flight in Tashkent. He was carrying drugs he had obtained in Thailand and was to sell them in Holland. He was kept in jail for a month with no opportunity to contact his family in Manchester, England. He appeared before a tribunal of judges and was condemned to hard labor for five years. Only after being sentenced was he allowed to write one letter a month to his family. In prison he was, like other inmates, given a mitten-knitting machine and required to turn out a certain number of pairs each twenty-four hours. Failure to produce the required quota resulted in increased prison time. If a knitting machine broke, there were no spare parts. Prisoners were required to devise ways to repair their own machines. The usual way was to steal parts from the machines of other prisoners. This was difficult to do as prisoners slept with their machines, took them to the toilet and to the mess hall. "A man with a broken machine was a dog with rabies. You had to protect yourself from his bite."

He remained in the middle seat and when we were served lunch, he wolfed his food down and asked for more. At Heathrow a plainclothes policeman boarded our plane and accompanied him to make his connection to Manchester. I could never again look at a pair of mittens without thinking of this encounter.

MIDDLE
EAST

On to Lebanon

In my role of UBS translation coordinator I was required to participate in the regional translation administrative meetings that were held in the Americas, Asia, Europe and Africa, teach in translators institutes, edit *The Bible Translator*, represent the interest of the world-wide translation program to the UBS executive committee, confer with national Bible Societies and interpret and explain UBS policies to them. The more I faithfully performed my UBS function, the further I fell behind in my role as a husband and father.

I did not fail to appreciate the opportunities to visit much of the world and to keep abreast of developments in nations as different as Sweden and Swaziland, Austria and Australia, Brazil and Belize. A trip to the Alaskan Eskimos gave me an opportunity to visit my nephew, Robin Pegau, who worked for the Alaska Game and Fish Department. He took me by sled and snow mobile to herds of musk oxen north of Nome where he was studying their feeding habits in the snow covered tundra. In Japan I was taken by the Reverend Thomas Miyauchi on the high speed train to Sasebo and Nagasaki, places I had not revisited for twenty-five years. One itinerary in 1970 took me from London to Denmark to Alaska to Japan to the Philippines, Thailand, Singapore, Indonesia, Australia, Madagascar, South Africa, Brazil, Mexico, USA and back to London. At the end of this journey I counted eighty-two countries I had put a foot in, sometimes only the airport, but in others I spent days or weeks over trails or rough mountain roads. On a Scandinavian Airways flight from Tashkent to Copenhagen, the plane had few passengers and the cabin was nearly full of cargo concealed under dark coverings. I asked a stewardess if I could take my pillow and blanket and stretch out on top of the cargo. She hesitated for a moment but then gave me permission. I slept soundly atop the cargo for three hours. When finally I returned to my seat, I inquired about the cargo only to learn that it contained boxes of poisonous snakes being flown to a snake serum center in Sweden.

In April 1972 Olivier Béguin, the Swiss General Secretary of the UBS, died after a six-month battle with cancer. We had been looking for someone to serve the Middle East as translations consultant and Marie and I had discussed a move in that direction as a possibility for our family. We began to study Arabic and Marie made a trip to Beirut, Lebanon, to scout out the situation. Annie would be 19 by the time we left England and wanted to remain there to do her university studies. Susie was nearly 16, David 12 and Maria 10. After a visit to our families, we made the move to Beirut at the end of August, 1972.

Lebanon at that time was a time bomb waiting to explode. Fifty years earlier France had taken over the country's political affairs. The Maronite Christians in the mountains cooperated with France, accepted French as the language of education and generally prospered. The Muslim population on the other hand did not benefit from the French presence in the way the Christians did; nevertheless, the country remained peaceful until 1958 when portions of the Muslim population rebelled against government plans for political and military alliances with the West. In the face of a threatening civil war, the president, a Maronite Christian, requested the US to send in the marines who landed in July, restored peace and departed in October. In 1968 The Palestine Liberation Organization (PLO) raided northern Israel from bases in southern Lebanon and in return Israel attacked. The presence of large numbers of Palestinians in Lebanon became a source of tension between Christians and Muslims, the latter defending the PLO's right to make war on Israel.

When we arrived in Beirut, life in the city seemed normal. We rented a fifth floor apartment in the Raouche area only a block from the Mediterranean and next door to a Lebanese bakery where we often awoke with the warm Mediterranean sun on the east and the aroma of freshly baked bread on the west. David and Maria enrolled in the American school only three minutes walk from the apartment. Susie joined us and enrolled in the Beirut College for Women soon to be known as Beirut University College (BUC).

My area of responsibility began in Turkey in the west and extended to the Pakistan-Indian border in the east. The languages of this section of Babel included Turkish, Modern Syriac, Balochi, Brahui, Punjabi, Urdu, Pashto, Iranian, Kurdish, Sindhi. The main language of the Middle East is Arabic and I would concentrate more effort on this project than on all the others combined.

An earlier attempt to organize a new Arabic translation had failed because the committee of translators and reviewers was far too numerous. The historical complexity of the Eastern churches is such that it is exceedingly difficult to convince them to work together. In the Middle East there is represented virtually the entire spectrum of world-wide Christianity. There are, for example, both the Eastern (Byzantine) and Oriental (non-Chalcedonian) Orthodox churches, Catholics of both Latin and Oriental rites, the Assyrian church of the East, Anglicans, many Protestant denominations as well as a large number of sectarian groups. Some of these churches are among the oldest in Christianity. Others arose out of theological and political disputes in early centuries. Later ones are the result of proselytizing in the nineteenth and twentieth centuries. It requires profound optimism to think that these ancient churches are interested in working together even to have a common Bible.

Some of the Arabic speaking churches grew to become

protectors and defenders of a Protestant Bible known as the Van Dyck version published in 1860. Among these is the Coptic Orthodox Church in Egypt where the head of that church carries the title *Pope and Patriarch of the Great City Alexandria, Libya, Pentapolis, Ethiopia and all Africa. Father of fathers, Shepherd of shepherds, Pontiff of pontiffs, Thirteenth Apostolic and Ecumenical Judge.*

My approach was to enlist a well-known writer to draft the translation and a qualified biblical scholar to assure faithfulness to the Greek New Testament. Thus was created the team of Yusuf El Khal of Lebanon and Abouna Naguib, professor of New Testament in the Coptic Catholic seminary in Maadi, Egypt. We provided copies of the drafts for various church leaders and engaged professional writers and biblical scholars to review the translations. I met with the two men whenever I could. Abouna Naguib, who later became Bishop of Minya, came to Lebanon during his vacations to work closely with El Khal.

After our final session in Maadi, Egypt, in 1975 the entire New Testament manuscript was completed. By this time the war in Lebanon had shut down the Beirut airport and so we arranged for El Khal to go to Cyprus and take a boat to the Maronite port of Jounieh in Lebanon.

El Khal boarded the *Phoenicia,* a thirty-foot converted launch, in the port of Limasol along with a dozen other Lebanese. All Lebanese knew the *Phoenicia* as the most luxurious hotel in Beirut. Luxurious was not a word used to describe this old tub. The voyage was advertised as an eight-hour night run to the Christian port of Jounieh. If all went according to schedule, they would debark in Jounieh about sunrise. The passengers, who soon found they had many friends and acquaintances in common, shared their news with each other and tried to adapt to the pitching and rolling of the *Phoenicia* whose motor droned and vibrated through the night. A steady rain was falling and the wind blew in squalls toward the north making it difficult to keep the boat on course. It was about 3.30 a.m. when El Khal pulled his small suitcase close, holding it between his feet. His mind was never far from that manuscript it held. Then he heard the motor sputter and die. The Greek pilot tried again and again to restart the engine but it would not respond. It had been known that the radio ceased to transmit earlier in the night although from time to time it crackled and picked up messages sent between Greek ships. With the motor dead and an angry wind howling on the sea, it seemed to the passengers that the boat was turning about and drifting aimlessly. El Khal remembered the stories of Christ quieting the waves on another sea and he thought of Saint Paul who had ridden out just such a storm on the very same sea as this. These accounts he knew well from having translated them more than once. He lifted his suitcase and held it close. This frail converted launch was no match for an angry Mediterranean. If we go down, he thought, how can I save this translation that represents over three years of many people's labors?

Passengers were scanning the tiny portholes searching for a sign of a passing ship, or anything that might give them hope. The Greek pilot put his head in and said that they would wait until daylight and try to determine their position. In the meantime he would continue to work on the recalcitrant engine. Everyone knew that drifting out of control could mean that the boat might end up in a port controlled by the opposition. That could mean imprisonment or death.

At the first light of dawn several went on deck and scanned the eastern horizon; however, the rain and darkness made it impossible to identify the landscape. By seven a.m. they could identify the mountains east of Jounieh, but their excitement vanished when the pilot showed them how fast they were drifting northward. No radio, no engine, a stormy night at sea and now a day to drift helplessly into what they feared would be certain death in Tripoli. "What about Sheikka?" someone asked. "It's still in the hands of the Christian forces . . . ." Everyone agreed that reaching the port of Sheikka south of Tripoli could be their salvation. Throughout the day the passengers of the *Phoenicia* scoured the sky through sheets of rain as the hills faded and reappeared. The men took turns manually turning the propeller shaft as the pilot steered the boat in the direction of the Sheikka harbor.

By five o'clock in the afternoon the Sheikka lighthouse was in view and hopes of rescue were riding high. From the deck of the boat passengers took turns shouting for help. Wet and exhausted, they sat in the cramped cabin. At least they were in the outer harbor, seasick but safe from the fury of the raging sea. The men had blisters on their hands from turning the shaft. Uncomfortable as they were in wet clothes, they prepared to spend a second hungry night on the *Phoenicia*.

About 9 p.m., as if daylight had suddenly leaped upon them, searchlights from the shore lit up the little boat and before anyone could scramble to the deck, a clatter of bullets rained against the bulkhead. The firing stopped, than a second hail of bullets came, this time more accurate, ripping into the boat and spewing glass and splintered wood everywhere. Again there was a pause, as if the shooters were reloading for another volley. Passengers, huddled on the floor, waited tensely for the next round which might take the *Phoenicia* to the bottom. Instead of shooting they heard an engine; a boat had pulled alongside. A loudspeaker called out, "Everybody out on deck with your hands in the air." Not knowing what would happen, the passengers stumbled out into a blinding light focused on them. A voice called over, "Yusuf El Khal, is that you?" El Khal called back, "Yes, of course. We were trying to get to Jounieh. Turn that light out of our eyes."

When the passengers had all been transferred to the military boat, the leader looked at El Khal and inquired, "Are you wearing a bullet proof vest under your shirt?" El Khal unbuttoned his shirt and gently lifted out his manuscript. "It is more than a bullet proof vest," my friend, "it's the armor of the Lord."

The *Phoenicia* was towed into port, repaired and refueled before setting out for the return trip to Cyprus.

A Provocative Act

The American Community School in Beirut had an international flavor among its students as some of these were from embassy and business families representing a number of different countries. Although this internationalism produced a lively exchange of ideas in classes, English was the language of everyone and the American curriculum set the tone for all learning. Consequently, the ACS students formed a cultural enclave of Americana in the heart of an Arabic, French and English speaking city. After a year, Marie and I decided to investigate an alternative education which would enable David and Maria to adapt more effectively to the life of Lebanon. Because our children had been raised in Africa and England, we were certain they had the flexibility to make the shift to the Lebanese way.

David accepted without hesitation the opportunity to enroll in Brummana High School, an institution in the mountains operated by British Quakers for the benefit of Middle Eastern students who came from such places as Kuwait, Yemen, Saudi Arabia, Iraq, Jordan, Syria, the Gulf states as well as from Lebanon. Instruction was in English, except in Arabic language and literature courses. The language of the dormitories was predominately Arabic and in a few months David felt at home in the language. When Maria saw how her brother could bargain with market people, inquire for directions, make friends with our neighbors, she too decided to continue her schooling at Brummana.

While our young folks were busy with school, Marie and I enrolled in Arabic conversation courses at Beirut University College. Because Arabic and Hebrew are related Semitic languages, I found it a great advantage that I had studied Hebrew, if only for reading. We soon discovered that many Lebanese shopkeepers would speak to us in French or English even if we addressed them in Arabic. There is a tendency for Lebanese people to play their international card when they encounter non-Lebanese. The spoken language tends to be considered an in-group means of communication. We later found that Egyptians, on the other hand, preferred to use Egyptian Arabic with everyone, foreigners and nationals.

Our march through the Babel of the Middle East brought us in contact with new kinds of people and sometimes unexpected cultural events. For example, in our Beirut neighborhood we discovered a number of Druze families. The Druze are a Muslim sect found mainly in Lebanon and Syria whose rites and beliefs are not propagated among outsiders. I found I gained very little information when I tried to learn about them. However, one account we learned concerned the extent to which these people will go to protect and preserve the sense of family honor.

The Jabbar family, like most families in the area, is ruled by the oldest living male and disobedience is not tolerated. It seems the Jabbar family had a grown daughter who was secretly seeing someone unacceptable to the fathers of the family. The young lady was warned to stop seeing this person but she failed to heed the warning. It seems her love for her mate was stronger than her fear of death. After some time, she was given a final warning but still could not give him up. They continued to meet secretly. One member of the family, her own brother, was assigned the chore of ending her life. Late one night after a rendezvous with her forbidden lover, she was returning to the family home. A shot rang out and the girl died immediately.

In Lebanese law a matter such as this is called a crime of honor. It is judged by a court that rules on family crimes.

Someone—not necessarily the one who pulled the trigger—serves a short jail sentence. The convicted person is looked upon as a family hero because he has paid the price of upholding the family honor.

In Lebanon, which has the largest proportional Christian population in the Arab world—traditionally the Maronite Catholics make up half the population—there is little or no objection against Christian bookstores or the printing and distribution of the Bible. Outside Lebanon where the Christian population is relatively small—Egypt 10%, The Gulf 1%, Iraq 3 %, Jordan 6 %, Kuwait 3%, Saudi Arabia, .8% and Pakistan 2%—it is sometimes dangerous to operate Christian literature shops and Bible stores.

Before I began making trips to Pakistan to work with translators in such languages as Urdu, Punjabi and Brahui, an attack that sent two men to the hospital took place at the Bible Society shop and depot on Anarkali Street, a busy commercial area, in the bustling city of Lahore. A fanatic, who happened to be a Muslim, burst into the quiet Bible shop and fired two shots into the clerk. When Hector Masih heard the shots, he rushed from his office into the shop where he found his clerk lying on the floor. He attempted to disarm the man but the gunman turned his pistol on Mr. Masih and fired into him at point blank range before running out and disappearing into the crowded street.

With a bullet lodged near his own heart, Mr. Masih lifted his wounded clerk and carried him outside to his car, drove to the hospital and then collapsed. Surgery on the clerk saved his life, but doctors judged that Masih's bullet lay too close to his heart to risk an attempt to remove it. Mr. Masih, who is now eighty-five years of age, carries the bullet to this day.

Many witnesses were able to identify the assailant and he was eventually apprehended by the Lahore police. When this case went to court, the Lahore judge ruled that the presence of the Bible shop in a Muslim city was a provocation. The gunman was given a suspended sentence.

How to put out a Fire

The massacre of Igbos in Jos, Nigeria, in September 1966 had exposed us to the darkest side of the human soul, at least that is what we thought then. The collapse of Lebanon and its descent into the hellish abyss would surpass anything we had yet seen. Our lives would never again be the same.

From September 1972 until April 1975 we managed to live a fairly normal life in spite of the deadly struggle going on about us. From time to time there were shootings and reports that it was unsafe to drive on certain streets for fear of being taken hostage by local militias. The Lebanese, whose identity cards revealed their religion and thus exposed them to being kidnapped or killed in revenge, were beginning to black out that part of their identity. When we had to cross town, taxi drivers usually knew the safe streets to follow.

Marie, who had enrolled at the American University of Beirut (AUB) to obtain a teaching certificate in primary education, was busy with her studies. The three children were full-time students and I was able to travel in and out of the Beirut Airport, unless trouble flared up around the Palestinian refugee camps on the airport road. However, April 13, 1975, marked an event that would change everything. A busload of Palestinian Feydayeen (commandos) and their supporters were passing through the suburb of Ein Rummaneh where Christian Phalanges party leader Pierre Gemayel was attending the consecration of a new Maronite church. Thinking that the Palestinian fighters were preparing to attack, the Phalangist opened fire on the bus killing 27 and wounding 19. This was the spark that ignited a war that could not be stopped.

How, we may ask, could a country known for its tolerance and freedoms give way to complete anarchy? Some say too much social and economic injustice. Still others say too much religious fanaticism while others claim that too much freedom leads to anarchy.

There is no doubt some truth in each of these views. However, there is more. From 1943, Lebanon's independence from France, there have been seventeen recognized religious groups, each demanding a bite out of the nation. The three largest of these are the Maronite Christians who hold the presidency, the Shi'ite Muslims who are given the Parliamentary Speakership and the Sunni Muslims who name the Premier. The country has been divided among interests held by greedy politicians who have done little or nothing to build a nation.

Furthermore, this tiny nation has always been a place of asylum for people seeking a home; for example, Armenians, Kurds, and, since 1948, Palestinians driven out of what became the state of Israel. Some 450,000 Palestinians poured into Lebanon, organized politically and began to arm themselves. When the Israelis attacked Palestinians in the south of the country, thousands of poor Shi'ite Muslims fled north and created a poverty belt around Beirut.

Petrodollars poured in from oil rich Arab countries and soon Kalashnikovs and ammunition were in the hands of nearly everyone, even children. Every neighborhood had its own militia, its own sandbag barricades in the streets, its own newssheet and its own cellar full of hostages who were often shot, tied behind cars and dragged through the streets. The Lebanese police were often forced to give up their arms and the central government lost every semblance of control. Shops were looted and bank vaults blown open.

Contributing to Lebanon's anarchy was the Cairo Agreement

of 1969, which was intended to regulate the activities of the Palestinian Resistance. In fact, however, it served to increase the distrust felt by many Lebanese, particularly Christians, toward Palestinian extremists. In May 1973 the Israelis made a commando raid in Beirut killing several Palestinian leaders. The Palestinians accused the Lebanese and as a result the Lebanese Air force flew air strikes against Palestinian positions.

Snipers with telescopic sights began to occupy many of the uncompleted high-rise structures from which they shot and killed anyone moving on the streets below—often women and children trying to find food to buy. Many Lebanese lost their lives without ever knowing what killed them or why.

Peace delegations sent by the Pope and others flew in and met with leaders only to depart with nothing accomplished. Frequent cease-fires were called—no fewer than fifty-five—and observed only long enough to reposition or resupply for the next murderous round. Not until January 1976 when Syrian troops entered Lebanon was there a cease-fire imposed on all fronts. The "Green line" was established by Syria along the Damascus road separating Muslim West Beirut and Christian East Beirut. The US State Department officially recognized that "Syria had played a constructive role"; however, Syria was unable to impose more than a temporary peace, and battles raged throughout the country until November—ten months later—when eight thousand Arab peacekeeping forces from Syria, Saudi Arabia, Egypt, Kuwait, the PLO and Lebanon—and two hundred and fifty tanks and other armored vehicles entered Beirut. The estimated toll was: 40,000 killed, 100,000 wounded, 5,000 maimed, 500,000 homeless or displaced, 300,000 had emigrated and the destruction was estimated in billions of dollars.

Part of Marie's training at AUB required her to teach English to Palestinian children in the Sabra refugee camp. Sabra along with the Shatilla camp was the area where fighting frequently prevented me from reaching the airport. Eight years later in 1982, after the Israeli invasion of Lebanon to drive the PLO from the country, Christian right wing militias attacked the Sabra and Shatilla camps, while the Israeli commanders looked the other way. The International Committee of the Red Cross is the only independent organization said to know how many people were massacred in the two camps. Their staff buried 210 bodies: 140 men, 38 women and 32 children.

But to return again to the events of 1974, because life was more normal in the mountains than in Beirut, we decided to move to Brummana where David and Maria were in school. To make the move, I arranged with the driver of a large truck to help me carry out the furniture from our fifth floor Beirut apartment. When fully loaded, the driver and I set off for Brummana, normally a half to three quarters of an hour drive. According to the driver, there had been no shooting reported in the Tell Zaatar section. We passed out of West Beirut into Ashrafiye and crossed the Jisr El Bacha and started up Mkalles road near the Palestinian camp of Tell Zaatar. Suddenly the crackling of bullets was like a swarm of bees around us. I knew these shots were too close to be safe. The driver jammed on his brakes and we leapt out and crawled under the truck. The moment I got beneath the truck, I smelled gasoline, which I saw dripping from a gas line onto the hot tarmac. While staring at the gas leak, I heard the pop of a striking match. My insouciant Lebanese driver was not going to lie about without a cigarette. I reached over and snatched the fag from his lips and flung it away from the truck, an act that brought the man's temper to an instant boil. Fortunately, my Arabic studies had failed to include the slime bucket of epithets he doused on me. When the firing had stopped and we were again enroute, he remarked, "What the hell, in this country the gasoline is so watered down, if you throw it on a fire, it will put the fire out."

Monastery

It is only reasonable to ask why we would remain in Lebanon when at nearly every turn life was becoming threatened. The answer is that we lived with the hope that tomorrow the killings would stop and things, having got so bad, could only improve. Furthermore, we had Lebanese colleagues and friends who through it all were trying in the good intervals to live a normal life. Thousands of good, honest and innocent people were appalled by the brutality and were trying desperately to live decent lives and to help others. Our European and American friends felt very much as we did and were determined not to abandon ship while there was still hope.

Nevertheless, hope was fading as the downtown district of Beirut burned out of control. Marie, who had completed her teaching certificate in October, 1974, began teaching in September, 1975, at the American Community School where she had seventeen second graders: Japanese, Indians, Pakistanis and Americans. Due to the intensive fighting in West Beirut, she had to live in a school dormitory and was unable to get home to Brummana. By December the situation had worsened and the school was forced to close. During a short lull in the fighting she managed to reach home.

Susie, who had been staying in a dormitory at BUC waiting for classes to begin, learned that BUC would not open and the prospects of opening later were growing dim. Therefore, Susie and I flew to California where she enrolled at Chapman College in Orange. Brummana High School closed for Christmas vacation and organized a convoy of taxis to travel at a safe moment to Beirut and to the airport. Marie, David and Maria were in the last taxi. In Beirut they spent the night with Carol and Ben Weir. Ben, who was later taken hostage for eighteen months, knew the conditions around West Beirut and, thanks to him, Marie and the children got to the airport and flew out to London.

The Reyburn family was finally out of Lebanon, but scattered. David and Maria enrolled at Ackworth School in Yorkshire, a Quaker school related to Brummana High School. Annie also was in England. Marie and Susie were in California and I was about to become a guest in the Coptic (Egyptian) Catholic monastery in Maadi. Father Antoine Naguib, professor of holy scripture at the monastery/seminary and member of the new Arabic translation project, had always assured me I would have a home in Maadi if the need ever arose. With a copy of the manuscript of the new Arabic translation under my arm—the original manuscript had been carried by Yusufu El Khal on the embattled *Phoenicia*—and my tattered suitcase in my hand, I walked up the steps of the building that would be my new home for the coming months.

The monastery in Maadi serves mainly as school and seminary and is located in a residential section of a suburb of Cairo. The building has three stories and was constructed in the 1930's. The Coptic Catholic church had resulted largely from Jesuit missionary efforts in the 18th and 19th centuries and the patriarchate was established in 1824. Msgr. Stephanos, the Patriarch and son of a former Egyptian Ambassador to the U.S., was made a Cardinal in 1965. The church, at the time of my sojourn in 1976, had some 100,000 members. The church has four bishoprics and more than a hundred schools in upper and lower Egypt, a hospital in Assiut, medical dispensaries and clinics and several orphanages. Although the ancient Coptic language is still sung in the liturgy, Arabic is increasingly used.

Maadi is a quiet area where the British colonials had built

wide streets and large homes. The sidewalks are lined with ornamental shrubs and particularly oriental sycamores—a fig-bearing tree such as Zacchaeus is said in Luke 19.4 to have climbed in Jericho to see Jesus. The monastery is built in two wings with the chapel in the center. The ground floor is used for classrooms, kitchen and dining hall while the two upper floors are used as living quarters for monks, priests, teachers and students.

I was given a room on the second floor that I learned later was the room kept for the Patriarch when he visited the institution. The room was plain, almost bare in its simplicity. However, from the first day two items caught my attention. The first was the very large bathtub—there was no shower—and the second was a large pair of long johns that hung on the back of the bathroom door. I assumed these belonged to the Patriarch but was surprised to think it ever got cold enough in Egypt to wear them. Eventually I learned they were not worn to protect from the cold, but rather to protect from the sight of nakedness when taking a bath. This attitude toward the human body was confirmed for me later while attending an ecumenical conference in Ethiopia. Two Russian orthodox bishops appeared at the swimming pool at midnight in their long underwear and indulged themselves in a refreshing swim.

The early morning darkness in Maadi was filled with sounds much like those in Beirut or a hundred other cities—the barking of dogs and the crowing of roosters. But daybreak in Maadi brought me slowly to life by half a dozen minarets each beginning moments apart, making the loudspeaker calls to prayer a traffic jam of thunderous voices.

> *God is great* (repeated four times)
> *I bear witness that there is no god but God*
> *I bear witness that Mohammed is the Apostle of God . . .*
> The call ends as it begins with *God is great* (repeated
> four times)

The chanting of the morning liturgy in the chapel took over where the minarets left off. I could set my watch; it was 6.30 a.m. As each day began, so would it end—the intermingling of Islamic praise and Christian adoration.

With eighty students around, I was given a splendid opportunity to recycle my Arabic. Lebanese and Egyptian Arabic are very different, far more different than, say, British and American English. I would suggest a difference such as between Brazilian Portuguese and Latin American Spanish. In addition to the spoken language, Arabic has a written form based on the classical language and the students in Maadi were required to read written Arabic precisely and to pronounce it correctly. To this end a seminary student was selected each noon meal to read aloud an article or a passage from the Bible while the other students and priests quietly listened as they ate their lunch. An error in the reading would cause the director to stop the reader, make him correct his mistake before continuing. It was not uncommon to see sweat on the brows of these young men when they had finished their public reading.

After classes in the afternoon, students swapped their robes for shorts and played soccer. The priests and monks had no games and their only exercise was walking and chatting along the dark corridors or on the flat roof at night. There under the stars in their black robes, they reminded me of moths flitting to and fro in the dark.

I had noticed on certain nights several berobed priests carrying their chairs and converging on one man's room. I assumed this was a meditation or perhaps making plans for the next morning's chapel prayers. I later learned that the resident of that room had a television and World Champion Wrestling was the drawing card. They also liked Tom and Jerry cartoons, westerns and especially I Love Lucy.

While I was in Maadi, President Sadat made one of his four-hour long speeches to the Egyptian Parliament. Sadat's oratory was famous and he drew huge television audiences whenever he spoke. His discourses ranged from the high literary to the most common man-in-the-street vernacular. Along with a room full of priests, I watched Sadat's speech in March, 1976, when he announced that he was breaking the agreement signed with the Soviets in 1970. The cameras then shifted to the members of parliament who leapt out of their seats and went wild with excitement. Telecasts signed off at midnight with a short sermon from a Muslim cleric and with quotations from the Qur'an on the screen.

While in Egypt, I was able to organize a team of Orthodox and Protestant biblical scholars to review the new Arabic translation of the New Testament. In September Marie, who had been interviewed and hired in the U. S., came to Maadi to teach at Cairo American College. Abouna Naguib helped me find an apartment a few blocks from the school. My monastic life, interesting and stimulating as it was, now was happily at an end.

Visa for Vietnam

The Vietnam war, the longest war in which the United States ever took part, began in 1957 and ended in 1975. The American losses of 58,000 dead and 365,000 wounded were small compared with the South Vietnamese deaths that exceeded 1 million and the North Vietnamese deaths estimated to be nearly a million. That conflict, which dumped four times as many bombs on Vietnam as had been dropped on Germany in World War II, cost the United States 150 billion dollars and caused nearly ten million South Vietnamese, nearly half the population, to become war refugees.

I had not expected to be in Vietnam; however, the UBS had decided to hold a training course there that would be conducted in English, Vietnamese and French. Jan deWaard and I were asked to head up the French courses for French-speaking Europeans and Vietnamese catholic priests.

As was often the case, I had to determine where I could obtain a visa before traveling to Saigon, now Ho Chi Min City. William Smalley, who was the organizer of the conference, informed me that I could easily obtain a visa in Bangkok, Thailand, where he was living. We were instructed to be in Dalat, an hour flight north of Saigon, on 1 March 1974. Consequently, on 26 February I flew into Bangkok from Beirut and the following day presented myself at the South Vietnamese Embassy and applied for a visa. The consul examined my passport and in a moment handed it back and walked away. Perplexed by his abruptness, I asked if there was something wrong. Disappearing into his office he called back, "communist!" I asked that he explain. He reappeared for a moment in the doorway speaking in French, "*Vous visitez les pays comunists. Pas de visa.*"

My attempt to explain that having been in eastern Europe did not make me a communist helped me not in the least. There was no one else in the office I could consult and so I took my communist contaminated passport and headed for the American Embassy. Perhaps a sympathetic ear would find a way around this impasse. I had to be in Saigon in two days.

At the American Embassy I asked to see a consular officer and was shown to a row of partitioned offices opening from a long hall. As I approached the closest one, a middle aged man was leaning back in his swivel chair. A sign on his door announced that he was vice consul J. D. Smith. I knocked and was waved in by a large hand wrapped around a copy of Time magazine. After explaining to consul Smith that I could not get a visa to Vietnam because I had visa stamps from communist countries, I inquired if I could obtain a new passport and how long such a procedure would take. Smith stared straight at me without speaking, so I explained the reason I had to go there. Perhaps his mother was a Southern Baptist and training Bible translators would strike a chord. Instead it struck to the very blood and bone of bureaucracy and Smith stretched and yawned all the while quoting from a well memorized handbook of procedures. In short, impossible. My passport, he soon detected, had more than six months validity and therefore had to be sent to Washington. This could take four to six weeks. If I had wanted to avoid going to Vietnam, consul Smith had given me the perfect excuse. But I wanted to go in the worst sort of way. It crossed my mind to make Mr. Smith an offer, but locked up in Bangkok for trying to bribe a US embassy official did not seem ethically consistent with my job. Consul Smith shrugged his beefy shoulders, "That's the way the bamboo bends, Mr. Reyburn."

Out in the hall again, I sauntered along going nowhere in

particular until I passed another open door where a bespectacled lady vice consul was bowed over a thick volume on her cluttered desk. In those days people had no computers to stare into. I knocked and when I was seated, she pushed her glasses to her forehead and focused intensely on me. I told her my tale just as I had reported it to Mr. Smith. When I finished she was tapping her ring-ladened fingers on her desk. From a drawer she extracted a folder, ran her eyes down the page then remarked, "Ah, that's good. They're open till four today." I was wondering who "they" meant when she added, "That's the Viet place."

Taking my passport she examined it quickly then told me to go to the cashier and get a receipt for ten dollars. I rushed off to do her bidding, not being entirely sure that Smith would not drop in on her for a chat and undo what I hoped the lady consul had in mind. Back with the receipt, I handed it to her still wondering if she would suddenly recall the standing operating procedure and throw on the brakes.

"How about 2.00 pm? That should give you two hours to go to the Viets" she opined. I wanted to hug the good lady, but did not want to raise any suspicion that she was doing almost immediately something her colleague a few doors away said would take weeks.

"I'm pretty sure I can manage it if you can have it ready by two" I said as I left her office. I was nearly flying as I went down the hall, but then realized I was approaching stickler Smith's open door so I shifted down into dejection mode, nodded weakly to the man behind the desk doing his bamboo bends, recovered my aplomb and left.

At the South Vietnamese Embassy Mr. Nguyen Do Son took my virgin passport, leafed through then sniffed it, almost allowing a shadow of a smile to escape his lips. I was still enjoying the euphoria of slipping through American bureaucracy when the wheels of my plane screeched on the Saigon runway.

CANADA
AND
LATIN
AMERICA II

Peace Pipe

The small log church in the woods at Sandy Lake, Ontario, Canada, was packed. I had just addressed a conference of Cree Indian leaders from Northern Manitoba and Ontario. My topic was "A Cree Survey." The Canadian Bible Society had requested me to make a study of the Cree language area and to determine what kinds of translations were needed and how they should be printed—in the Cree syllabary or in Roman type.

James Evans, a Wesleyan missionary who arrived in Canada from England in 1840, invented the Cree alphabet—a syllabary bearing no resemblance to English letters. At his station on the west shore of Lake Winnipeg, Evans learned the Cree dialect of that area, known as Western Cree. Desiring to teach the people to read their language, he had to find a way to write it and then to produce printed pages. Having no paper, ink, type or press, Evans had to come up with some ingenious solutions. He determined that the language would require 42 letters or symbols. This number was only half as many as Sequoia needed to write Cherokee. He set out very much like Sequoia carving his 42 symbols out of wood with his pocketknife. With these he fashioned clay models, melted the lead linings from his English tea chests and poured them into the clay molds. In this way he obtained lead copies of each symbol. The resourceful Reverend Evans then took a press used for treating animal furs, made his ink by mixing soot and fish oil. For paper he used the soft inner bark of the birch tree, sewed these with leather strips and bound the "printed pages" in deer hide. Little wonder that the Indians said, "The birch bark began to speak the words of the Great Spirit."

The chairman of the conference at Sandy Lake thanked me for my talk and invited questions from the audience. It was August and the weather was hot; black flies and mosquitoes were everywhere. People had traveled long distances and I could see that many of the older men were catching up on missed sleep while I spoke. There were people whispering to one another and after a while a large elderly Indian rose to his feet, cleared his voice several times and shook his fist in my direction. "That guy says he's gonna do way with our language." He turned to face the audience, "But I say he ain't gonna do it. We ain't gonna let him do it, are we?" There was a responsive rumble of No's. Encouraged by his supporters, he moved into the aisle. "Brother," he was pointing at me, "do you know where our language came from or when it was invented? No, you don't. Well, I'll tell you, God made it at the tower of Babel." The speaker was pleased with the applause that rang out. He turned to face his listeners. With a finger he pushed back his upper lip to reveal two missing front teeth. "You know how I lost them teeth?" He turned around so I could see his missing teeth. "I lost 'em fightin' for my language, you hear, and if I have to, I'll lose the rest of 'em fightin' agin to save my language." Another hearty applause filled the room.

Of course, I had said nothing to warrant his charge that I was going to get rid of his language. I was delighted that someone was willing to fight to save it. The chairman rushed in, speaking now in Cree, and explained that we needed to know if we should continue printing the Bible in the syllabary or if it would be better, since the language is not being taught in the schools, homes or churches, to print it in Roman, that is, in English letters. "Or perhaps both," I added.

The chairman's question landed on the audience like a flaming match on gasoline. The traditionalists, like the previous speaker, were on their feet all shouting at once. They were clinging to the symbolic vestiges of a way of life that was speeding by and leaving them behind. These were the older folk for whom the language and its writing were matters of life and death. When finally the hubbub had spent itself, I asked to speak. "How many of you, I asked, "have always spoken to your children in Cree?" Three or four hands were raised. "How many of you have taught your children to read the syllabary?" Ten hands shot up and eight of them quickly came back down. "How many of you have talked to your children in English so they could advance in school?" The room was alive with raised hands, even if some had to look around before putting up their hands.

The reality among the Cree was much like I had seen among smaller languages all over the world. Many of these languages are going down to the grave with their older speakers, like the disappearance of so many species. I spent two nights at Sandy Lake sharing Stanley McKay's pup tent. Stanley is a Cree-speaking Indian pastor and university graduate. He expressed to me his concern for his church. The United Church of Canada provides cultural orientation for their missionaries going overseas, but nothing equivalent is done for those who are sent to work among Canadian Indians. As a result, he said, many of these missionaries suffer cultural shock and withdraw because they have not been adequately prepared to face the Indian reality. "Indians," he observed, "are looked upon by both church leaders and laity as simply poor country people."

As I traveled through Ontario, Manitoba, Saskatchewan and Alberta provinces by plane, bus, car, boat and train, I carried with me a questionnaire aimed at finding out how well the Cree read in the different scripts, which scriptures they owned and which ones they read. I was interested in their family and community life and the gap that separated the elders from the youth, men from women, what they were doing to pass on the language to the youth and attitudes of the youth to their parents' native tongue. At the conclusion of the survey, I passed on my recommendations to the Canadian Bible Society.

I was everywhere captivated by the scenic beauty of the

countryside. Nearly every time I took to the air, another lovely lake arose out of the woods. One lake that left a lasting impression on me was Trout Lake, Alberta, where I encountered Roman Catholic missionary, Paul Hernou.

Here was a man who did not fit in any sense Stanley McKay's description of the missionary suffering from cultural shock. Hernou, a Belgian Oblate father, carried the moniker "Bear" and Bear he was. With his black crew cut hair, his thick black beard and his stocky frame wrapped in a black soutane, he could easily be mistaken for a bear lumbering over the trails of Trout Lake. Hernou had grown up as a Flemish-speaker and was well aware of the struggle of his people in Belgium to defend the use of their language. He was, therefore, sympathetic with every effort to increase the use of Cree, always under the threat of the constant encroachment of English. He was a culturally sensitive missionary whose church building had the form of a huge tepee. He approached the Cree as a learner, sought the advice of the elders and tried to make the gospel meaningful to the Indians' way of life. He sat in the local council circle and took his turn with the peace pipe. In this land where sheep were unknown but horses were ubiquitous, his predecessor, Father Van der Steen, had translated John 1.29 "Behold, the young colt of God that takes away the sins of the world."

Father Hernou had taken me to several Cree families along the shores of the lake so that I could conduct my questionnaire. We were chatting in French and making our way back to his cabin, when two young Crees carrying rifles suddenly stopped us. One lifted his rifle and pointed it at Hernou. They had been drinking and were unsteady on their feet.

"Hey, Bear, I can shoot a hole through your head," one of the youths said, waving his gun barrel in Hernou's face. Bear understood how shame worked among the Cree to control their behavior. It was this he had in mind when he responded. "Yes, I know you can. And if you missed when this close," Hernou pointed toward the weaving gun barrel, "there would be laughter all around Trout Lake."

"Well, I'm gonna shoot you anyway." Saying that, the man levered his bolt and threw a round into the chamber. I heard the safety latch click off. From where I stood, it looked like the Cree survey was just about to end. Hernou spoke again, "Does a powerful hunter like you need a gun to kill old Bear? Why you could kill me with a stick, like killing a jack rabbit."

"Shut your mouth, Bear, I'm gonna shoot you and your friend both."

Hernou asked him, "Will that make you a big man? Will the elders in the council sing your praise because you shot us at point blank range?"

"When I shoot you, you'll be a dead bear, wont he?" he said nodding to his companion. "We're gonna make a bear rug out of you." The two Indians laughed.

I could see the sweat glistening on Hernou's forehead. He spoke softly to me, *"Allez vite, mon ami, et ne regardez pas en arrière."* I stepped around the two and walked briskly toward a bend in the trail and did not look back, as instructed. I was tense from anticipating the bang of a rifle shot, maybe a bullet in me, maybe in Hernou. From the bend in the trail I peered out and watched as Hernou brushed the muzzle of the gun barrel way from his head and swung along the trail toward me in his plodding gait. Together we watched with great relief as the drunken pair staggered off in the opposite direction.

The following morning we heard someone cough outside the cabin. Hernou said, "That is the Cree way of knocking on your door. Oh, by the way, what is your opinion of my translation of Revelation 3.20 'Behold, I stand at the door and cough'"? Outside the caller coughed again and Hernou opened the door to find the two young men who had confronted and frightened us on the trail. They came in and sat down while Hernou and I continued our conversation. After some time, I asked Hernou if they did not want to say something. His reply was, "They will when they are ready. I think I know what it's about." Later while Bear was talking, the young man who had threatened to shoot him suddenly broke into the conversation.

"Bear, you know why we came?"

"Yes, I think so."

"Well, Bear, you know my head is hot."

"So you have a hot head." (This is a metaphor for embarrassment.)

"I don't like to have a hot head."

Hernou went to a shelf and brought down a long pipe, filled it with tobacco, lit it and took a couple of drags. He then passed it to his visitors who pulled smoke and blew it from their nostrils. Then they passed the pipe to me and I did the same, not without a chesty cough. Later we shook hands all around and the young men departed. It was clear that forgiveness was expressed by sharing the pipe, an act far more meaningful than mere words. I had learned in Lolo how reconciliation between enemies is effected through eating from the same bowl.

Hernou addressed me as *mon frère* and went on to say, "I'd like you to hear how I say Matthew 6.12 (Forgive us our debts as we forgive others) 'Smoke the pipe of peace with us as we smoke it with others.'" The Canadian Cancer Society may feel on health grounds that this is an unfortunate rendering, but for the Cree at Trout Lake it is packed with meaning.

Marching to a

Different Drum

The years 1979-80 were times of great changes. The Iranian revolution began and students seized the US Embassy in Teheran. The Soviets invaded Afghanistan. The Gdansk shipyard in Poland went on strike and the communist government recognized the Solidarity Union. Iraq invaded Iran for the start of an 8-years war, the US being the main supplier of Iraq's arms. Beatle John Lennon was assassinated in the street in New York City and Archbishop Oscar Romero was shot down while saying mass in a hospital in San Salvador. In Nicaragua the Sandinistas overthrew the US supported dictator, Anastasio Somoza Debayle, and were soon engulfed in a war with the Contras who were financed and equipped by the US. Under the rule of General Pinochet in Chile, thousands of people were disappearing and right-wing death squads in El Salvador carried out a litany of assassinations, mass murders and mutilations. The Guatemala government was murdering its Indian population.

The war in Lebanon prevented us from returning there and so the UBS asked us to go again to Latin America. After Marie completed a refresher course in Spanish, we settled in San José, Costa Rica, from where I traveled north through Central America and south through Panama and South America. Costa Rica, that had done away with its army in 1949, was unlikely to have a revolution. Frankly, we were exhausted from revolutions and civil wars and were happy to make San José our home for the next four years.

Twenty-four years had passed since we had left Latin America and we had to reacquaint ourselves with this changing continent. For example, in Chimborazo, Ecuador, where there had been almost no converts to the evangelical faith at the time of our departure in 1955, now there were active churches scattered across the high Andes with more than five thousand believers and a community of more than twenty thousand. Quechua Indians whose lives had been dominated by drunken fiestas, fights and illness were now sending their children to school, saving their money and becoming entrepreneurs, owning trucks, busses and cars. Cement block houses with windows and electricity were replacing darkened mud and thatch houses. The Indians saw the drinking of fermented chicha made from the century plant as the vice that made them easy victims of land grabbers and loan sharks. In one of his commentaries on the New Testament, William Barclay tells of a Welsh coal miner whose drinking father had become a follower of Christ. When asked by skeptic miners if the young man believed in the story of Christ turning water into wine, he replied, "I don't know about turning water into wine, but I do know that in my house Christ turned whiskey into furniture." This was also the case in hundreds of shacks in the Ecuadorian Andes where faith in Christ had transformed intoxicating chicha into education and hope for the future.

In nearly every country of Latin America the evangelical churches were growing at a phenomenal rate. From Mexico to Argentina it was not the older denominations that were multiplying, but rather national Pentecostal movements. These fundamentalist bodies were spirit-centered and often concerned with the social issues their people faced. Biblical symbolism played a vital role in their worship and, like most evangelical churches, they clung tenaciously to the traditional version of the Spanish Bible, known as the Reina-Valera, a revision of the 1569

Bible translated by Casidoro de Reina. Many such churches have stubbornly resisted revisions of this Bible and refuse to read modern versions that are based on older and more authentic manuscripts and are expressed in the Spanish used in today's literature and speech. This reactionary attitude, while not unknown in other parts of the globe—a typical example is the adherence by Orthodox and Protestants to the Arabic Van Dyck Bible in Egypt and the Middle East—enables defenders of the traditional Spanish version to draw a clear line between themselves and Roman Catholics. Because evangelicals in Latin America remember times of persecution, they often feel that the Bible is a Protestant book, their private domain and most showed little interest in the documents advocating the study of the Bible produced at the Second Vatican Council—1962-65.

When I have pointed out to evangelical pastors that "The Constitution on the Sacred Liturgy—one of the documents from Vatican II—permitted "easy access to the Holy Scriptures for all the Christian faithful," they would sometimes remind me that Vatican I in 1869 approved the doctrine of *papal infallibility*. Therefore, they would ask, "Why should we pay any attention now?"

In 1968 the United Bible Societies and the Catholic Secretariat for Promoting Christian Unity jointly issued a document titled *Guiding Principles for Interconfessional Cooperation in Translating the Bible.* In a short while, there were numerous translation projects around the world in which Protestants, Roman Catholics and in some cases Orthodox scholars were working together harmoniously and by 1987 interconfessional Bibles and New Testaments had been published in one hundred and sixty-one languages. Latin American evangelicals, with certain outstanding exceptions, were often opposed to these interconfessional efforts. For me personally, this was painful because in Africa, Europe and the Middle East I had for years been working closely with such teams of translators. In nearly every case I had witnessed a genuine desire on the part of Roman

Catholic scholars to deal truthfully and honestly with the text and to make a clear distinction between translation of the text and doctrinal comments about the text. I had been invited to lecture in Catholic seminaries, and had discussed translation issues with Vatican officials, scholars and local priests.

It was extremely gratifying for me to see that Catholic Bishops, anxious for their constituencies to study the Scriptures, gave their endorsements to the modern Spanish Bible *Dios Habla Hoy* and to the new Brazilian Bible *A Biblia na Linguagem de Hoje*. Numerous Bible Study groups were forming throughout both Spanish and Portuguese Latin America, mainly among Roman Catholics but also among non-Romans.

The rejectionist attitude of many evangelicals struck me as bigotry and unChrist-like. It was, indeed, discouraging to find that some national Bible Society leaders were themselves unsympathetic with any kind of ecumenical effort. With their memories of the past, they could not bring themselves to be reconciled with their old enemy, the Roman Catholic Church.

By 1984 thirty-two years had passed since we had left the US. Our children had become adults and given us two grandchildren—eight at the time of this writing. I had worked in more than a hundred languages in as many countries. The world had become my workshop and I had a familiarity with the people and places across the earth. I had counseled and taught Bible translators in nearly every variety of Christian faith from Russian Orthodox to Roman Catholic to Pentecostals, to the Cherubim and Seraphim of Nigeria and the Kimbanguist of Congo. Our friends were Muslims, Jews, Christians, Buddhists, Animists and Atheists. As international citizens we could no longer fully identify our thoughts and feelings with one nation, one economy, one political system or one expression of religious conviction. We were at home everywhere and nowhere.

It is, therefore, not surprising that we were often out of step with most of the evangelical faithful in Latin America and when Roman Catholics behaved as if they had never heard of the Second

Vatican Council—and many of them hadn't—we were also not marching along with them. The atheists and free thinkers who considered themselves liberated from all religions were too often arrogant and superior. Clearly, it was time for us to go.

At the time of our departure from Costa Rica, colleagues Heber Peacock and Robert Bratcher had summer cottages on the shores of Lake Nottley in Union County, Georgia, close to the borders of North Carolina and Tennessee. They invited us to join them. I continued to travel to Latin America and to the Middle East, where the new Arabic New Testament we had worked so hard—often against the opposition of the Bible Society of Egypt—to bring into existence, was being widely used throughout the Maronite churches in Lebanon and, at the time of writing, the entire Bible in this modern version is widely read on a web site.

At home in Georgia, Bratcher and I were preparing *A Translator's Handbook of the Book of Psalms*. By 1990 I had ceased traveling and was able to concentrate fully on the writing of Old Testament helps. These are books that a translator with a knowledge of English can use to get verse-by-verse information dealing with exegetical, textual, linguistic, literary and cultural aspects of the text. A survey of translators around the world had shown that the Handbooks were among their most valued tools. In addition to the *Psalms* (1991), I wrote Handbooks on *Lamentations* (1992), *Job* (1992), Genesis (1997), and *Proverbs* (2000), the last two done in cooperation with Euan Fry of Australia. In spite of being half a world apart, we worked well together, thanks to computers, email and floppy disks. These five books, published by the United Bible Societies in New York, contain a total of 4,033 printed pages.

While I was busy in front of the word processor, my talented partner Marie was teaching literacy to adults who had dropped out of school and was organizing a two-county program against domestic violence. This work originated following a murder trial in Union County, Georgia, in which a woman had shot and killed an abusive husband. A group of concerned citizens came together and created S.A.F.E (Support in Abusive Family Emergencies) and elected Marie as the first president of the board. S.A.F.E. has for twelve years been providing shelter, social and legal services, crisis intervention, counseling for hundreds of battered women and children as well as education in the public schools. Churches, civic clubs and individuals have been made aware of the problems of domestic violence and many battered women have been empowered to make good decisions for themselves and their children.

Having lived in Central America and with our daughter Maria working in Nicaragua, we understood the injustice being done by President Reagan's support of the Contra war. We took an active part in opposing his policies. Marie also helped organize a peace walk whose purpose was to raise funds for prosthetic limb replacements for victims on both sides of the Nicaraguan war. She joined others in Washington D.C. at Peace Pentecost in 1985 to protest in front of the State Department and, when arrested, went quietly to jail where these protesters joined hands through the cell bars and shook the jail singing The Hallelujah Chorus. The guards and many inmates felt abandoned when these peacemakers were freed.

With the help of several others, she began a local affiliate of Habitat for Humanity. Today there are three Habitat houses in the two counties.

Her most recent initiative has been the S.A.F.E. thrift shop, a store where everything from contributed clothing to computers are sold to help finance the domestic violence program. Volunteers provide nearly all the hands required for transporting goods, sorting and arranging items, working the cash register and the many other tasks required to operate and sustain the business. Although most of the funds received to operate S.A.F.E., which now has nine employees, come from government and foundation grants, the thrift store provides a substantial part of its budget. Marie and friends have worked to raise additional money by putting on a community chili supper each March, one of the many ways that keeps the needs of the organization before the public's eyes. As one volunteer remarked to me, "It is hard to refuse to be a volunteer for Marie's many efforts when you see how hard she works herself."

In May 1997, forty-five years after our first arrival in Guayaquil, Ecuador, I retired from my work as a translations consultant for the United Bible Societies. We had seen three of our children become teachers and one a computer programmer. They are spread from England to northern Indiana, South Georgia and Nicaragua. And today we watch, sometimes at a distance, our eight grandchildren and wonder prayerfully where their marching may lead them.

END

Printed in the United States
703800001B